16.95

Mullock

AN ENGLISHMAN
AT HOME
AND ABROAD
1829 - 1862

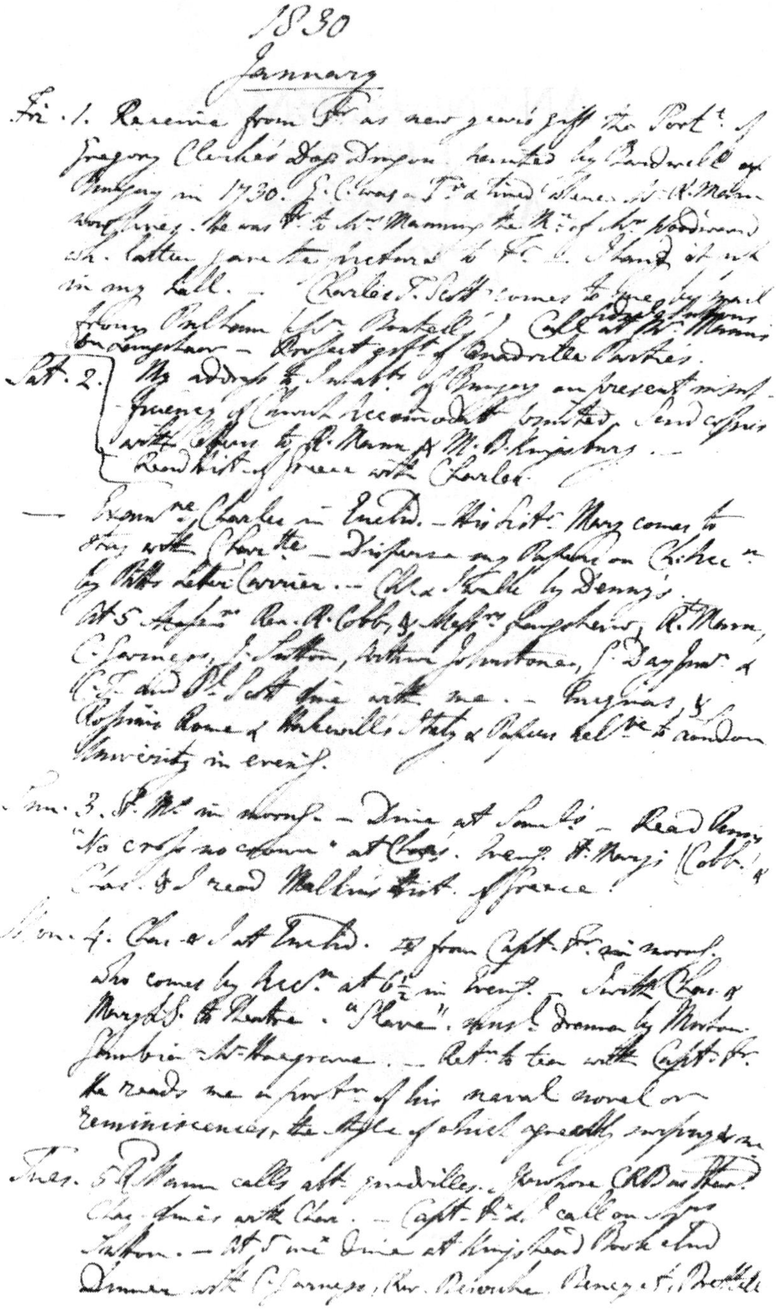

Facsimile of a page of J B Scott's Diary

AN ENGLISHMAN AT HOME AND ABROAD 1829 - 1862

Extracts from the Diaries of
John Barber Scott
of Bungay, Suffolk

Edited by
Ethel Mann & Hugh Cane

Additional Notes
Christopher Reeve

Morrow & Co
Bungay, Suffolk
1996

First published
Morrow & Co, Bungay, Suffolk 1996

Limited edition of 299 copies

Copy number . *101* . .

ISBN 0 948903 43 0

Designed & typeset by Morrow & Co, Bungay, Suffolk

Printed & bound by Ipswich Book Company Ltd.

CONTENTS

ILLUSTRATIONS

Frontis: Facsimile of a page of the Diary

PREFACE

It is now sixty-five years since Ethel Mann, a descendant of the Scotts, published the first part of this diary, though she had intended to complete the work soon afterwards. Although she had prepared her extracts by 1937 she never published them, and after her death in 1947 the extracts passed to her daughter. They were lost after the daughter died in 1970, but fortunately discovered in a Yarmouth bookshop the following year.

The original diary, which is now in the Suffolk Record Office in Lowestoft, consists of seventy-seven small notebooks closely written in small crabbed handwriting, and it must have taken Ethel Mann months or years to read through them and extract what she regarded as the most interesting. Much had to be omitted, and even in the first year, 1829, of this second part we hear hardly anything of Scott's activities as Town Reeve, or chief citizen, of Bungay.

John Barber Scott was born in Bridge House, Bungay, on February 24th 1792, the son of a prosperous merchant. He died at Waveney House opposite on September 10th 1862. For most of those seventy years he lived in Bungay and, being of independent means, was free to follow his many interests - the pursuit of knowledge, continental travel, public education and the social round at home and elsewhere, untrammelled by wife or children.

Lilias Rider Haggard has summarised his character and achievements in her admirable preface to "An Englishman at Home and Abroad (1792-1828)" so I will not enlarge on the finer details. These further extracts of his diary begin when Scott was thirty-six, Town Reeve for the first time, and settled into his second house which he inherited from his father. He has much to say on local, national and international events and the many notable personalities that he met at home and abroad, though nothing so dramatic as his encounter with Napoleon on Elba in 1814. His main local activity was centred on furthering public education, then in its formative years under church and state. He was much involved with both our ancient churches and in 1860 completed the restoration of Holy Trinity. He was particularly interested in archaeology and local history.

The citizens of his native town showed their appreciation of his public work by appointing him their Town Reeve on seven different occasions.

1

Acknowledgements

I am grateful to the following contributors:

Commander Mark Cheyne, nephew of Lilias Rider Haggard, who rediscovered the lost diary and presented it to Bungay Museum.

Christopher Reeve for his encouragement and additional notes on the domestic section. Also for his explanation of the 1835 cartoons and the Church Rates Prosecution.

Paul Roe for having found the cartoons in Norwich many years ago and donated them to the museum before we realised their significance. He has drawn the views of Bridge House, Waveney House and Scott's "Ruined Tower".

John Meade for the portrait of his great grandfather, General Robert Meade of Earsham Hall, friend of J.B.S.

Col. Henry Smith of Ellingham Hall for information on his ancestor, 'Tiger Smith', and the 1852 painting of Ellingham Hall.

Carol Skoulding for the portrait of J.B.S. as a child. She also has the oil painting of his father, John Scott, illustrated in the first volume of *An Englishman at Home & Abroad.*

Sean Leahy for his photographic work for the illustrations.

My thanks are also due to the Bungay Society, the Bungay Museum Trustees, and several individual sponsors who have contributed to the cost of publication.

Editorial Note

Notes and commentary, printed in italics and incorporated in the text, remain as originally inserted by Ethel Mann. Those in the foreign sections were contributed by a certain P.W.Walsh who has disappeared without trace. They are so useful however that it seemed best to leave then unaltered. Additional notes incorporated in the text have been added by the present editor.

Bungay,   Hugh Cane
Suffolk
March 1996

PART ONE

1829-1839 Ten Years at Waveney House

At the time these Diaries were written the Scott family were living in Bungay. J. B. Scott, lately returned from a tour on the continent, was at Waveney House, the home of his late uncle Samuel Scott who died in 1825. The widow and her unmarried daughter Charlotte had settled themselves in the old Bridge House, and its former occupier, John Scott the elder, was at Outney Cottage.

Charlotte, now aged twenty-five, was a great invalid suffering from spinal trouble with loss of power in the lower limbs. She had been visited by Sir Astley Cooper[1] on the advice of her medical attendant, Dr. Crowfoot of Beccles[2], in February 1828 but was no better, and this year Dr. Charles Clarke was consulted. He gave his opinion that her complaint probably arose from excess horse exercise. "I should be a rash and foolish man" he added, "to say she will certainly get well, but were it a subject to bet on, I should bet she will do so".

Some years previously she had had a bad accident. A horse sent on trial had thrown her, and her old uncle and guardian, John Scott, Senr. had ordered it to be returned to the dealer the following day. This did not please her and being determined to try it again she gave orders to her groom to have it saddled and ready for her very early the next morning before anyone was about. She was thrown a second time and was injured for life.

This was not known to her family until some time later and up to the time of Dr. Clarke's visit and after, they appear to have been quite ignorant of the cause of her ill health.

1829

January 5. Applications for my late gardener's place, but I do not care for the men I have interviewed today. One asks £20 per annum board and lodging and the other 15/- per week without either. Finally when William Baker, brother to my servant James, who died last week, offers himself as his successor, I approve and agree to give him 15/- per week, a cottage rent free and terms for his fuel.

Three days later Elizabeth Reid comes as cook. Wages ten

guineas in quarterly payments to be made up to £12 a year, tea, sugar and washing allowed, which is what she asks.

January 6.   My worthy friend Robert Stone of Bedingham Hall dies in bed early this morning, and without any previous attack of his usual complaint, the gout.   He was up and pretty well yesterday, receiving his tenants rents.
       He is the last of the old botanists in this neighbourhood - Woodward, Sir James Smith[3] and Ashby having predeceased him. He was benevolent and extremely interested in natural history.   His friend Sir James established the Linnaen Society and was its first President.

January 9.   Attend the annual meeting of the Dispensary. Dine at Franklins with Howes, Betts and others and thence to General Meade's[4] at 8. Theatricals till 12, dance till 2 and then supper and dance again till 6 in the morning.

January 12.   Mrs Penrice, who died at Yarmouth on the 5th, buried at Redenhall this afternoon. The procession passed through Bungay at 2$\frac{1}{2}$ and consisted of the hearse drawn by four horses, two mourning coaches and four, one carriage and four (the Fountains) and eleven others.

January 15.   Mrs Padden, widow of Thomas Padden who was perpetual curate of St. Mary's Bungay in 1767, dies of an apoplectic stroke in the 85th year of her age. Mrs Willoughby Rackham is her daughter.
       Until the end of this month, Scott is constantly engaged with the many festivities in the neighbourhood which took place at this time of the year. Also he is busy making calls on his friends and acquaintances, canvassing for votes for the Athenaeum.

January 27.   Walk to Flixton and call on Alexander Adair[5], now in his 90th year, full of life and anecdote, breakfasting at 12. Later a party of young people to dine with me and at 8$\frac{1}{2}$ we all go to a ball at Beccles.

February 3. London. Having brought up my canvassing letters for election to the Athenaeum from Norfolk, Suffolk and Cambridge, set about delivering them. First hear from the Hon. John Shore[6] of the Catholic Emancipation Bill to be proposed by Wellington and Peel[7] as Ministers. This to my great joy. In the evening to the opera with George and Lady Holland[8]. Peel unpopular.

February 5. The King is recommending Catholic Emancipation!!!

February 9. Am balloted for at the Athenaeum. 224 voted for me: 6 against. The largest majority ever obtained in the society. 199 was the maximum previously gained. Dine at the U.U.C. and wait till Capt. Cook comes to inform me thereof. The same evening were elected General Grant and Macpherson Grant (Embassy at Turin) Dr. Mayo, Mangler, R.N., and Mr. Courtney, son of the President of the Board of Trade.

February 13. With Charles Roberts (cousin and deputy Keeper of the Tower) Henry Sharp and Woods Jun. to the Royal Institution to hear Faraday's[9] lecture on 'Action of Molecules of all kinds in water' and the following evening dine with Professor Phillips, F.R.S.[10], the distinguished chemist who first introduced Faraday to the Institution.

February 20. Returned home yesterday. Call at the Forsters, Chambers of Hedenham, Sandby, Cooper, Elswood and the Sucklings. General conversation - a running fight on the Catholic question.

March 5. This evening Mr. Peel introduced into the House of Commons, in a speech lasting four and a half hours, the measure for admitting Catholics to equal civil rights with Protestants.
Gower of Flixton calls to ask me if I will take the apprentice allotted to me or pay the fine of £10.

By the Poor Relief Act of 1601 Overseers of the poor were employed with the consent of the Justices, to put out poor children as apprentices where they shall be convenient. From the disinclination to receive such apprentices, it became necessary in 1696 to make the reception compulsory or pay a fine. This order was not abolished until 1884.

March 11. Ipswich. By Star coach where I examine Whiting's plan for Sir Edward Kerrison's[11] house at Oakley. Wilkenson, Rector of Holbrook *(his schoolfellow and lifelong friend)* meets me and we proceed to Woolverston, where we dine with Charles Berners and his brother, the Archdeacon, Ralph Berners, Cooke, and Campbell and Dr. Forster of Shotley. We discuss the Catholic Bill with congratulations. Excellent cooking and wines.

The next two days are occupied in helping Wilkenson with his house and grounds. They cut down trees, move shrubs and lay out plans for the garden, also arrange for the alteration of a large barn into a stable, coach and brew house.

April 15. To Mr. Fitzgerald's at Wherstead Lodge (father of the poet). See his paintings. From thence to Ipswich where I meet Charles Roberts. We stop two nights here and dine the first evening with Admiral Page and meet Mrs Cockle, Mrs Rope and Mr. Baum.

April 17. Good Friday. "Hot Cross Buns, one a penny two a penny, Hot Cross Buns" is called in the streets from 5 to 9 a.m. After breakfasting at the White Horse, Admiral Page arrives and brings some of his Egyptian curios, amongst them a French Almanac published in Cairo, with the trial of Kleber's assassination in it.

Kleber was a celebrated French general who went to Egypt with Napoleon and was assassinated by an Arab in 1800.

Page then takes us to see a carved room at the Tankard public house which formed part of the ancient residence of Anthony Wingfield in Henry VIII's time. Attend the service at St. Mary's Tower, where is a magnificent organ. Robert Cobbold preaches and afterwards we leave for Bungay, arriving at 6 o'clock.

April 18. Charles Roberts stays with me and in the evening our cousin, Edmund Barber comes from Burnham via Norwich where he saw three men hanged this morning for sheep stealing.

The next few days are spent in seeing friends and on the 23rd to Lowestoft and examine the steam engines, dredging machines and excavations of the Norwich and Lowestoft canal which was begun in 1827.

April 23. Meet Francis Cunningham and J. Wegland. The Catholic Bill becomes law.

April 25. Yarmouth. Walk to the Monument before breakfast. Later look at the church and the new Chain Bridge over the Bure, built by J. S. Scoles at the expense of Robert Cory and costing £4000. It was opened the day before yesterday. Meet Scoles himself on the bridge. After calling on the Dawson Turners and Mrs Fisher, Sen. we leave for Bungay and Charles returns to London the following day.

May 12. Tiverton. Arrive here this day at 12 o'clock by coach from Exeter having been invited to the marriage of my god-daughter, Anne Barne. John Barne meets me and conducts me to his mother and we walk to New Place, overtaking Mr. Barne, Sen. on our way. Mrs Barne scarcely looks a day older than when we parted in 1810, figure just as good but her husband is grey-headed and lame with rheumatism. I was introduced in succession to the whole family. Catherine, Mary, Elizabeth, Anne, Fanny and Charles, who is a clergyman, and to Henry. Much pleased with them all and in three hours we feel as if we had known each other for years. Dine at 2½ and afterwards was introduced to the bridegroom to be, Frederick Owen Patch. In the evening my interesting godchild walks with me in the grounds of Worth House and back to Exeter. This was one of the evenings of my life that will never be forgotten.

May 13. After breakfasting at 8½, Anne in an eel-blue dress with a white hat and feathers, extremely becoming and looking most lovely and interesting, accompanied by her father, Margaret Osmand and Elizabeth Barne leave New Place for the church in the first carriage, Frederick Owen Patch, John and Ellen Barne in the second and Mrs Barne, Catherine, Fanny and myself in the third. Charles, Henry and Mr. James meet us there, Charles performing the ceremony admirably. Mr. and Mrs. Paton, Mr. and Mrs Wood, Capt. and Miss Baker join us at breakfast. There were a thousand people in the churchyard and 2000 more lined the streets, they behaved decorously and showed much interest and respect for the house of Barne. At 10½ the bride and bridegroom left for Bath. Sixty friends of Mrs Barne called from 12 to 4 to congratulate her and eat cake and drink wine. Charles and I walk to Mr. Raxor's garden and at 4 o'clock join the corporation at dinner. I was almost overpowered by the events of the day before I went there, and the heat, wine, and exhilaration and noise did the rest. At 9 p.m. Osmand and John Barne led me home! How I joined the ball at New Place, danced with Catherine a quadrille and with Ellen a country dance steadily and sang "Heigh Ho" most ludicrously with Margaret Osmand, I know not.

May 17. Sunday. Too unwell to dine or go to church. Lie on the sofa alone. Margaret comes in and taunts me with "Heigh Ho" and observes that the sham pain is being succeeded by real pain. At 5 o'clock accompany Catherine to Chettiscombe, 2½ miles away to take tea with Mrs Barne's father who is 84 and with Capt. and Miss Ellen Barne.

May 18.   Mrs Barne and a large party of us drive to Broad Clyst to see the excellent horticultural gardens and nurseries belonging to Mr. Veitch. Thence to Sir J. Acland's. In the evening to the theatre and see S. Blitz, an excellent conjuror.

May 19.   Call on the Dunsford's Sen., and Jun., and on Mrs Woods who receives congratulations from her friends on her nephew's marriage. Examine the church and an illuminated M.S. of Litanies made by a monk in 1738. Capt. la Roche and Charles Barne dine with us. I am leaving Tiverton tomorrow.

Bungay

June 24.   John Bedingfield[12] of Ditchingham married to the Hon. Mary Henniker, daughter of Lord Henniker of Shoreham.

June 26.   Died at Ringsfield, the Rev. Gunton Postle, Rector of that parish, and in the adjoining village of Barsham, Samuel Lillingstone, aged 72, at the house of his son, the Rev. J. Lillingstone.

July 20.   Drive William Mann[13] to St. Olaves from 8 to 10 a.m. Meet there J. J. Bedingfield and his son James, Recorder Alderson and his son Robert, Cooper, Sandby Jun., Mr. Mann and Richard. Embark on Mann's boat 'Fly' and breakfast on board. Sail to Breydon and to Yarmouth Water Frolics. Plowman of Oulton in his boat 'Maria' beats Col. Harvey's August and three others. A tremendous thunder storm comes on with torrents of rain. Dine under Burgh Castle. Much mirth all day. Arrive at Yarmouth at 7 p.m. and land in Mr. Preston's garden whence we see the boat race and Mrs Mann gives us coffee on board at 91/2. The Misses Bacon etc., join us. I sleep at the Crown and Anchor and leave next morning for Bungay with William Mann who breakfasts there with me.

August 13. Norwich. To the Cathedral where were assembled 2000 children who had been educated at the Norwich Charity Schools. The singing of the Anthem, Te Deum and Psalms was very fine.

September 17.   Samuel and I to Lowestoft. We examine the excavations and work at the new harbour and talk with engineer Cubitt who shows us his model of the gates acting both ways. Simple and beautiful.
This day Edward Kerrich, late of Harleston, married to Mary Evelyn

Susan, second daughter of the late Richard Fuller, of the Rockery, Dorking.

September 23. The venerable pastor[14] of the Independent House, Bungay, dies aged 84. A truly humble, pious Christian. He was born and educated at Manchester but had spent the last fifty-seven years of his life in Bungay. During his time here he was forty-two years regular minister and fifteen years occasional preacher to the Independent Dissenters.

September 24. Charles Childs[15] called to show me the edition of Ainsworth's Dictionary which his firm have just finished printing in Bungay.

September 30. At 12 leave Bungay and join Sir Thomas[16] and the Rev. R. D. Gooch and accompany them to Southwold where we hear that Henry Gooch had expired at 2 o'clock this morning. For three weeks he had eaten nothing solid and had lived entirely on rum and milk. Previously one bottle of brandy and one of gin had been his daily allowance.
He was 51 years of age, kind and humane in disposition and of very retentive memory particularly for poetry, especially Horace, Shakespeare and Byron. Want of prudence was his stumbling-block.

October 16. Meet the Committee at the Theatre where it has been decided to hold the dinner for J. J. Bedingfield. R. Mann appointed President. Butcher[17] and Bewicke, Vice-presidents. Tickets placed for seventy-nine guests. Dinner on the table at 5 o'clock. An excellent farewell speech was given from J. J. Bedingfield and Lord Neville, R. Butcher and others address the meeting which lasts till midnight. The dinner was given on the retirement of John James Bedingfield from his Magisterial capacity and for the many services he had rendered to the town and neighbourhood.

November 2. This day at Richmond, aged 25, Hannah, wife of the Rev. Gilbert and eldest daughter of Richard Mann of Bungay, dies. She had only been ill a few days and was going on tolerably well when, in consequence of a fit of coughing, she broke a blood vessel and died immediately. E. B. Frere calls to tell me of her death.

November 24. R. Mann breakfasts with me and talks of his daughter's death and of his plan for pulling down the house used for St. Mary's parsonage and adding the ground to the churchyard. Also of mine for double duty in both churches. In the evening a tremendous storm and much damage done at sea. Wind north-west and afterwards a heavy fall of snow. The East window of St. Mary's and the one at the Catholic Church blown in.

November 29. The Rev. Thomas Sworde preaches his farewell sermon. An extremely beautiful one from Acts XX, verse 25. "Ye all, among whom I have gone preaching the Kingdom of God, shall see my face no more". It excites deep feeling and regret.

November 30. John Bedingfield and his wife arrive at Ditchingham.

December 1. Procure a holiday for the school boys, it being the Town Reckoning Day[18]. Accounts till 2½ and then the Town Meeting, when I lay before our townsmen the simplification of their accounts. For this and my donation to balance them I am unanimously thanked.

December 3. At 4 p.m. go to H. Wilson's of Kirby to dine. Meet Miss Upcher, Miss Sandby and the two Miss Bacons and attend the three last to Beccles Theatre where *Black Eyed Susan and Master's Revival* were performed for the benefit of David Fisher[19]. Much pleased with the performance and delighted with the Miss Bacons.

December 4. John Cobb, the new vicar of Bungay St. Mary, does duty for the first time. Several of the boys from Barkway's school come and dine with me after the service and later we walk to Fries Hill, Mettingham from whence we see the sea.

December 14. Cambridge. Arrived here yesterday. Inspect the rival plans for a new Museum Library with Cockrell, Williams and Rickman. Call on the Master of Emmanuel and dine at Corpus Hall with Shelford. Prizes distributed. Much talk with Master Lamb and Professor Henslow.

December 16. With Miss Forster and Professor Henslow by coach to London, having laughed at the latter's jokes all the way. Evening to Covent Garden to hear Fanny Kemble in *Belvedera*. My pocket picked at the Pit entrance of a purse containing £36.10.

1830

January 1. Receive from Father as a New Year's gift, the portrait of Gregory Clarke's dog 'Dragon' painted by Bardwell [20] of Bungay in 1730. Clarke was a tanner and lived in the old house in

Bridge Street where Mr. Mann now lives. He was the father of Mrs Manning, whose daughter married J. J. Woodward[21] of Ditchingham Lodge, Norfolk. In 1801 the Woodwards left the neighbourhood and went to Walcott Hall, Diss, when Mrs Woodward presented the picture to my father.

Bardwell was a well-known local artist in the early part of the 18th century. Several of his portraits of the Suckling family are in the Oxford Museum besides others in St. Andrews Hall, Norwich and in various collections in East Anglia.

January 2.　　Since the beginning of November I have been trying to evolve a plan for effecting double duty in both our churches and today sent out a printed address to Richard Mann and Kingsbury, Churchwardens of St. Mary's and to others in the parish.

January 10.　　Archdeacon Glover[22] preaches morning and evening in favour of my address and the next day he calls with Messrs. Cobb and Mann to talk about the scheme, wherein he thinks raising the money and the interchange of ministers form difficulties.

January 12.　　Deep snow. To an evening party at The Grove where Mrs Mercer at the piano, David Fisher and William Mann at the violin, Roland Wilson at the hautboy and others discourse most eloquent music of Mozart, Beethoven, Weber etc. Mrs David Fisher sings.

The Fishers were professionals and the proprietors of several theatres in Norfolk and Suffolk.

January 13.　　Snow continues to fall. The mail arrives at 12 noon instead of 9 a.m. by chaise. The star coach comes in at 11 a.m. with six horses and is six hours late. Neither the Halesworth nor the Norwich coaches were able to reach Bungay. Walk to Denton with Robert Mann and in the evening go to the theatre. Frost and snow continue.

February 4.　　The Suffolk County meeting at Ipswich to petition Parliament relative to the national distress. I, to the Tuns, Bungay to meet Messrs. Kingsbury[23], Butcher, Cobb and Bewicke as a committee for the distribution of coals and flour to the poor. The subscription was £95 and by the 1st of March all was spent but £1.19.

1830]

February 6.   Charles Ray, surgeon in the East India Company's service dies at Manningtree, aged 39. Amiable and much loved. He was formerly apprenticed to Launcelot Davy of Bungay.
In the evening to Norwich to hear William Cobbett[24] lecture for 2½ hours on the state of the nation. The chief cause assigned is the diminution of currency. On the 13th he gives a second lecture when he suggests that the remedy for the present state of the country is to take ten million of church property per annum for the expenses of the Government and the reduction of the National Debt. On the 16th Cobbett comes to Bungay and lectures at the New Theatre.

April 12.   This was the last day on which King George went out of his apartment alive. This night he became very ill and continued so until his death on the 26th June.

May 5.   Drive to Shadingfield Hall from 6 to 7½ and spend the whole day in cutting and pruning trees, forming walks and laying out the grounds. Sleep there and drive back the next morning.

Thomas Scott, his cousin had owned the Old Hall here. About 1806 it was taken down and a modern house built near the original site by T. C. Scott his son, who also inherited an estate at South Cove from his father. There is a good drawing of the Old Hall in Suckling's History of Suffolk.

May 20. Whitsunday. Prayers for the King who is suffering much pain and has been in great danger all this past week.

June 9.   The Swing Bridge near the sea at Lowestoft Navigation Works opened.

June 11.   Finish scheduling the 'Town Writings' which I deposit in good order and with the schedule in St. Mary's vestry in the presence of Dyball[25] and R. Mann, Churchwardens. Leave Bungay for London.

June 13.   To St. James Palace to see the bulletin which was better. To the Athenaeum New House and canvass for the one hundred members and on the 21st with Sedgwick, Peacock, Coddington and others endeavour to select the most worthy one hundred out of eight hundred candidates for admission. Afterwards with Mrs. Phillips (wife of the artist) and his sisters to Lambeth Palace, now being rebuilt by Blore[26] in the Gothic style.

June 26. Before leaving my rooms this morning was informed of the death of George IV. The King died at Windsor Castle at 1/4 past 3 this morning after a severe illness of 77 days and a reign of ten years, four months and twenty-eight days. His complaint dropsy, accumulation of fat round the heart and a partial ossification of the heart itself. He was in his 68th year. His brother William Henry succeeds to the throne by the title of William IV.

Breakfast at the U.U.C., all shops and houses partially closed. Bells tolling in every part of the metropolis. People crowding and talking in the streets, looking unsettled and enquiring about the past and future. Wait long in St. James Court-yard seeing Privy Councillors, Peers and City Authorities go to the Palace to proclaim the King and take oaths to him.

June 27. Sunday. Read memorials of the late and present King in various newspapers. At 2 p.m. go with the Phillips' to view Soames curious house and museum in Lincoln's Inn Fields where we stay till 5 o'clock.

These were afterwards bequeathed to the Nation.

June 28. From the balcony of the Athenaeum view the procession of Guards and Heralds proclaiming William IV. At 3 o'clock meet the Phillips' at the gate of Buckingham Palace, which with its gardens, we see entirely in two hours with a permit from Pennethorne, Nash's nephew. Great skill is shown in the execution of the details and much taste in the design of some of them. The general design is not convenient or harmonious. The cost in details must be immense and without proportionate effect. The simple parquet flooring of the Picture Gallery cost 30/- per foot; its dimensions are 165 feet by 30 ft. It contains 4950 square feet and cost £7425!

July 1. With Thomas Phillips, the antiquary, examine his historical MSS relating to Bungay and Wangford, and on the 3rd see Gage who offers to copy from his notes any relative to the same.

At this time Scott was making enquiries concerning the history of Bungay and the Hundred of Wangford generally. These, with many other notes which he collected, he gave to Alfred Suckling for his History of Suffolk which was published in 1846.

July 15. All shops closed and no work done after 11 o'clock.

At 11 a.m. Prayers but no sermon at St. Mary's. I drive to the Freres and then call on Captain Sutton. The Rev. Charles Barlee of Wrentham dies this evening after a short illness. He became unconscious while on horseback at Pakefield yesterday evening.

August 1. This month there was some excitement about the Suffolk Election. The result was declared on the 11th. Sir H. Bunbury 1057 votes C. Tyrell 1007 and Sir T. S. Gooch 626. The two former elected.

August 7. At 3 o'clock set out with a party of friends for Wherstead Lodge the residence of Mr. Fitzgerald M.P. where 170 people assemble at a gay and splendid fete. Promenading in the gardens and a dinner off cold viands in a marquee and in the dining room. Dancing in the drawing room and fireworks in the evening.

August 21. Drive to T. C. Brettingham's new house and estate at Brockdish and spend the day there with him, his wife and Mrs Allsopp.

September 6. Robert Cobb breakfasts with me and we go by Star Coach to Ipswich. Explore Fonnereau's Park, St. Clements and St. Helens. Then drive in Wilkenson's gig to Holbrook where we stay with him. Find the grounds much improved, they are really beautiful. Dine at Archdeacon Berner's with Mr. and Mrs Western, Messrs. Jarrett, R. Berners, Croft etc.

September 27. The Rev. Samuel Reeve dies aged 45, son of Thomas Reeve, formerly Master of Bungay Grammar School.

October 6. To Halesworth and fix at Mrs Crabtree. Dine there with Mr. and Mrs Meadows, White and Miss Revans who is staying here and Dr. Whately[27] (afterwards Archbishop of Dublin). At 7 o'clock we all go to church and the latter lectures on the Catechism. Afterwards have a long talk with him on political economy.

October 7. Edward Holmes joins us at breakfast and at 11 to church on the occasion of the opening of the newly built National School at Halesworth when Dr. Whately preaches an admirable sermon.

October 9. George Suckling, eldest son of the late Horace Suckling of Barsham, dies this evening in his 29th year.

October 15. To a ball at Bury. Five hundred present, amongst them were Wilkenson, Ireland and his wife, Bennet and his daughters. Rust and daughters, Gooch, Shaws etc., I dance with Miss Jones (Mrs Shaw's sister) the Fitzgeralds etc. The belles were Miss Catherine Godfrey and Mrs Purvis, daughter-in-law of the Speaker, Manners Sutton. Ball over at 3 a.m.

November 13. At 6 o'clock this evening a stack was wilfully set on fire on the premises of Mr. Lamming. Eight stacks, a barn and a stable were consumed. The owner of the property is J. Farr.

November 24. Drive to Brooke from 12 to 1 to see Mr. and Mrs Holmes in their new house. The former very weak and ill from partial paralysis. Sit with him in his own comfortable study for an hour and then he took me all over the house and seemed the better for it.
At this time there are melancholy accounts of fires and violence in the south of England. The universal topic of conversation is the insubordinate and democratic state of the poor - in the south and east we are almost in the horrors of civil war. In consequence of the many alarming fires in divers parts of the kingdom the King's Proclamation offers £50 for the capture of rioters and £500 for the conviction of incendiaries and orders are issued by the Secretary of State for swearing in of Special Constables.

November 30. Magistrates Sutton, Garden, Bedingfield and others sworn in as Special Constables and on the 3rd of December we are called out.

December 7. Town Reckoning dinner at the King's Head. Forty-two present. William Mann the incoming Town Reeve and Pearse Walker the out-going. I speak of the state of the country and of the necessity of improving the condition of the poor and my belief that all will come forward and unite in the protection of lives and property, if unfortunately it should be required. Much cheered. Separate at 12. The new Town Reeve and I patrol till near 1 o'clock.

December 11. A debate in the House of Lords on the distress of the country.

1831

January 1. Charlotte walks with me through Lincoln's garden at the back of Bridge House to Outney Cottage to wish father a Happy

New Year. The first time for four years that she has been so far. God be praised!

Here follow daily accounts of dinners and other entertainments usual at this season.

January 14. At 10 attend a Dispensary meeting to discuss the establishment of bed and nurse for the town. After a consultation thereon it was arranged to consider the question and a decision to be made one month from the present date.

It was more than fifty years later, in 1887, that the Bungay Nursing Institute was founded from the interest of £3000 left by Samuel Scott, his cousin. This provided a nurse to attend upon the sick poor of both parishes at their own homes.

February 8. A riot at Shipmeadow House. The Special Constables were called out. To the Tuns rooms where the magistrates, Garden, Sutton and J. J. Bedingfield convict five of the men who had assaulted the Governor. They were sent to Beccles jail and tread-mill for three weeks.

March 11. The first plan for reforming Parliament introduced by Lord John Russell.[28]
I am much interested just now in hearing of Mr. Tower, who has been staying with the Forsters, being cured of numbness in his arm by strychnine and am anxious to discover if the treatment may be of any benefit to my cousin Charlotte. Meade has whooping cough.

April 3. Charlotte goes to church for the first time since her illness and receives the Sacrament as do Samuel, Charles Roberts and myself. In the afternoon, after the service Charles, Berwicke and I walk round by St. John's and St. Margaret's hills. The former has been lowered six or seven feet, thus furnishing work for the unemployed.

April 4. Call on Sandby and his bride. Then to Brooke Hall where John shows us his trees he has transplanted and the new road and explains his plan for a piece of water. Mr. Holmes (his father) sees us for half an hour, looking like death. Return home to dinner at 6.

April 6. Very busy yesterday and today, placing garlands and ornaments in the Assembly Rooms for a supper party at the Tuns,

with William Mann, Charles Roberts and Cobb. Charlotte goes to see the preparations.
After dining at Samuel's go again to the rooms at 6½. Receive 96 friends there to tea, coffee, ball and standing supper. All seem pleased. Dance till 3 o'clock.

April 9.   Nichols the incendiary executed at Norwich.

April 29. The Rev. John Holmes of Gaudy Hall dies this day age 55.

April 30.   Dine at my own house, the first time since the 7th on account of my housekeeper's illness. From Leman's and Musket's room at the King's Head see a mob of boys insult and pelt the passengers on the Star coach. Is this Barbary or England?

June 3.   London. With Shelford to Paganini's first concert at the Opera House. Surprised and delighted beyond measure, as was everyone else. The extraordinary skill and the charm of his execution, together with his mysterious personality excite the most wonderful sensations.

June 4.   Evening to the opera and after the first act to Phillips RA and meet Hallam[29] the historian, Professor Brande[30] and Marston the orientalist.

June 5.   Leave London for Tiverton where I am met by F. O. Patch who escorts me to his house. Find dear Ann in good health and very pretty.
Soon off to New Place where I meet Mrs Barne and the girls and later John Barne.   Charles is at Exmouth, Henry at Oxford and George in London.
During my stay at Tiverton meet many of the Barne's friends and on the 21st ride to Cadbury Castle, the romantic Roman fortress anciently called Camelot, where King Arthur held his court.   From this point is a splendid view of Exeter, Wellington and the surrounding country. Leave tomorrow for Scotland where I intend to remain until the middle of August.

The first entry of any interest on Scott's return is his visit to William Kirby[31] the entomologist. Kirby was a member of a well-known Suffolk family, his uncle being Joshua Kirby, friend of Gainsborough, Hogarth etc., and publisher of various architectural drawings. His grandfather (1690-1753) was author of the "Suffolk Traveller".

17

September 19. Leave by 'Star' at 7½ for Barham Rectory, which place I reach at 12 o'clock by invitation of the Rev. William Kirby who shows me his collection of insects. It is his birthday and he is 72. Lady Middleton, Countess Brownlow, Lady Cust and others come to see him. He takes us to inspect the improvements at Barham Church. In the afternoon Wilkenson arrives at 4½ to dine with the family party. Fourteen of us in all. Return to Holbrook with Wilkenson where I stop the night.

September 20. Inspect the improvements in his house and grounds. Archdeacon Berners drives me to his new parsonage at Arwarton and I dine with him at 6½. Charles, Hugh and the Rev. Ralph Berners and his bride are there. The latter a daughter of Colonel Cuyler.

September 21. Much rain. At 5½ Wilkenson drives me to Kesgrave Hall, Mr. Shaw's place. We dine here, a party of eighteen. Mr. and Mrs. St. George, Mrs. Phillips and her daughters, the Woods, Clarksons, the Rev. S. Crofts and others. Singing in the evening of Scottish, English and Italian songs. Wilkenson and I walk to Miss Capper's house at Martlesham and sleep there. Explore Miss Capper's house and grounds and then to breakfast at Kesgrave. Shaw shows us his gardens and we plan a new approach to the house. He with the rest of his party return with us to Holbrook where they look over the gardens, the house and the Infants School. All dine at the Rectory after a most enjoyable day.

Bungay

October 8. At ½ past 6 this morning the Lords reject the Reform Bill by a majority of 41. Against, 199. For, 158. The news reaches Bungay on Sunday morning the 10th. The bells commence ringing on account of rejection and I, to prevent a riot, go to the belfry and stop them.

October 12. Mr. Holder, formerly organist at Bungay, calls to see father. He has now an income of £2000 a year.

October 27. Begin to build the summerhouse in my garden on the banks of the Waveney and adjoining the Bath House.

This Bath House was built after the same plan as that by the river on the Common and had a supply of hot water as well as cold. The cold bath was in the open on a level with and supplied by the river.

The hot one in an adjacent building was heated by what was then considered a very up-to-date method.

November 9. Admiral Sutton sells Ditchingham Lodge to Captain Travers for £2750, fixtures included and 40 acres of land.

November 14. Hannah Butcher goes to stay with Mrs Sutton who is in a great fidget and the Admiral half off his head at having sold his home.

After remaining there two days she returns to Charlotte Scott.
Miss Butcher was born at St. Margarets Ilketshall, near Bungay, and was related to the Butchers of The Grove[32]. She seems to have been an extraordinarily kind woman and always at the call of her friends whenever they were in difficulties. In 1815 John Scott, the elder was greatly attached to her but determined not to make a second marriage unless a debt owing to him of some £33,000 was paid off, fearing he would be unable to provide adequately for his son and possibly a second family. Later the debtors were declared bankrupt and his losses were so great that he gave up all idea of marrying again, although I find from the diaries that his property was estimated at £50,000 at the close of 1817.
Miss Butcher, however, continued a firm friend to the family and on the death of Samuel Scott, a younger brother of John, she appears to have made her home with the widow and her children who were devoted to her. She died the 23rd November 1861, aged 83.

December 2. Call on Admiral Sutton and find him very low and agitated. This was the last time I saw him. From now on he became decidedly worse and Miss Butcher returned to the Lodge to be with Mrs Sutton.

December 25. Christmas Day. Cold, frosty and fine. To Trinity Church. John Sutton comes to see me with bad news of the Admiral who went to London on the 17th with Mrs Sutton, an attendant and two servants.

December 26. Dine at General Meade's with Lady Cremorne, her husband and sons, the Dallings, Sandby's etc. 'Coach' after tea and then dancing until 1 o'clock.

December 28. After breakfast drive to Chester's at Denton and go on with him to shoot at Longwood, Topcroft.
J. Bedingfield, Capt. Dalling and Meade join us. A fine day and

pleasant. Dine at Chester's at 6 and home at 1 1/2.

December 31. Mr. Rivers Drake of Earsham Park returning from Norwich this evening was stopped at Hedenham by two footpads and robbed of his watch. The same evening a cottage at Bergh Apton was burnt to the ground.

1832

January 1. Congratulations to father and my cousins. To St. Mary's Church. All dine with me including Miss Butcher. Much talk of last night's robbery and others.

January 2. Congratulatory visits to friends. Dine at General Meade's; music, piano and harp by Miss Schutz and then dancing till 1 1/2.

January 6. Evening, to dine at Earsham Hall. All the usual party. Being Twelfth Night, dress in character. Waltz and then romping Italian Opera, Masquerades etc., till 2 1/2. Whilst I was away Wilkenson arrived at my house by coach and spent the evening with the Kingsburys.

January 8. Sunday. Wilkenson to Trinity Church where he preaches an admirable sermon on 'the power of faith'. Miss Butcher and the Scott party dine with us. *P.M.* to St. Mary's. Robert Cobb preaches his Peace sermon and it is a really good one but his manner prevents Wilkenson from attending to a word of it. We walk to Earsham and tea at the Kingsburys. The three little Margitsons there - very clever, merry girls. Some talk of establishing a Girls School at Bungay.

January 11. At Brooke. Wilkenson and I arrived here last evening and found Mr. Holmes better. Look at his new kitchen garden and Sayer's farm and the plantation. John is worried about poachers. At dinner meet the Chambers, Fellowes and his two sons, the Margitsons etc.

January 16/17. Sucklings auction at Woodton. Many people attend. Books sold the second day. Purchase the Indian paper proof of Lodges Portraits for £27. They cost originally £53.10.

January 23. London. Outside an abominable bus to Woolwich. Dine with Col. Jones and meet my cousins Maria and Cholomley

Roberts for the first time. At 10 go with them to the Woolwich Artillery Ball. Five hundred there. Dance till 4 a.m.

January 24. Breakfast at 11 and then walk to the Dockyard and inspect "The Thunderer" which was launched last August in the presence of the King and Queen.

January 26. Leave London by the Ipswich "Blue Coach" with a learned and political coachman and a polite pedlar. To Holbrook to stay with Wilkenson and am astonished and pleased with his improvements since I was here last September, both in the garden and house. We spend all the next morning planning further alterations and in moving shrubs. Then to Woolverston now Archdeacon Berners' home. Dine and sleep here. Kindly received.

February 1. Family prayers before breakfast. Twenty servants present. Afterwards the Archdeacon shows me over his house and we talk of more improvements. Return to Ipswich at 12 and on to Bungay with young Charles Reeve, who is going to Barkway's school there[33]. Though late I dress and go to a Quadrille at 9 o'clock. Bruce and Fulcher stewards. Miss Day of Tuddenham was the belle. Dance with her.

February 2. Call on father at 10 to congratulate him on his 76th birthday. Then to see Charlotte and tell her of last night's ball. Miss Padden brings Miss Day to see my prints. The latter a fine girl. Dine with Garneys[34] and ten others and go to the Theatre.

February 4. Call on Miss Padden and Miss Day and escort them to the Castle. Then drive Fulcher to St. Cross where the late William Clarke had been rector since 1789 and we look at his books. Evening to the Theatre. The play bespoke by the Bachelors of Bungay. Go with the Meades, Sandby and Holmes.

February 10. Dine at General Meade's with Sandby and Cautley to keep Annie's birthday.

February 20. The Rev. Courtney Boyle Bruce receives the living of St. Cross and Homersfield from Alexander Adair.

February 21. The Rev. Thomas Holmes of Brooke Hall dies at 2 o'clock aged 72 or 3. He was the son of Thomas Holmes and Sarah, the daughter and heiress of Thomas Seaman of Brooke. Two years previously he had removed from Bungay and built the house and

21

laid out the grounds of his residence near the site of the Old Hall. He left two sons by his first wife (Charlotte Lyon) and one by his second (Margaret Tuthill) and several daughters. John succeeds to the property and is unmarried.

February 22. Mary, daughter of the late Matthias Kerrison[35] of Bungay and wife of Lieut. Gurbatt dies at Boulogne. She was formerly the wife of R. Rabett of Bramfield.

March 15. A letter from Wilkenson announcing his intended marriage to Jane, daughter of John Fitzgerald of Wherstead Lodge.

April 23. Go to the vestry meeting and advocate the petition of forty-five house-holders who ask for pews. I propose a plan for providing accommodation in our two churches for the Church of England members of the 3734 inhabitants and suggest:-

1. That in each parish, non-parishioners should vacate their pews.

2. A new arrangement of the parish of St. Mary's be effected.

3. And double duty be established in both parishes.

This well received. Richard Mann and Samuel Scott appointed Churchwardens on the express understanding that they should do all in their power to carry out these alterations. Robert Cobb offers to perform double duty if heads 1 and 2 of the above regulations be carried out. Archdeacon Glover advises the whole measure. A very large meeting, the vestry was quite full. Dine at the King's Head afterwards with the Ministers, Churchwardens etc., of St. Mary's.

April 24. To a vestry at Trinity parish. Apply, as do the other parishioners, for pews. Brettel[36] and Burtshall nominated Churchwardens. I give notice of the proceedings at St. Mary's vestry and urge the same for this parish. Evening, dine at Chesters with the Bedingfields, Mr. and Mrs. Spencer of Starston and Mrs. Umphelby newly come to Denton House, lately the Etheridges.
About 9 o'clock the same evening, Mary Ann, widow of the late Major General Kelso[37], died at her house in Bungay (Rose Hall). For ten months she had suffered from dropsy. At the last she died of complete exhaustion. She possessed wit and originality.

May 5. Cornish the sweep suffocated in Rathbone's chimney at Geldeston.

22

May 7. Lord Lyndhurst's motion for enfranchising before disfranchising carried against the ministers by a majority of forty-five in the Lords and on the 9th Earl Grey and his colleagues' resignation is accepted by William IV.

May 15. Wilkenson was to have been married this day to Miss Fitzgerald but the marriage was prevented by her being taken with the measles. Drove Stoddart[38], who is staying with me, to look at Mrs Costerton's new house at Ditchingham (Holly Hill Lodge) whence is a fine view of the sea.

May 16. Hear of Earl Grey's[39] return to the ministry. To the Norwich Horticultural meeting at the Corn Hall. A very brilliant show in flowers and visitors.

May 26. Read of the progress of the Reform Bill through the House of Peers. A melancholy exhibition of the loss of independence by the Lords. The first correct evidence of the overthrow of the constitution.

May 29. J. B. Wilkenson married to Jane, daughter of John Fitzgerald M.P. of Seaford, at Trinity Church, Marylebone, London.

June 1. Admiral Sutton dies at 9 this morning at Woodbridge, after 6 months of mental and bodily illness.

June 4. The Reform Bill passed by the House of Lords this evening after a mockery of debate.

June 8. Mr. and Mrs. Frederick Patch arrived from Tiverton to stay with me.

During their visit they are shown the principal attractions of Bungay and the neighbourhood, including Flixton Hall and Mettingham Castle. They go by chaise to Ixworth Abbey where they are met by Mrs. Cobb and John who show them the Cedar Walk, the Crypt and the rest of the house. Thence to Bury and inspect the churches and the botanical gardens, now transferred to the Abbey grounds. Scott remarks "an admirable change". Then drive to the charitable Lord Bristol's mansion and proceed to Cambridge.

June 20. *London.* The anniversary meeting of the British Institution where Lord Jamboro, Northwich and Messrs Ridley,

Colbourne, Baring Ball and self discuss Wilkins' project for a National Gallery at the Mews.

William Wilkins, 1778-1839, was a native of Norwich and an eminent architect, one of his chief buildings was the National Gallery which provoked much criticism from his contemporaries. Perhaps his most remarkable achievement was his family of thirty-two children by the same wife!

June 26.   Start by coach from Algate at a 1/4 to 6 outside. My neighbour was Mr. Quilter, the spouting yeoman who returned Tyrell for Suffolk - much argument with him.

June 27.   Bungay Reform Festival[40]. Go with father to see the dinner which was held in the principal streets. 2,480 attended at the cost of £140. A fine day and much gladness and good order. Sports and fireworks in the evening.

July 13.   The Wilkensons come to stay with me and on the 15th, Sunday to St. Mary's where Wilkenson reads and Howarth, who is staying at the Mann's, preaches admirably. At 2 o'clock Mr. Fitzgerald, the member, Miss A. Fitzgerald and the Kerrichs arrive and dine with us at 4. All to St. Mary's in the evening. The Wilkensons leave the following afternoon for Worlingham, Lord Gosfords, and I to dine with the Frere's.

August 6.   David Fisher of the Norfolk and Suffolk Company of Players dies at Dereham aged 73. His name and person are associated with my earliest theatrical amusements. He was born in 1759 and having a fine voice took to the stage as a profession, was very successful and became the proprietor of fifteen theatres.

August 16. Sunday. Yarmouth. To church in the morning and Pellow preaches; afterwards to Dawson Turner's and meet Francis Palgrave, Bernard Barton, the poet and Fitch of Ipswich, the antiquarian.

August 17.   This day at the house of her brother, Samuel Ashby[41] of Olland Street Bungay, Mrs Henly, late of Denton House dies. She was buried at Denton on the 22nd.

August 20.   The alterations at St. Mary's commenced and while they were in progress two Holy Water basins were discovered. The Church is to be entirely repewed.

October 10. Richard Reeve M.D. of Bracondale, brother-in-law of Benezet[42] by his first marriage and of Mrs Dreyer by his second, dies this day aged 64. George Sandby Junr. takes possession of the late Mrs Kelso's house in Bungay (Rose Hall).

Musical parties and many dances take place as usual at this time of the year at the Meades, Travers, Chambers and other houses in the neighbourhood.

October 16. To a gay ball and supper at the Old Hall, Hedenham, given by Major Travers. Mrs Bridgeman and Miss Rose Wadman play and the three Yelloly's and Mr. and Mrs Tom Steward sing. Capt. Eaton Travers (afterwards Rear Admiral) Dr. Cox and their wives, the Butchers, Mercers, Sandbys, Garneys, Slades, Storeys and Betts among the party. After supper dancing till 10 o'clock. All very merry.

October 18. At 7 p.m. to another party at the Travers for juveniles. Much amused watching the servants ball which took place the same night after supper. Music and jigs till 1 o'clock.

October 19. St. Mary's Church was re-opened this morning by Archdeacon Glover. In effect it is much improved and the accommodation greatly increased, also double duty is today first established in the parish of St Mary's. In the afternoon to Trinity Church where I take possession of the new pew allotted to me which was lately Mr. Kingsbury's. Am now more than half way through with my plan for double duty in both churches. Write to Benezet the vicar of Trinity praying for double duty and enclosing my letters to and from the Bishop with regard to it.
J. W. Holder, M.D., formerly organist at Bungay, dies suddenly in the street in London aged 71.

November 3. Write to the Bishop of Norwich praying for double duty at Trinity Church.

December. In the beginning of this month the deaths occurred of Gwynn Etheridge, late of Denton House, on the 4th after 24 hours illness. He was staying with his friend J. Cotton at Weybread; and on the 8th at Denton Lodge of Mrs. William Vachell, sister to Mrs Sandby.

December 17. The East Suffolk Election. Candidates Lord Henniker, R. N. Shawe and Sir Charles Broke Vere. Riots at Beccles and Sir Thomas Gooch grossly attacked and insulted. The two first were returned.

December 20. Yarmouth. Walk to the Market Place and vote for Peach and Cholmondly. The Election is being carried on with great good humour.

December 22. Daughter of Richard Mann dies of typhoid fever at their house in Bridge Street, aged 20. Her mother and brother have been seriously ill for several weeks but are better. Charlotte much distressed and does not come downstairs today. Offer my house to Mr. Mann's sons and Robert comes to me from Holbrook. The funeral is to take place on Friday the 28th.

December 31. With Robert Mann sit the old year out and the new year in but observe it not.

1833

January 1. At 12 noon to a concert at the Assembly Rooms to hear Jacobristch sing. Dine at General Meade's and dance till 1 o'clock.

January 3. Anne, the daughter of Henry Wilson of Kirby married to the Rev. J. M. Johnson of Scoulton, Norfolk.

Various meetings occupy the second week of the New Year. One for the Book Club accounts with a dinner at the King's Head afterwards takes place on the 8th, and on the 11th is an annual meeting and dinner for the Dispensary. The 17th Scott devotes the day to Town business and examines who should pave the streets and on the 21st at the Town meeting establish the non-liability of the Feoffees to repair the pavement, and an offer is made to the surveyor of £10 for that purpose. 26 for 7 against.

March 15. Bury Assizes. Arrived here last night to attend the Special Jury and go at 11 this morning to St. James church. The High Sheriff, Sir Thomas Gooch, escorts the Judges Vaughan and Holland thither. Matthews reads and Charles Gooch preaches well. At 11 1/2 to the Court where there was an overflowing attendance of Grand and Special Jurymen. Cause - Finch v Beckham for assault. It lasts from 2 till 11 p.m.

March 16. At the Nisi Prius Court at 9 o'clock. Scarlett v Steele.

Lasts till 3 p.m. then to the Crown Court. Robbery of Montague's desk at Beccles by his servant, Sam Tubby, for which he gets transportation. The following day Sunday, I spend at Thetford.

March 18.   To the Nisi Prius Court at 9. Rackham v King & Garrod, editors of the Suffolk Chronicle, which case lasts till 8 p.m. Judgement for the Plaintiff. At 8 sworn on Special Jury to try Fenton v Hurst whether a thrashing machine is determinable for rent or exemption as a necessary implement of husbandry. We finish at 11 p.m. Verdict, machine is not exempt. Leave for Bungay the following day.

March 27.   Dine at Yelloly's at Woodton Hall. Twenty-four to dinner and as many more afterwards. Dance till 2 o'clock. The next night a grand ball at the Holmes' of Brooke. Lady Suffield, the Beauchamps, E. Bacon, E. Preston, H. Berney, Meades, Irbys, Bedingfields, Sandbys etc. Home at 5 o'clock.

April 5. Good Friday. Service at Trinity Church only in the morning and at St. Mary's in the afternoon. No duty in the evening.

April 9.   The paving of the streets of Bungay commenced. The next day Archdeacon Glover and Richard Mann join me and view the piece of land voted for the new burial ground. We then walk to the Old Theatre with the idea of converting it into a school house.

April 11.   At 3 p.m. to Beccles and dine with the Portreeve, Crowfoot, and fifty-five others. Speeches and compliments. Rout at Mrs Crowfoot's afterwards.

April 16.   William Crowfoot of Beccles married to Emily Miller, daughter of Miller the publisher of Albemarle Street and niece of Mrs Stone of Bedingham. Archdeacon Berners is staying with me and in the afternoon drive him to Flixton. Evening to a lecture at the Assembly Rooms, the fourth of a series given by Dr. Warrick on Galvanism, Electricity and Magnetism, which he proves to be identical.

May 9.   Messrs. Mann, Bewicke, Butcher and Elswood meet at my house to draft up rules for the suppression of vagrancy and then we call on various inhabitants in the town and ask for their support. Afterwards see Magistrates Garden and Bedingfield at their room. The rules are approved and the next day an order is given for them to be printed by Messrs. Childs.

June 12 to 29. At this time Scott is in London where he has many engagements with his numerous friends. He goes to the exhibition of paintings of the three last Presidents - Reynolds[43], West[44], and Lawrence[45]; to the British Museum and inspects the splendid new Halls for sculpture, minerals, books etc; with Robert Southey[46], the Poet Laureate, his son and daughters to look at the M.S. of Pope's Homer; and on the 20th with Charles Stoddart to view Wilkins' model for the new National Gallery at the Woods and Forests offices.

The Sunday following with Rodwell of Ipswich to Camberwell Camden Chapel to hear Melville, whom he notes preaches on Christ's descent into Hell with close reasoning, critical erudition and impassioned eloquence. The evenings are spent at the Athenaeum or at the Opera. If the latter George Sandby is usually his companion.

August 1. Bury. To the Crown Court where I have been summoned for the first time by the Sheriff Sir Thomas Gooch, to attend the Assizes as Grand Juryman. Enquire into bills until 6 1/2 and then discharged. Dine with the Sheriff and spend a pleasant evening.

August 2. Jolly of Yaxley tried for arson and found guilty. Verdict, death. Sixty were present at the Sheriff's dinner this evening.

August 11. Miss Amelia Kettledy Johnson, the daughter of Sir Williams Johnson of Aberdeenshire, resident in Bungay for the last twenty years, dies at the house of her sister-in-law, Mrs Uvedale of Needham, Suffolk. She left Bungay only last July.

August 13. Take the Pages, who are staying with me, to Southwold where we arrive at 3 1/2; James Robinson illuminates his gardens with 2000 lamps and opens them to the public with a Dutch Fair. He enters them, drunk, to the tune of "See the Conquering Hero Comes".

August 14. Robinson borne on a triumphal chair round the town and Gunn Hill, with a Bard playing, surely he must be insane! Edward Holmes comes with a party of twenty-eight to pass the day at Garrods. I have been invited but refuse as I have the Pages with me.

August 15. Lowestoft. Drive Mrs Page and Mrs Suckling, who has lately lost her daughter (Mrs Flavell) to Lowestoft. Go to the consecration of St. Peter's Chapel by the Bishop of Winchester. A fine service and an admirable sermon. All much impressed, £57 was collected. Then take leave of the Pages. They dine with Sir Thomas Gooch and I to the Queen's Head with Cunningham, the Bishop, Lord Arthur, Weyland, Millman, Cator, Bevan, Porcher etc. sixty-two in all. Afterwards to the Porcher's grounds at Normanston where the school children have tea, sing and are lectured by Messrs. Dallas and Carns. It was a very pretty sight with the setting sun, the tranquil lake and the gleaners and reapers processing through the trees.

August 16.   Sleep at the Crown. The Consecration of St. Peter's, Yarmouth, today to which I drive between 10 and 11 o'clock. More crowds and pomp than yesterday but less quiet and devotion. Selections from the Messiah were performed. The service lasts till 3 o'clock. Dine and stop the night with Capt. Fisher.

August 26. Bungay.   Prepare for a discussion on establishing a school in Bungay and go with Cobb and George Sandby to a meeting at St. Mary's vestry. Messrs. Kidd, Childs, Bobbit[47] and myself appointed to enquire what pecuniary assistance can be raised and what are the opinions of the inhabitants about a National or a Lancastrian School.

September 2.   A meeting at the Fleece at 10 o'clock about the education of the poor, when it is decided that a National and a British (Lancastrian) school be established. The former was essentially a Church of England school while in the latter, the Bible without note or comment, was the only religious book used.

As there was no Government legislation on the subject, public instruction was promoted by personal donations and by the British and Foreign School Society, started in 1805, and the National School Society of the Church of England in 1811. It was not until 1835 that other agencies began to influence the spread of education in this county and Bungay and Wrentham seem to have been amongst the first, if not the first places to obtain aid from the Treasury.

Sept 10/11.   Cobb, Kidd and I have been collecting for the National School and have £120 towards it. Write to Shaw, M.P. and Wigram[48], the Secretary of the National School Society for promoting the education of the poor. At a meeting a few days later Cobb and I are appointed Secretaries of the School Committee. Bewicke has now become the sole licensed curate of Trinity Parish and Kidd is canvassing for the Chaplaincy of the House of Industry.

September 14. Draw out plans for the schools and see Botwright and Nunn about estimates for them. On the 29th to London to see the Bishop of Norwich (Bathurst) now 90 at his house in 12 Bedford Street. He signs our application for aid towards the National School and asks if the Bishop of Dublin is the Incumbent of Bungay? I return by Buckingham Palace, the Guards New Barracks and Westminster Abbey. Attend the service there at 3 p.m. and am irritated by the verger but calmed down by the music and solemnity of the surroundings. See Charles Stoddart at the Naval and Military Museum of which he is Secretary; then return and dine at the University Club.

September 30. Call on the Rev. J. C. Wigram at 11. He admits the application for an Infant as well as for a National School and requires a memorial. I draw one up for the Lords of the Treasury for aid and send it to Cobb for signature. Dine with Stoddart and Capt. King and go to Drury Lane. Macready[49] acts excellently in Byron's Werner; a very interesting tragedy.

November. While in London visit several schools and amongst others one on Stoat's Circulating System, Francis Eldon's school at Vauxhall and Mrs Hart's Infants School in the City. Return to Bungay on the 13th.

November 18. Bungay. Preparations are being made for the Infant's School and a temporary room has been prepared in a house belonging to Mr. Butcher, which Bewicke, the two Miss Butchers and I open this day at 10 o'clock. Susan Barrett, our Infant School Mistress and Sarah Alden from Lowestoft, arrive at 9 o'clock, I having sent my servant for them. Nineteen children attend between the ages of 3 and 6. Draw up rules and order several articles required with the help of Miss Alden who is at school at Lowestoft. On Christmas Day a letter comes from Wigram announcing a grant from the Treasury of £181.7. for our schools.

November 22 The first night this winter of Fisher's Company performing at Bungay.

From now until the end of the year there is the usual succession of dances and dinner parties, the latter of which are often followed by the Theatre and a play "bespoke" by residents in the town and villages adjoining.

1834

January 1.   As a Director of Shipmeadow House first attend the quarterly meeting. Sandby Jun. in the Chair. Arnold returns with me and his son Charles also. They stay with me till Saturday and Hunter Rodwell joins us later.

January 2.   A very wet morning but we go out and look at the Castle. In the evening a party of ten to dinner and Stoddart arrives only in time to go with us to a ball at the Assembly Rooms. J. J. Bedingfield and I stewards. One hundred and forty present. Tea etc., and then dancing. Take my guests home to supper, returning afterwards and break up at 6 a.m.

January 4.   Breakfast at ¹/2 past 10. The Arnolds leave at 12. The Stoddarts, Rodwell and I to the Coffee Room where we meet Bedingfield, Frere and others.Walk round by Hedenham and Earsham. Evening Theatre. The play 'bespoke' by Reunion of Ladies and Gentlemen at Earsham House.

January 5.   Hunter Rodwell leaves by the "Star" coach. Stoddart and I to Trinity Church. Then look at the site for the National School and talk of the plans. Evening to St. Mary's. The first time I have been there since George Sandby preached admirably, and William Frere sings extremely well.

January 23.   To Wrentham Parsonage to stay with the Rector, Clissold. Meet there Mr. and Mrs.Bosanquet, now of Kensale. The latter plays the organ and sings. After dinner talk of Penny Clubs, the letting of land to the poor for gardens and of Animal Magnetism.

February 11.   Mrs Williams of Yarmouth, mother of Mrs E. B. Frere, buried at Ditchingham today. She was 64.

March 12.   Harvey and Hudson's Bank at Bungay robbed of about £4000 between 7 and 10 p.m.

March 17.   Alexander Adair of Flixton Hall dies this day at his house in Pall Mall aged about 91. Mrs Adair died in 1814. He succeeded to the Flixton estate in 1783 and married the same year.

March 21.   The Poor Amendment Bill, Tithe Commutation Bill, and the Church Rate Abolition Bill all introduced this week and under general discussion.

March 22.   Augusta Birch niece of Robert Butcher (The Grove) and late of Bungay, dies this evening at the house of her brother-in-law, Mr. Balfour, after about fourteen days' illness.

Thomas Charles Scott of Shadingfield Hall, after attending a meeting of Commissioners of Kessingland Level in his office of Treasurer, was thrown from his horse and severely injured in the head. I went to see him on the 19th and found him in a torpor and dangerously ill. Crowfoot had been three times during the day. Wrote to his son, Walter.

Until the 23rd Mr. Scott continues very ill and Walter does not arrive until the 24th, being in a very bad state of health himself. By the 29th both are improving although the father is still in a drowsy condition.

May 13.   The foundations of the National School laid without any ceremony. God grant the institution may produce good to thousands, injury to none.

May 29.   The Right Hon. Lord Woodhouse of Kimberley dies aged 93.

June 21.   A splendid thunderstorm. Redenhall Church steeple struck by lightning and considerably damaged.

June 24.   This afternoon the children from the Infant School, thirty-six in number, come with their teacher to sing and recite before Charlotte, Miss Butcher and Cobb (curate of St. Mary's). Afterwards they play in the garden and have tea and cakes in the kitchen.

July 1. London. Breakfast at St. George Street, Hanover Square and accompany Mr. and the two Miss Phillips to the Abbey to hear the Messiah exquisitely sung but not astonishingly performed. The King, Queen, Duke of Cumberland and Duchess of Kent with the Princess Victoria there, also Wellington, Brougham[50], Tallyrand, the Archbishops of Canterbury, York, Armagh, and everybody of note in London. A splendid sight. Dr. Hill joins our party (the traveller). Return tired and dine at the Athenaeum.

July 8.   To Eldon's school in the morning. Afternoon to a concert given by Mrs Frere from 4 to 6. Laura Tuthill, Mrs Groom, Mr. Nobell, Mrs Roche and Mrs Frere sing delightfully. The Fitzgeralds, Phillips, Mrs. Bridgman and Wilkenson were amongst the guests. Very pleasant. Walk home with Laura Tuthill and dine with Sir George (Tuthill) Mrs Holmes and Margaret. Evening to the Opera and hear of Lord Grey's resignation. On the 17th a new Ministry was formed with Lord Melbourne as Prime Minister.

August 6. Bungay.   To Shadingfield and find T. C. Scott quite recovered from the accident he had last March, but his son Walter is still in bad health and, although he looked well in the face when I arrived, he had no voice and the next day was not well enough to see me.

August 11.   George Norman Cracknell drowned in the Orwell while bathing, aged 17.

At this time Scott is very busy superintending the erection of the National School and seemed to have planned and carried out everything connected with its site, fittings etc. He had been empowered by the National School Committee to look for a Master and Mistress and went to London in July for this purpose.

September 8.   This day was opened the Infant Department of the Bungay National School in the newly built School House opposite the Drift.   One hundred and one children under 7 were admitted. The boys schoolroom and the rest of the premises are not yet finished.

September 15.   The school buildings were finished on Saturday last and opened today, Monday. Cobb, who breakfasts with me, presides at the Boys School and I at the Girls. Admit 80 boys and 42 girls. Our new Master, J. Abel, who arrived on Saturday, appears to be a great disciplinarian.
Terms for one child 2d per week; for every additional child 1d. To be paid every Monday morning. Sittings in the church for the children have already been arranged with the churchwardens.

September 20.   The Rev. Thomas Collyer[51], inducted to the living of Holy Trinity. The same day Clissold, Rector of Wrentham, comes to see our schools, dines with me and leaves in the evening.

The National School at Wrentham was also erected this year at the cost of £745.14. Of this sum £131 was granted by the Treasury and

£80 by the National School Society. Scott and Clissold had frequent meetings and consultations about the building and management of these schools.

September 29. Yarmouth. At 4 o'clock dine at the Town Hall with Major Isaac Preston and 360 others. Tea with Capt. Gwynee. At 10 to a ball at the Bath House. Dance till 2.

October 7. Dine at Dr. Yelloly's with Capt. and Mrs Loftus who are living at Whissonsett, near Fakenham. They have been living at Mr. Butcher's cottage at The Grove for the past year.

October 12. Father threw his purse containing £40.10. into the fire by mistake this morning and is much vexed thereat.

Early in December Mr. Scott, Sen. was taken very ill and Dr. Crowfoot from Beccles was sent for. He seems to have recovered for a time but never regained strength. From this date the diaries of J. B. Scott cease until October 1838.
On October 4th 1836 J. B. Scott had been dining at the Sandby's of Denton and on his return found his father was again very ill with violent sickness. Soon after he became unconscious and died the following day in his eightieth year. He was buried in the churchyard of St. Mary's on Wednesday the 10th.
It is not known why there is a four-year gap in the diary and it is unfortunate that we have no record of Scott's involvement in the prosecution of the printer, John Childs, for non-payment of Church Rates. (see Appendix). It is also regrettable that we do not know Scott's views on the Municipal Corporation Act of 1835 which abolished the Portreeve of Beccles in favour of an elected Mayor. Diary entries at that time might have solved the mystery of the survival of the Town Reeve of Bungay - an office which is now unique in the United Kingdom.

1838

October. The diaries are continued from the beginning of this month when Scott starts for Cheltenham.

October 3. From Paddington to Maidenhead by the Great Western. The passengers were complaining of the slowness of locomotion, because we were travelling only twenty-four miles an hour. At Cheltenham stay at the Queen's Hotel, a magnificent place with two hundred beds.

*From thence he goes to see his mother's relations, the Roberts of
Drybridge, near Monmouth.
At this time Henry Roberts was living in the old family house there.
He had married Margaret, daughter of Allen Jones of Hay Hill and
had five children, two of whom, William, a solicitor at Coleford and
Margaret had both married Probyns, daughter and son of the Dean
of Llandaff. The son was in the East India Company Service and
was now at home with his wife and six children.*

October 4.   In the morning to see Mrs Tom Probyn, my second
cousin, and in the afternoon to tea with the Balfours with Margaret
and Caroline Probyn.

October 6.   To Longhope to call on the Archdeacon who is
cheerful though blind and find Susan Roberts there. Then to see
Mrs and Mr. Durnester. Stop half an hour at Ross and look at the
Cross and the inscription about the Plague in 1637 which dear
father used to talk about but which I had forgotten. In front of the
tomb of John Kyrle, the man of Ross, solemnly resolve to devote
my means to the benefit of my fellow creatures much more than I
have hitherto done.
Proceed by fly to Monmouth and find the party there had not yet
finished dinner (7 p.m.). Besides Mr. and Mrs. Henry Roberts and
Eliza there are now at Drybridge Mrs William Roberts, Charles
Cholomley and Annie.

October 7. Sunday.   Look round the garden and think of my
former visits in 1811 and 1824, inspect the ancient little Chapel at
St. Thomas newly restored by Wyatt in Norman style and attend
service at St. Mary's Church. The Rev. G. Roberts is vicar and the
Church Aid Society has furnished him with a curate.
The next few days are spent in exploring the various places of
interest in the neighbourhood - Raglan Castle, Troy House and the
Forest of Dean, which latter contains 2,000 acres of woodland. A
splendid store for future navies. I never saw straighter, cleaner or
finer oaks.

October 12.   From 11 to 1 o'clock with Gee Roberts and Major
Marriott at the Monmouth Union Guardians Sitting.Thirteen
present. Proceedings and discussions very similar to our own at
Shipmeadow, except that the chairman decides too much without
putting the question to the Board. No new house here so that the
Smallpox patients are in the same room as the other sick.

October 13. Take leave of my friends at Monmouth and travel by coach along the Wye whose beauties from here to Chepstow are much greater than memory or imagination had painted them to me. The coachman offered to stop while I went inside the ruins of Tintern Abbey, a fine specimen of the second or decorated style of English architecture. It is admirably kept, green grass forming the floor and the sky the roof of this once splendid edifice. The remains of the Castle of Chepstow are amongst the most striking and picturesque in Britain. The tide at Chepstow Bridge rose about thirty-five feet during my walk but it is said to vary even to sixty feet at Spring tides.

October 14. To Newport but did not arrive in time for church as I hoped to have done. Newport contains 14000 people. Sixteen chapels and only two or three churches. 'The Church has slept too long'. It now rained and blew exceedingly but we continue our journey to Cardiff and passed by Sir Charles Morgan's enormous but ugly brick house near Newport. Many fine chestnuts, elms and oaks were in the extensive park adjoining, also some deer and a fine piece of water.

October 15. From Cardiff at 6½ a.m. into Glamorganshire, cross the Taff and then to Newbridge where I call on Edmund Scott Barber and find him and his wife and children at breakfast. Later we explore the beauties of the Rhonda Valley on foot and those of the Taff Vale with the aid of Barber's two pretty Welsh ponies. He is second in command over the works connected with the Taff Vale Railway. The bridge of Ponty Prydd was built in 1750 by Edwards, a Welsh farmer. It is a singular and picturesque specimen of art and consists of a single stone arch, 140 feet in span and 50 ft. in height and looks as light and aerial as a rainbow. The Rhonda Bridge of the railway, the centring of which is not yet removed, is a three arched skew bridge, the centre arch being 104 ft. in span. We went up the lovely fall of the Rhonda and then to the still more beautiful fall or falls of the Taff, near the light bridge which conveys water in a feeder to the canal, but the viaduct over the Daff was the great wonder of the excursion. It consists of six arches 365 feet long and on a curve of 25 chains radius. At the west end of it is a tunnel. I went with Barber to the highest point of the scaffolding of this viaduct and was agreeably pleased by the work itself and by the manner in which he exercises his power over the many workmen under his command.

October 16. Edmund drove me to Cardiff from 7.30 to 9.30 this morning. Crawshaw and his huge works to our right and the cattle Koch on our left and the railway works along the whole route furnished some of our conversation. The morning was too wet and windy to view the Marquis of Bute's new harbour and the weather was so stormy I resolved to return to Chepstow and on to Bristol by coach where I arrived at 6 o'clock and slept at the Buck Inn.

October 17. Leave Bristol by coach. A fine view of Clifton was enhanced by the morning sun. The elevated chain suspension bridge across the Avon, 630 feet long designed by Brunel, is suspended in its progress by want of funds. Only one pier is cut out but the work is expected to be resumed shortly. *(It was eventually abandoned).* Passing through Taunton I had time to look once more at the fine steeple of the Cathedral and to be pleased with the flourishing appearance of this neat town. Passing by Mr. Adair's property we proceeded to the town which gave its name to the great military hero of this age. Soon after entered Devonshire and passing through Samford Peverell reached Tiverton at 3 p.m.

After seeing Patch, establish myself at his house and Mrs Patch being at Taunton on some business of importance I walk to New Place. My dear Mrs. Barne is all kindness as she ever was; Catherine still an invalid, Elizabeth frank, good and eccentric and Fanny, my dear little playfellow when I left Exeter in 1829, is now a fascinating and elegant girl of three or four and twenty. Henry Barne is curate at Taunton and John married to Lucy Dunsford and has a little boy three months old.

October 18. My godson, John Barne Patch, was born on the 5th of March 1834 and his little dark eyed sister, Susannah Mary, commonly called 'Betty Bunch' or 'Buffy' came into this world only on the 1st July 1836. With John Barne and Mrs Patch inspect the new Union House and look at the National Schools, which are not well organised. We all dine at New Place at 4 with the exception of Barne and Patch who return from Exeter later and join us in the evening. My heart swells, as it has often done during this tour, when I think of father. All his friends and mine are delighted with his portrait[52], which I have had engraved. He was one of the best and kindest of men.

October 22. Leave Tiverton with much regret. At Taunton talk for five minutes with Henry Barne but did not mention his proposed marriage with a woman twenty years older than himself, which is distressing his family.

October 23. From 7 to 10 explore Bristol and its shipping and Clifton with its rocks and the works for its suspension bridge, 250 feet perpendicular above the Avon.

A very pleasant journey to Maidenhead on the coach box of the Regulator - fine horses and good driving, the forest of Marlborough is a pleasing mixture of oak, beech and birch on a smooth grass surface. I regretted we had only four miles drive in it. It belongs to the Marquis of Aylesbury who is in difficulties, though the rental is more than £1000 a year. His late wife's love of gambling occasioned this. At Maidenhead we entered a carriage on the railway and were whiffed the twenty-three miles to London in fifty minutes. The thumping, rumbling noise was so loud, we could not talk. In mere rapidity a railway is desirable but in every other respect is far less agreeable than travelling by the aid of our good old friend the horse. I anticipate much evil from the monopoly which is and will be created and fear we shall travel worse in the future than we do now and dearer too. At 8 o'clock establish myself at 2, Suffolk Street and tea at the University Club.

October 26. Breakfast with Charles Roberts at the Tower. Evening to the Adelphi to see the Indian dancing girls. An interesting spectacle in a national point of view but not particularly so for grace or beauty.

October 27. This evening to Covent Garden to see *The Tempest* splendidly staged but like most of Shakespeare's plays, to me, heavy in the acting. Macready a fine Prospero.

October 28. Sunday. After breakfasting at my Club go to St. Bride's Church, half an hour before the service. Find it very difficult to find even standing room and hundreds went away. Melville preached astonishingly - attention was rivetted and feelings excited in the most extraordinary way. I looked round after the sermon was over and everybody seemed to have been crying. The subject 'The Wedding Garment' - the object - Fund for a new church in the parish of St. Giles. Leave town by coach at 2 o'clock and 10 reach Bradford Parsonage where I find T. C. Hughes awaiting me. The rest of the household had gone to bed.

October 31. Much pleasant chat at breakfast about the boys future and The Grove property. At 10 leave these good friends with every wish for their happiness and return to Bungay after a month's absence.

November 7.   See Muskett, the Duke of Norfolk's Agent, about the exchange of land for the enlargement of Trinity burial ground. Miss Butcher leaves Charlotte for Bradfield and Alfred Hughes [53] comes to stay with me. He translates the second book of Caesar till 12 and then we examine some sketches by Cooper, the animal painter.

From now onwards Scott appears to have undertaken everything connected with Alfred's education, both in England and abroad.

November 16.   Much talk with Samuel about business and other matters preparatory to his going to Foster and Unthank, attorneys in Norwich.

November 25. Sunday.   While I was at the schools a messenger comes to tell me that Mr. Butcher has been taken ill with a fit. Go at once to The Grove with Alfred and Miss Butcher and find Drs. Crowfoot and Webb[54] in attendance. At 3. o'clock leave for Bradfield where I arrive at 10½ p.m. to inform Mrs. Hughes of her father's illness. Stay there three hours and at 1. leave in chaise with Miss A. M. Butcher. We take the mail at Ipswich at 3½ and go as far as Yoxford and then by chaise to The Grove where we find Mr. Butcher rather better. On the 29th I am able to write to Mrs Hughes giving a favourable account of him, but he continued in a very weak state and it was not until a fortnight later that there was really any great improvement.

December 1.   Dine at the Gardens of Redisham with Capt. and Mrs. Carpenter, the former talks of his new propelling engine for vessels.

December 24.   This day Lieut. Col. Stoddart, my old school-fellow, was made prisoner by the Ameer of Bokhara and began to endure the most horrible cruelties from that mad tyrant.

Christmas Day.   To sacrament at Trinity Church in the morning and in the afternoon to hear George Sandby preach at St. Mary's. Gas first lighted there at the altar and in the galleries. The choir sing well. Spend the evening with the Samuel Scotts and Miss Butcher.

December 30. Sunday. To Trinity Church morning and afternoon and to St. Mary's in the evening when the latter was entirely lighted by gas. Sandby preaches. Three duties are now performed at St. Mary's and two at Trinity. Contrast this with the year 1828.

1839

Music ushers in the New Year and for the next ten days there are dinner parties and other gaieties almost every evening.

January 20. Sunday. Walk to the Margitsons to hear about John going to Bradfield to be with the Hughes as a pupil. Evening to St. Mary's where the Bishop of Norwich (Stanley) preaches to a congregation of 1100 on Brotherly Love.

January 24. A vestry meeting of Trinity Church. Charles Childs present and shows that the Independent Chapel should not be rated. Mrs. Judd, Miss Whitear and W. Holes call and go with me to the Silk and Crepe factory at Ditchingham. Six hundred and fifty girls and children are employed and everything in very good order.

February 13. Inspector Mitchell comes to me. He has been deputed by The National Society to inspect our schools. Show him the churches, castle and British School and the following day he and I to the Boys school, from 9 to 12. Afternoon to the Infant School where Mitchell examines and reads to the boys. Evening to the Theatre to hear Colonel Thompson, late M.P. for Hull, lecture on the Corn Laws. A failure.

February 15. Again to the schools. The Inspector considers the Boys School a first rate one - the Infants very good and the Girls School second best of the fifteen he has already inspected, although their arithmetic is bad. He left by the Yarmouth coach at 7 this evening.

February 16. Mr. Hughes arrives and stays half an hour with me. He in such bad health that he is going abroad with his family and it is decided that Alfred, who has been with me since the 12th February, shall accompany them to France. I grieved at parting with him.

April 5. Mr. and Mrs. Cobb leave Bungay for Ditchingham. The former has been curate at St. Mary's more than nine years. Mr. Cookesley takes his place and preaches for the first time on Sunday the 14th. Forcible style and a beautiful voice.

May 2. Saxmundham. Arrived here last night and am staying with Robert Mann, he shows me his church and I walk to Little Glemham, he riding. See Gibson's recently erected statue of Dudley

North. Life size, sitting in chair - nature, ease and life. No appearance of artifice. One of the finest statues I ever saw. I am thankful Suffolk possesses such a treasure. The Mausoleum too in which it stands is beautiful. Call on young Thurlow, a sculptor, and trust that he and young Nursey of Bungay will each hang a wreath on the triumphal arch of their and my native county.

May 18.   To Bradfield where I join the Hughes and the following day, Sunday, John Hughes aged 1³/₄ years is christened. John Ambrose and I are his godfathers. Remain with the Hughes until their departure and take leave of them on board the Rotterdam steamer, the Giraffe, the morning of Saturday 9th. God bless them all. Return to Bungay on Sunday evening arriving about 7. o'clock and spend half an hour with Charlotte and Miss Butcher.

May 30.   Drive to Lowestoft. Walter Scott married to Anna Everard. Flags, guns and garlands decorate the town. The Scotts and Everards go to the church in five carriages. Francis Cunningham performs the service impressively. Twenty-five to breakfast. The bride and bridegroom leave at 1 o'clock for Aldeborough.

June 2.   Mrs Cracknell of St. James South Elmham, late Miss Norman, dies after fifteen months illness from dropsy.

June 5.   At Girlings, the butcher in Earsham Street, see the neer *(the fat enclosing the kidney)* of an ordinary sized bullock which weighed 147 lbs, the other being of normal size.

June 6.   A tremendous thunder-storm, like cannons firing close to one. The Old Theatre at the back of the Castle Hills struck and widow Mays killed by lightning.

June 18.   Mrs Scott and Charlotte move from Bridge House to Outney Cottage and Miss Hannah Butcher goes with them.

June 26.   Hear today of the death of J. Lillistone, Rector of Barsham. Last Monday the 17th, I left him in good health. He burst a blood vessel in consequence of sea sickness on his way to the Rhine and was brought back to London, where he died.

July 1.   The alterations are proceeding at Bridge House. The boundary wall between the premises and the Castle Lane is being built and today the foundations of the Ruined Tower on the

Waveney is laid. Keying on both sides of the river is going on. I had previously had the channel widened. Whiting, the architect from Ipswich, is in charge and has fourteen workmen employed.

July 7. Drive to Shadingfield to breakfast. Spend most of my time talking with John and Henry Scott on their journey to Australia. They are starting tomorrow for London and Plymouth and their parents are much depressed at parting with them. At 8 p.m. bid adieu to the two travellers, John aged 25 and Henry 23, and return thoughtfully home.

July 22. View James Utting's painting of the Crucifixion which he is presenting to Ditchingham Church.

July 30. An evening party at the Kingsbury's, Brettinghams, Allsopps, Cooksleys and Monsieur Brettel who married Hartcup's sister there. Meet Brettel and his wife again the next evening at dinner at the Margitsons. He talked French the whole evening and seems a very gay and volatile man.

August 4. Drive from Ipswich, where I stayed last night with the Walter Scotts, to Holbrook and receive a hearty welcome. Meet Miss F. Freestone and Mr. Hirschfeld, a German Jew there. Wilkenson preaches twice and Hirschfeld gives a lecture to the school children. Return to Walter in the evening.

August 5. The first Ipswich Assizes. Fifty grand jurymen attend to make twenty-three.
Attend on the the Special Jury and leave Ipswich on the morning of the 8th.
Up to this time the Assizes and Gaol deliveries for the County of Suffolk were held at Bury both in the Spring and Summer. From now the Lent Assizes are to be held at Bury and in the Summer at Ipswich.

August 24. Yarmouth. I came here on the 24th and this morning the 26th meet Abel, our master at Bungay, and with him inspect the hospital and schools. Dine at Isaac Preston's with E. Woodhouse, the Pillews, Gunthorpe, Prestons in abundance and John Lacon who last week gave his brother £70,000!!

September 11. To Cookesley's and Hartcup's[55]. At the house of the latter hear of the sad fate of poor Brettel. *(See July 30th.)* When in Bungay he was very anxious to be in Dieppe in time to meet his brother who was returning from Mexico and he hasted home for that purpose and learned that his beloved brother died within sight of his native shore. The shock so affected him that he became blind and insane.

September 13. Hear that Montagu of Beccles has died from the bite of a serpent in India.

November 10. Sunday. To the schools and then to Trinity Church. In the evening to St. Mary's Church to hear Scudamore[56] preach on the authority of the clergy. A thorough Oxford Tractarian; just such doctrines as the Roman Catholics maintain. I deeply reflect on the principles of Christianity.
On the 24th hear that Marcus Hughes is gazetted Ensign in the 69th regiment, and go to The Grove to tell his grandparents the news. On the 26th Calvery Bewicke was married to his cousin Emma Bewicke and three days later they arrive at their house at Barsham. (The White House).

December. The ugly white and red back kitchen and all the offices next the river on the Bridge House premises have now completely disappeared and Charlotte and Miss Butcher come to see the view opened out by their removal. Our farm house on the Flixton Road and The Grove can be plainly seen from the library windows.

PART 1 (1829-1839)

Ten Years at Waveney House

References

1. Cooper, Sir Astley (1768-1841). Surgeon to Guy's Hospital. Operated on George IV. Author, works on anatomy and surgery.

2. Crowfoot, William Henchman(1780-1848). Second generation of four Beccles surgeons all named William. Memorial in St. Michael's Church, Beccles. His death is recorded on p187 and the Doctor Crowfoot mentioned on p217 is his son, William Edward, who died in 1887.

3. Smith, Sir James Edward (1759-1828). Botanist & author.

4. Meade, General the Hon. Robert. Fought in the Peninsular War (1808-1814) where he lost his eye. Appointed Lt. Governor of the Cape of Good Hope and visited Napoleon on St. Helena on his way home from South Africa.

5. Adair, Sir Alexander. A descendant of Sir Robert Adair, of Ballymena, Ulster. He had inherited the Flixton Hall estate from his uncle, William Adair, in 1783. The estate had previously been owned by the Tasburgh family, from whom William purchased it in 1753.

6. Shore, John (1751-1834). Govern. Gen. of India. Author.

7. Peel, Sir Robert (1788-1850) Founded Police Force and Conservative Party (1831). Prime Minister 1834, 1839 and 1845. Repealed Corn Laws.

8. Holland, George Calvert(1801-1865) MD (Edinburgh). Adopted Homeopathy and studied Mesmerism. Author.

9. Faraday, Michael(1791-1867).
Natural philosopher. Discovered magnetoelectricity, 1831.

10. Phillips, Richard (1778-1851). FRS. President of Chemical Society. Author of chemistry works.

11. Kerrison, Sir Edward (1774-1853). Son of the wealthy Bungay trader,

Matthias Kerrison, he had a distinguished army career. See biographical note in *An Englishman at Home and Abroad 1792-1828*, page 244

12. Bedingfield, John. John James Bedingfield was a local magistrate and a friend of Scott's. The Bedingfields were a long established local family. Based in Ditchingham, they also seem to have held property in Bungay. The family coat of arms, dated 1572, was found on an old mantelpiece in the ancient building opposite St. Mary's Church, now Bowtell's. In the 18th century they were patrons of the Bungay Theatre, and James Bedingfield was a founder member of the Gentlemen's Club. Mr Bacon Bedingfield owned Ditchingham Mill until his death in 1792. The family are frequently referred to in Scott's diaries.

13. Mann Family.
Richard (1777-1844) was involved with the Staithe Navigation and lived in Bridge Street House (in which Chateaubriand had been a former resident). He was Town Reeve in 1820 when he presented a silver medal to be worn by the Town Reeves as an emblem of office. This was to commemorate the Coronation of George IV. In 1836 he ordered the removal of the old cage for the detention of prisoners under the Butter Cross. His son, William Mann, (1806-1878) was in business with his brother, Richard, as a coal and corn merchant at Wainford Mill. They established a maltings there in 1856. He was Town Reeve six times between 1831 and 1863. His brother was also Town Reeve six times - between 1844 and 1872. Henry Mann, another brother, was an East India merchant and father of Robert Campbell Mann who married Ethel Norton, author of *Old Bungay*. There is a stained glass window commemorating various members of the family in St. Mary's Church.

14. Shufflebottom, The Rev. Robert. Minister 1771-1817.

15. Childs, Charles (1807-1876), son of John Childs who owned Bungay printing works. Charles took over the management of the business on his father's death in 1853. Although John Barber Scott and his brother Samuel had been engaged in bitter conflict with John Childs over his refusal to pay rates to the established Church of England, they seem to have maintained a reasonably friendly relationship with Charles, who had a milder disposition. Charles himself was taken to court for non-payment of rates in 1840, but successfully defended his case. He was Town Reeve in 1870. His chief hobby was music. He organised a choral group from among his printing works employees, and Edward Fitzgerald recalls how much he enjoyed attending one

of their concerts. He is buried in the old cemetery, together with his wife and son Edgar.

16. Gooch, Sir Thomas (1766-1851). The Gooches were an old established local family. They owned Staithe Navigation in 1770 and Bardolph's Mill which was destroyed by fire in 1779. The property was sold to Matthias Kerrison in 1783.

17. Butcher, Robert (1764-1844), was born in Earsham where his father ran the Norfolk Distillery. He became a local landowner and in 1809 purchased The Grove, the mansion on the hill above Flixton Road. The house was later demolished and replaced by Upland Hall.

18. Town Reckoning Day. The Town Reeve's final duty at the end of his year of office. It was followed by a dinner of the Feoffees (Trustees of the Town Charities) when they appointed a successor for the ensuing year.

19. Fisher, David (1760-1832), actor and producer. See biographical note in *An Englishman at Home and Abroad 1792-1828*, page 238.

20. Bardwell, Thomas (1704-1767), artist. His origins are obscure: Ethel Mann thought that he was related to Thomas Bardwell of Woodton, servant to the Suckling family, but it is now thought that he was perhaps the son of a farmer of Worlingham. In his early career he produced some local views, including a depiction of the Bath House at Ditchingham, and a view of Hedenham Hall which is still in situ over the mantelpiece in the house. Among his major commissions were the nine portraits of Mayors of Norwich, c. 1747-65, hung in St. Andrew's Hall (referred to by his most recent biographer, M. Kirby Talley, as "among his most miserable creations"). In 1758 he published "The Practice of Painting and Perspective Made Easy" printed by Miller of Bungay. He was buried in Bungay and there is a memorial plaque beside the West door of St. Mary's Church. His fine self portrait is in the Ancient House Museum, Thetford.

21. Woodward, John Jenkinson (1744-1820).Born in Huntingdon, he was the son of Benjamin Woodward and Frances, daughter of Thomas Manning of Bungay. He came to Norfolk in 1770, lived at Ditchingham and practised as a lawyer in Bungay. His chief interests were botany and local history, having inherited a number of old Bungay records from his father-in-law.

22. Glover, Archdeacon George. Archdeacon of Suffolk, a pluralist and

Perpetual Curate of St. Mary's from 1829-1850. He married Susannah, daughter of Eliza and Daniel Bonhote, as her third husband. After her death he surprised everybody by marrying, at the age of seventy seven, a much younger wife (see page 185). On November 2nd, 1850, he was succeeded at St. Mary's by his son, the Reverend William Glover, M.A.

23. Kingsbury, Matthew Brettingham (1766-1837).
The Kingsburys were solicitors in Bungay. The family had owned Waveney House since 1734 and in 1801 Matthew Kingsbury inherited it from his mother. It was sold to John Scott, father of John Barber Scott, in 1813.

24. Cobbett, William (1763-1835). Essayist, politician and agriculturalist. MP Oldham 1832.

25. Dyball, William. Town Clerk and a churchwarden of St. Mary's. It is recorded in the local press that on December 8th 1849 at the Town Dinner, following the annual meeting for the auditing of accounts, when Richard Mann was elected the new Town Reeve "the Vice Chair was occupied for the 56th time without exception by the Town Clerk, Mr. W. Dyball, whose health was drunk with the usual honours". The Dyball family were engaged in trade as grocers and silversmiths but they also had artistic abilities. Joseph Dyball, who died in 1818, is recorded as being a painter; the old water colour of the Market Place in the eighteenth century was painted by J. Dyball: and Ethel Mann recorded that she owned a drawing of the old Corn Cross by William Dyball.

26. Blore, Edward (1787-1879) Architect and artist. Architect to William IV and Queen Victoria.

27. Whately, Richard (1787-1863). Rector of Halesworth 1822-1825. Archbishop of Dublin 1831-1863. Author.

28. Russell, Lord John (1792-1878). Statesman. Prime Minister 1846. Reformer. Author.

29. Hallam, Henry (1777-1859). Historian, barrister & author. Vice-President, Society of Antiquaries.

30. Brande, William Thomas (1788-1866). Professor of Chemistry at the Royal Institution.

31. Kirby, William (1759-1850). President of Entomological Society 1837, to which he bequeathed his collection of insects.

32. Butcher Family of The Grove. In *Old Bungay* page 151, Ethel Mann refers to a Mr. Butcher, ancestor of the Butchers of The Grove who, in the eighteenth century, was one of the principal buyers of hempen yarn. The weaving of this yarn was an old Bungay cottage industry.

33. Barkway's School was, of course, Bungay Grammar School. The Reverend Frederick Barkway (c. 1801-1875) was Deputy Head Master from 1824 to 1858. He was elected Town Reeve for two periods of office, 1866 and 1874; the only clergyman recorded to have held this honour.

34. Garneys, Charles (1781-1849) Practised as a surgeon from his house in Trinity Street for over 50 years. His three sons, Thomas, William and Henry all became doctors and worked with their father at various times. He was Town Reeve of Bungay three times, being 88 on the last occasion in 1847, two years before his death.

35. Kerrison, Matthias (1742-1827). Became owner of the Bungay Staithe and Navigation in 1783. He built up a considerable trade, dealing in coal, timber and corn. He used his accumulated wealth to purchase estates in Norfolk and Suffolk inherited by his son, Sir Edward Kerrison. When Town Reeve in 1812 he replaced the Corn Cross in the Market Place with a new town pump.

36. Brettel, John. Bungay surgeon who practised in Upper Olland Street for at least 50 years. He was Town Reeve three times and died in 1842 aged 75

37. Kelso, Major General Robert (1760-1823). A memorial in Holy Trinity Church states that "this lamented officer served his King and country for 43 years in every quarter of the globe with distinguished honour and credit ..." and enumerates the various naval actions where he fought. He lived in Rose Hall and was a churchwarden of Holy Trinity.

38. Stoddart, Charles (1806-1842). Soldier and Diplomat. Beheaded by Persians in Bokhara.

39. Grey, Charles, Second Earl (1764-1845). Statesman. Prime Minister 1831. Parliamentary Reformer.

40. Bungay Reform Festival. The public dinner to celebrate the passing of the Reform Bill was very efficiently organised by John Childs, the printer. Forty-two tables, with tablecloths, were erected on both sides of the length of Earsham Street, the Market Place and St. Mary's Street where the poor, half of them children, were provided with beef, plum pudding and beer. A printing press was erected over the town pump where bills were printed and distributed. The proceedings and many toasts were punctuated by a flourish of trumpets and the firing of guns.

41. Ashby, Samuel. Ran a printing business established by his father, John Ashby (1753-1828) in the ancient building at the junction between Upper and Lower Olland Streets. Both he and his father wrote topical verses about Bungay events and Samuel also published the song *Old Bungay*, written in 1816.

42. Benezet, The Reverend Edward, Vicar of Holy Trinity, 1803-1834.

43. Reynolds, Sir Joshua (1723-1792). Portrait Painter. President of the Royal Academy which he founded in 1768. Buried in St. Paul's Cathedral.

44. West, Benjamin (1738-1820). Historical painter, employed by George III.

45. Lawrence, Sir Thomas (1769-1830). Painted George III, 1792, and other continental sovereigns. Collected drawings of Michelangelo and Raphael. Buried in St. Paul's.

46. Southey, Robert (1774-1841). Poet and man of letters. Friend of Wordsworth.

47. Bobbit, John. Had been a friend of Scott's from childhood. In Scott's earliest diaries, written in 1799-1800, in which only one incident a day is recorded, he wrote in his large, juvenile hand on Friday, April 1st, "I took a walk with John Bobbit". Bobbit became an ironmonger and was churchwarden of St. Mary's, as his father had been before him. With Samuel Scott he was deeply involved in the case against John Childs over the payment of Church Rates. He is caricatured in a cartoon on page **** .

48. Wigram, Joseph Cotton (1798-1867).Bishop of Rochester. Published religious and educational works.

49. Macready, William Charles (1793-1873). Actor, taking many

Shakespearean parts. Acted in France and America. Manager of Covent Garden and Drury Lane Theatres.

50. Brougham, John (1814-1880). Actor and dramatist.

51. Collyer, The Reverend Thomas. Vicar of Holy Trinity, 1834-1890.

52. Portrait reproduced opposite page 176 in *An Englishman at Home and Abroad 1792-1828*.

53. Hughes, Alfred. Travelling companion of Scott, the son of an old friend. He was born in 1825 and at first studied engineering. At the age of 24, however, he bought a farm near Bungay and in 1851 married Maria, the daughter of Colonel John Smith of Ellingham Hall. Six years later they moved to another farm on the Isle of Wight and in 1889 he succeeded his father as 9th Baronet. He died at his country seat at East Bergholt, Suffolk, in 1898. Maria lived to the age of 83, having borne him 18 children, three of whom died in infancy. She died at East Bergholt Lodge in 1913.

54. Webb, Thomas Ernest. Surgeon who practised in Broad Street for about 20 years. Town Reeve three times.

55. Hartcup, William (1814-1895). Born at Ipswich, he was articled to a firm of solicitors, Kingsbury and Margitson, in 1833, and was taken into partnership with Margitson in 1839. On Margitson's death in 1848 Hartcup took over the entire business. He lived at Upland Hall, which he had built on the site of The Grove in Flixton Road. He was made J.P. for Suffolk and played an active part in Bungay life, becoming churchwarden of St. Mary's, and Town Reeve for three periods of office, 1868, 1875, 1881. In 1893 he and his wife were presented by the townspeople of Bungay with a magnificent silver candelabrum to celebrate their Golden Wedding anniversary; this was presented to the town in 1958, and is still used at Town Dinners.

56. Scudamore, The Reverend William (1813-1881) Rector of Ditchingham from 1839 until his death. He was educated at St. John's College, Cambridge, where he came under the influence of the Oxford Movement. He was a strong supporter of the Ditchingham Anglo-Catholic Community of All Hallows. He restored the parish church and built, partly at his own expense, Pirnhow Church near the silk factory. He also built the village school next to All Hallows Hospital.

PART TWO

1840-1841 - Seventeen Weeks in the Rhineland

1840

January 9. Having made my preparation for leaving Bungay, I start for Ipswich by the "Star" coach and arrive at 12. Attend a committee meeting of the Suffolk Educational Society at the County Hall. Lord Bayning, Sir Charles Vere, Archdeacon Berners, etc. there. Grants were made to Sunday Schools.
Dine at Walter Scott's and tea at Admiral Page's and thence by mail to London.

January 12. Embark at 10. on board the "Victoria" steamer at the London docks. Among the passengers were a young Danish merchant, intelligent and well educated, a Mr. Duke, who thinks with me that natural differences of character are evanescent as compared to the great characteristics of human nature; and a Dr. and Mrs. Tancred, he a married Catholic priest with a family; i.e. he was first a priest, then a Protestant clergyman and in that state married, became a Catholic priest again with a dispensation not to be divorced.
At 7 p.m. began to feel very ill, but slept soundly till 2½.

January 13. Thinking it was 7 o'clock I got up. Found it bitterly cold on deck but walk there with the captain, an American, for two hours. At daylight, having left Flushing behind us, we glided up the very low-banked Scheldt. Reach Antwerp at 8½, but were obliged to break through three miles of ice to make our way to the quays. Our luggage was examined on board.
Go to Hotel du Parc, taking care of a school-boy who is going to Brussels and escorting Mrs. Tancred to the Cathedral.
Its area and five aisles give much grandeur though the architectural ornament is poor. The "Descent from the Cross" most beautiful, far more so than any engraving leads one to suppose. The expression exquisite but the face of the Christ commonplace, with nothing of divinity in it.
Dine with the Tancreds and we start together from Antwerp by rail at 4. parting at Malines. Slow travelling, only 15 miles an hour. Liege at 9. Tea at the Pommelette Hotel and at 10 start by diligence and reach Aix-la-Chapelle at 4½ a.m. Much examination at the Custom House till 5½.
Here Germany begins and I talk with mine host of a cabaret till 8.

All frost and snow but fine sunshine on our way to Juliers and Cologne. Cologne at 3. The Rhine half bound in ice. Walk along the river to the ramparts and talk with the landlord's son at Kaiserlicher Hof. A good day's practice, but I speak very much like a child of three years old.

January 15. At 8 1/2 leave Cologne in Schnell Post Wagen with a wine merchant, a lieutenant of infantry and a nun (Benedictine). All very talkative, in German only. The Rhine pleases me quite as much as formerly.

At 4 1/2 reach the Trierischer Hof on the Clemens Platz at Coblenz and was met at the door by Robert Hughes, who with his father happened to be in the hotel at the moment. With the latter to their lodgings, where in succession I had a very pleasant meeting with Mrs. Hughes, Marcus and all the dear children.

January 16. Breakfast with the Hughes'; hear the children take their lessons from their master, Uttner. Alfred dines with me.

January 17. Begin a German journal and decide to take lessons from Uttner.

January 19. Sunday. To the Jesuits' Church. Military Mass and divine music. My Dresden feelings of 1818 all revived[1]. Later to the Protestant Lutheran Church with Robert; a political eulogy on the King of Prussia on this his Coronation Day[2] and 200th anniversary of Prussian monarchy[3].

From now until the beginning of March, I spend my time principally with the Hughes, having my rooms at the Trierischer Hof, where Alfred joins me daily and we both take lessons in German.

Almost every day I take excursions with Marcus or Alfred, returning in the evening to our several quarters, and if not too tired after our long walks we go to the theatre later or meet friends at my hotel or the Hughes' house.

March 6. I plan a tour with Alfred and we start on board a steamer from Coblenz to Bingen - very varied scenery. We pass twenty-three old castles, Rheinfels and Schomberg are the largest and all are so picturesque that I cannot tell which is the most so. Reach Bingen at 1 o'clock and after table d'hôte, ascend the Elzen Hohe and Rupprechts Berg on the left, and Rochus Berg on the right bank of the Nahe.

The view from the latter is exquisitely rich and grand, with its mountainous hills, valleys, woods, vineyards and cornfields, and the glorious old Rhine, with its many islands, towns and villages to the number of thirty. These compose a magnificent whole, now rendered surpassingly beautiful by the blue, purple and gold tints of the clear sky and setting sun. Explore the remains of the castle and after an hour's chat in the Saal, retire to bed, having spent a most delightful day.

March 7. After further excursions in the neighbourhood, we embark on a Dusseldorf steamer and land at Mainz at 4 in the afternoon. Go to the Hollandischer Hof and in the evening to the Theatre which was elegant but not comfortable.

March 10. Return from the Platte to Wiesbaden by Sonnenberg through the forest. Promise Alfred that if he has no gun given him before he is seventeen, I will give him one for his birthday. Sonnenberg is a dirty village, its castle bold, imposing and extensive. Dine at Wiesbaden Hof, good and cheap. Look at the Kursaal with its 28 dark marble pillars. Longer but much lower and by no means handsome as that at Ems. The colonnades on either side good.

The Museum of Antiquities was closed, that of Natural History contains a good collection of animals.

Walk back to Mainz and after table d'hôte go along the quay to the Schloss-Platz and see the Prussians exercising. Then to the Museum, a dirty, dark set of rooms. One of the most interesting objects is a clock which shows the position of the sun, moon and planets and has gone for thirty-three years without varying one second. It is the work of a monk named Johann who calculated his work would take twenty years and executed it in two. He finished it in 1807 and would not sell it but gave it to the Poor House and died in poverty.

The collection of Roman antiquities found at or near Mainz is very interesting. It contains many monuments of Roman soldiers of the 22nd and other legions, but as works of art they are not very good and executed in coarse brown sandstone.

Thence by the modern burying-ground to Zahlbach, a village where there are many masses of a Roman aquaduct. They are 30 feet high (perhaps some of them) and 15 feet square; made of turf, sandstone, grey and red with here and there a few courses of large flat bricks all cemented with a strong mortar. Some of these ruins are nearly 3/4 of a mile long. A Roman burying-ground is close by.

Evening. Theatre.

March 11. Leave the Hollandischer Hof at 12, a pleasant,

53

comfortable, but, for Germany, a somewhat dear hotel. In a two-horse carriage with a Jewish damsel to Hallenstein, through very ugly country. Even Hochheim has no charms but those of its wines. At Hallenstein we take our seats in a railway carriage, speed about 22 miles an hour - the carriages are very good, machine-built at Newcastle-on-Tyne. Motion much steadier and noise less than on our Great Western. At 1/2 past 3 enter Frankfurt. Dine quite late and walk round the town and its beautiful streets and by the Main, etc. In the evening to the theatre. "Don Juan", Mozart's music, like everything good, pleases me more and more.

March 17.   Homberg; it is here the Princess Royal[4] of England died in January last. It is still a little Independent Principality. The plantations and gardens around do much honour to the taste of its late owner, who resided here so long. The Palace is extensive but ugly but the views of the hills are very agreeable. The mineral waters are rising in repute. The people around seem grateful for the kindness of their late Princess.
We dine at a neat inn here and walk to Frankfurt, having accomplished 28 miles to-day.

March 18.   To Bethmann's Museum of Sculpture and to see the casts in his garden. Ariadne by Dannecker, excellent. Have not been well but feeling rather better, we start for Heidelberg, where we arrive at 4 a.m. and to bed at the Prinz Karl Hotel at 5.

March 20.   Late up.   General walk through the streets p.m. Examine the noble ruins of the castle and the beautiful gardens attached.   Here is the Heidelberg Tun. It is 36 feet long and 24 feet in diameter.   It holds 283,200 bottles and cost £500; was three years in the making and was three times filled with Tithe wine but the Tithes are taken off and the Tun is leaky. It was constructed in 1751. Many fragments of the Middle Ages are carefully preserved in the castle, which is admirably kept. The gardens serve as a Botanical arboretum. The parts built and enlarged by Elizabeth[5], daughter of James I of England and wife of Frederick the Elector Palatine[6] and King of Bohemia, are particularly interesting to us as Englishmen. She had a lovely residence.

March 22.   To the English church, which is half used by Protestants and half by Catholics. It is full of interesting monuments. The altar with its Host and candles and wreaths appearing behind the simple, unadorned table of the Protestants. The same font and pulpit serve for both confessions. The two ministers agree well. The sexton explains their harmony by declaring that, provided they are regularly paid, it matters not to either which religion is uppermost.

After table d'hôte we go in a party to Konigstuhl, the loftiest hill in the district, and from the tower of the castle there, have a splendid view, but it was interrupted by a heavy snow storm. Thence we descended to Wolfsbommen, a beautiful spot a little way up a hilly glen; its Swiss houses, fine varied trees and pools of clear water, full of enormous trout some 20 inches long and 10 lbs. in weight, pleased us much. These trout are caught in the neighbouring streams and placed here and kept for sale. Some have been in the pool for eight years, and when very large sell for 4/- per pound to the Frankfurt gourmands.

March 23. Snow still falling so as to render excursions or continuation of our journey alike inadvisable. Alfred and I study "Ollendorf"[7] till 12 and then see the Botanical and Horticultural Gardens. Much German talk at dinner about German universities.

In the afternoon a procession of students passed through the town. Nine on horseback, three and three, wearing dragoon boots, leather breeches, velvet coats, sashes of pink, white or orange, and caps, black, white, green or red, according to their club, with swords in hand. Then a carriage and four with one student, the senior of the University, followed by a single carriage and six horses. In this were two in full dress, bare-headed and sitting in front and one plainly dressed student at the back.

Twenty-six other carriages followed, all open and each containing two students. Of these about ten were drawn by four horses and the rest by two. The last carriage of all had only one occupant, fully dressed with cocked hat. He was the second student of the university. This procession was in honour of the student in the carriage with six horses, who, having passed his examination this night, is leaving Heidelberg. He looked as if he felt the transition to be one from joy to care. His companions escorted him some miles on his journey. Many a beaker was quaffed and many a song for the welfare of the departing student.

To obtain a degree in Germany a student must complete eight semester terms in four years, but these semesters may be passed in any of the twenty universities in Germany. He can live quite up to the average of comfort for 300 thaler (£45) a semester or £90 a year. The expenses of a degree amount to £18 or £20, so that if a student becomes a B.A. and also a Doctor of Law, Physic or Theology, his whole university course will cost about £400. Heidelberg is famed for Medicine and Law, but not greatly for

Classics, Mathematics or Theology.
After seeing the procession we attend a funeral of a young musician, aged 20. The hearse was covered with flowers and about 80 friends followed in pairs - all in black but few with crepe. Men only. A Protestant minister attended. At the grave a band of wind instruments played a dirge. The minister then addressed the assembly and read some prayers and scripture from a book. 30 of the party sang a hymn and with another dirge the ceremony closed.

March 26.   Continued snow confines us again to the house and we talk much of England, but all in German. Two days later we leave our comfortable Prinz Karl Hotel and in a hired carriage we go the thirteen miles from Heidelberg to Mannheim in two hours through the snow. Inspect the cavalry stables and barracks with a very civil officer who takes us to his own rooms.

March 29. Sunday. To the English chapel in the castle. 60 present of whom 20 were children. p.m. View the new harbour, canal and warehouses. The Baden government wish to make Mannheim head of the Rhine Navigation; if this succeeds, the town will probably double its population, but its site is swampy and unhealthy.

March 30.   Alfred and I examined the drawbridge and then went to the designer and saw the models of the locks, which are like those of Lowestoft. Visit the tomb of Kotzebue and the grave of his murderer, Sand, which are in the Protestant burying-ground. That of Kotzebue[8] is a die supported by tragic and comic masks, resting on a stone cushion, which is itself supported by rough stones, all emblematical.

April 3.   At Kreuznach on the Nahe, where we arrived yesterday. After exploring the castle, we visited the market place. This was crowded with white-kerchiefed peasant women and tricorn-hatted men, who were selling corn and seeds in sacks, as in an English country town.
Ascend the Gans Hill, from which is a glorious view of the Taunus and see a large flock of geese called to bed by a well played bugle. Just below us, the Nahe is very beautiful - the noble porphyry rocks of Rheingrafenstein rise 600 feet, perpendicularly, from the river. There were cattle on their summit. On the opposite bank is the ruined Castle of Ebernburg, with others in the distance. Our walk through the woods was delightful and we enjoyed ourselves exceedingly, arriving by a very steep descent into the village.
Here we examined the creaking and long-jointed salt water pumps

of the Salinen, the buildings attached to them are very extensive. The water is raised 30 feet to filter down again nine separate times through a thick stack of faggots, the heavier salt water falls into wooden vessels or pans. Beneath, the fresher water evaporates among the faggots. Then the salt water is boiled, etc., and crystallizes as at other salt works. These salt springs are used also to drink from and to bathe in.

As a watering place Kreuznach is yet in its infancy; the town is very ugly and dirty but good new houses are rising near it and may form a future Ems. A hundred people supped, smoked and played billiards, dominoes and cards and listened to good Jewish music at the Pfalzer Hof in the evening.

April 4. A 2 1/2 we start by diligence with a Heidelberg student and a Prussian officer for Trier. At Oberstein is a church cut out of the rock with two castles on its summit; but, alas! coffee had more charms than the ruins. Hence we ascended a portion of the Hohe Wald - barren generally, but with extensive woods. The Duke of Oldenburg is Sovereign of Birkenfeld, where we stay two hours; thence by Hermeskirl, downwards to the valley of the Moselle. Near Trier it becomes rich, wide and beautiful. The Porta Nigra surprises and delights me in its grand Doric simplicity. I know no city gate in Italy to equal it.

April 7. Alfred and I walk six miles along the side of the Moselle to Conz, where we explore the scanty remains of Constantine's Summer Palace. Much more might be found by excavation here, as at Trier and in all the neighbourhood.

The view from this place most lovely with the bridge over the Saar where the quiet waters of the two rivers unite and red rocks and vineyards come into view, the latter covered with labourers - men, women and children with their horses and oxen. We cross the Saar and Moselle by ferry to Igel where we examine a very interesting monument of the Secundini[9], probably of the time of the Antonines, 70 feet high and covered with sculptures.

Walk back to Trier for 3 o'clock dinner and then see the library with its ancient MSS, paintings and Gutenberg's admirably printed Bible and many Roman and Middle Age antiquities.

Theatre in the evening to a well played comedy by Charlotte Birch Pfeiffer.

April 8. We visited the Amphitheatre yesterday and again this evening. The lovely, though melancholy pensiveness which I have often felt in Rome again returns in Trier, the Rome of Gaul and

Germany. While we viewed the ruins, the stillness of the evening was delightfully broken by a chorus of vinedressers returning from their labours.

April 9.   Up at 3 and on board the "Elizabeth" at 4. Leave the packet at Muhlheim and start across the meadows to the fort of Schloss Velding, which will scarce survive another year as a "noble ruin". At Cus is a place of refuge for aged tradesmen and others and a hospital founded by a native of the place.

In the vineyards, every man, woman and child was busy - some in finishing the pruning or in bending the vine branches back and tying them with willow twigs, some too in carrying the prunings to their houses. Others were collecting manure and placing it round the roots of the vines or in covering the earth with stones and slates which retain and attract the heat and preserve an agreeable temperature about the plants. All the labour of carrying along the vast vineyards of the Moselle is performed by means of baskets on the back, barrows, etc., being quite inappropriate to this hilly district.

At 7 we descend to the village of Tranbach, where we stop and sup with our very intelligent landlord and his family. The charge for two suppers with wine, two beds and two coffees was only 2s 3d each.

April 10.   At Marienburg we ascend a lofty hill whence we seem to see four rivers instead of one, so extraordinary are the windings of the Moselle at this point. We dine in a wooden hut attended by a happy, dark-eyed forester and his wife.

Leaving our knapsacks, we run down to the Alf and see the iron works where 100 men and five furnaces and sundry huge water-wheels are hard at work. The iron comes from distant parts of the Rhine and is used chiefly at Coblenz, Koln and Dusseldorf.

Proceed up the valley of the Alf and Ues to Bertrich, which is one of the most picturesque valleys I have seen. Rocks mostly volcanic. Trout abundant and salmon occasionally.

Major Falkonski, the Bath Director, shows us the hot springs and baths, descanting on their power against gout, stone, etc. He accompanies us to a curious basaltic grotto; the angles are worn away by water and the columns look like Dutch cheeses piled one above the other, so it is called the "Käse" Grotto. The Major then showed us the Falkenlei, a volcano, one half of which has fallen, though the other half stands erect. The place is a complete museum of volcanic products. There are said to be 27 extinct volcanoes in the Eifel.

We walk back to Alf by moonlight, delighted with the second day's Moselle tour.

April 11.   In a boat from Alf to Bremm whose tower was lately destroyed by fire. Echoes abound here and almost everywhere along the Moselle. Walk to Ediger, then boat again to Beilstein, where another picturesque ruin towers above the town. Cross the river, regretting that the Roman ruins were covered up again. At Sehl enjoy the most lovely view on the Moselle, almost the most beautiful I have ever seen.

As we walked slowly along, the romantic grandeur increased with the charming towns below and in the distance rises the lofty castle of Winneburg, the cradle of the Metternich family which still belongs to that Prince[10].

Through meadows, orchards, gardens and vineyards we went with the still stream on our right and the varied rocks on our left, whilst the golden hues of sunset were gradually succeeded by the silver of the moon.

April 12.   A lovely still morning. Palm Sunday. All are Catholics here. The peasants carry branches of box instead of palm.

Walk from Treis and cross the Muden and on to Berg Eltz - a castle preserved, not restored, as a Feudal residence, just or nearly as it was 300 years ago. A great pile of buildings of various ages varied with projections, windows and loopholes of all sizes and shapes and turrets and pinnacles without end. I counted 105 openings or windows on one side alone.

It is about 100 feet high and stands on a conical hill of 400 feet whose base is almost surrounded by a clear, rapid stream 15 yards across. On the other bank rises a hollowed hill 800 to 1000 feet in height. A stone bridge connects the castle with the neighbouring hill, on whose top is a small stone fort built to attack Berg Eltz.

The effect of this scene was surprisingly enhanced by the beauty of the day and by the groups of female peasants, neatly dressed in blue, red and white and children bearing palms (box branches) winding their way up the zigzag path or kneeling before the Stations of the Cross which leads to the chapel on the opposite hill.

We passed through the dark gateway to a narrow court; the warders were gone but the barking of a hound announced us, and the three children of the Graf Eltz's steward were commissioned to show us the dim, rock-floored room and the winding staircases, the rusty armour, carved bedsteads and the family portraits and pictures of tournaments which so appropriately hang on the ancient walls.

We unwillingly left this romantic place and wound our way back to the Moselle along a beautiful narrow valley, but were six times obliged to wade through the 15 yard river or brook which had flooded the surface of the road. At Moselkern we dined on bread and cheese and wine, in the neat Gasthaus of an old lady whose whole life had been passed here, but who has never seen Berg Eltz, which is only a few miles away.

From here we went to Ehrenburg where was another grand and lofty ruin, with five tiers of walls, on the top of a high conical hill and a sovereign tower in the midst. Thence to Cobern, passing other imposing and lofty castles, but the beauty of the Moselle diminishes as we return.

It was a clear moonlight night; the watchman's calls and the tinkling sheep bells with the barking of dogs were echoed from rock to rock. We crossed the Karthause and reached the residence of my young companion exactly at midnight, having performed 36 miles on foot to-day. I passed the rest of the night at the Hughes' and resumed my quarters at the Trierischer Hof on the morning of Monday, the 13th.

April 17. Good Friday. No bells are sounded in Coblenz; even the Military Mass bells are silent. Wooden clappers are used instead and the boys in the district, in imitation thereof, parade the streets all day long with rattling clappers.

At 10 to the Protestant church. It was crowded to excess. After the regular service and sermon the Communion service begins. The whole of the females first arrange themselves in pairs or threes and approach the left of the altar in procession, the organ playing and the choir and the whole congregation singing; the words are pronounced to six at a time and the bread given to each; they then pass behind the altar and at the other end receive the cup from the assisting Minister and return to their places. The men now approach the altar and receive in both kinds in the same way. Three hymns were sung during the administration. At least 500 of each sex communicated.

In the afternoon a procession of several hundred children, women and men paraded the streets, singing a doleful litany. These were Catholics with banners, candles and beads and priests. By all, Good Friday is observed at Coblenz with more sanctity than a Sunday, but particularly by the Protestants. Outside the town, however, the Catholics were working as usual.

April 23. Have not been well the last few days, but in the afternoon Alfred and I leave for Bonn by steamer at 4 and arrive at 7$^{1}/_{2}$.

April 24.   Amongst places we visited was the church of Kreuzber, beneath which is a vault with 25 bodies of monks lying in open coffins, said to be from 100 to 200 years old. The skin and clothes of many undecomposed. No artificial means have been used to preserve them. The air in this hall seems very pure. The beadle says he was born in 1742 and is therefore 98 years old.

The town contains a magnificent library and fine reading rooms. Bonn has existed as a university only since 1818. This is vacation so we see scarcely any students.

We leave Bonn on foot and walk along the Rhine to Godesberg. A lovely view from the castle. Ascend the 1055 feet Drachenfels and sleep at the inn at its summit.

By the English steamer "Victoria" to Coblenz arriving at 8 and stop with the Hughes' till 10.

May 1.   Having left Coblenz yesterday we pass Wesel this morning at 5 o'clock. Cold, cloudy and dreary.

Emmerich at 7. Stay half an hour there and at Lobith, on the Dutch frontier, from 9 to 10. At Tiel we ran aground and were delayed from 1½ to 6½. Reach Rotterdam at 8 o'clock, having performed I suppose, 288 English miles from Coblenz and going perhaps, on an average, 12 miles an hour, exclusive of the 8 hours stopped at various places.

Walk about the quays at Rotterdam and look at the statue of Erasmus and am more pleased with Holland and the Dutch than on my former visit.

At 10 start on board the "Giraffe" steamer and arrive in the Thames at 3 on Sunday morning. Land at Woolwich where Marcus Hughes meets us and we go to Colonel R. Jones. Up to London in the evening and get my letters at the Club, returning to Suffolk the following week.

BUNGAY

May. After an absence of 17 weeks in Germany Scott takes leave of the Hughes with whom he has spent much of his time since January. He brings young Marcus Hughes with him to Bungay on the 9th where they are received by Mrs. Scott, Charlotte and Hannah Butcher. All have tea with him at Waveney House and afterwards Marcus returns with his grandmother to The Grove. Stops the night there and starts off next morning to London and Shrewsbury and then to Ireland where he will join his regiment.

1840/41]

May 19. Samuel arrives from Norwich and tells me that his mother and sister wish to continue at Outney Cottage instead of taking a house near him in Norwich. He will come and stay with them for the weekends. This quite pleases me and we make plans for several alterations and, amongst others, decide to take down the barn adjoining.

May 20. To Shipmeadow House. Sir Edward Twistleton, at this time Assistant Law Commissioner for England, comes to investigate a quarrel between the Wangford and Blything Hundreds. In the evening to dine at George Sandby's with Twistleton, Beevor, Crowfoot and Cookesley.

May 22. Dine at Shadingfield and meet the Rev. D. H. Leighton, Arnold, Stead, Reeve, the Vincents, Clarkes, James Montague and the Bordens. Leighton, who has been for two years Chaplain at Baden Baden, is a good linguist and very pleasing.

During the rest of this year and the beginning of next the grounds adjoining Bridge House were completely changed. Here stood formerly an inn known as the "Cock" and the County Bridge adjoining was called the Cock Bridge. In recent years on both sides of the river were tan yards and buildings connected with them. These were cleared away, and the ground raised and laid out with grass and flower beds, the channel of the river made wider and walls built along each side of it. The walls between the new stables and Cock Lane and the ruins of the Water Tower were constructed.

1841

January. Draw up a plan of operations for the whole of 1841 and call on several friends. Prepare for the introduction of general vaccination into the Wangford Union, and on the 29th move a resolution at Shipmeadow to this effect.
From the first week in January the weather becomes intensely cold, I never experienced greater. On the 8th the thermometer went down to 34 below freezing point, 2 below Zero. The next day the thermometer at 10 and snow fell during the night and continued until the 17th when a rapid thaw and flood succeed, which render the Earsham Dam impassable for foot passengers. Bitter cold with alternate snow and thaw prevail until the beginning of March.

February 8. The master and mistress of the boys and girls schools too ill to attend. Give away coal tickets to one hundred and fifty-six families at their houses i.e. to my tenants, the inhabitants of the Almhouses, old people and widows and the parents of all the children belonging to the National School. Trust that thus my donation may not, as the general distribution did, serve for the encouragement of vice and immorality.

February 12. Sir Astley Cooper dies in London aged 73.
He was born at Brooke and was the son of Samuel Cooper, the Rector of Yelverton and Morley. He was a very handsome man and one of the most famous surgeons of his day. After he was created a Baronet in 1821 his extensive practice increased enormously and in one year his income is said to have exceeded £21,000.

February 16. In honour of the anniversary of Queen Victoria's marriage and of the christening of the Princess Royal, all the Bungay tradesmen close their shops so that the town looks as if it were a day of general mourning. No-one is to be seen in the streets nor any sign of rejoicing except the pocket handkerchief flag on the steeple.

Scott now consults the County Surveyor and in March starts lowering the crown of the County Bridge, and a little later we find him making a channel under the high road to take off the surplus water. Such was the licence allowed to private individuals in former days. Even the course of the highways and rivers were frequently diverted to suit their inclination provided they had money to carry out the alterations and could show they were not detrimental to the public welfare.
Thus the roads at Ditchingham, Wainford, Flixton etc., were altered some hundred years ago, and it must be owned decidedly for the better as they supplied more direct and shorter routes to the outlying towns in the district.

March 13. Lady Travers calls to tell me of the intended sale of Ditchingham Lodge. This month the cottages built originally by Mrs. Bonhote[11] *(see old prints)* between the castle towers and used by her as a summer residence, were removed so that the towers now stand alone and look much more majestic than heretofore.

April 10. Mrs. Butcher calls to announce the intended marriage of Anna Butcher to Mr. Saunders of Clapham and Fleet Street. The wedding took place on the 18th May following.

1841]

May 19. William Stewart of Yarmouth dies aged 81. The father of Lady Travers.

June 2. Archdeacon Philpot, Lady Berners and Mrs. Onslow call to see Bridge House and ruins. The latter are now completed; they have given me exercise and amusement for many days the last two years.

June 9. Capt. Edward Kelso married Miss Purvis, daughter of the late Barrington Purvis of Beccles.

June 10. *Scott is now in London, preparing for a further foreign tour. He has a talk with Colonel Hughes about Alfred Hughes' future and, in this connection, makes enquiries about the College for Civil Engineers.*

PART II (1840-1841) Seventeen Weeks in the Rhineland

References

1. Where J.B.S. attended the Italian opera frequently and cultivated his love of music.

2. Frederick William IV, reigned from 1840-61.

3. The rise of the Prussian monarchy dates from the accession of Frederick William, the Great Elector.

4. Princess Royal (1766-1828). Eldest daughter of George III, married Frederick, King of Wurtemburg.

5. Elizabeth (1596-1662).

6. Frederick (1596-1632), the acceptance by whom of the Bohemian Crown in 1618 precipitated the Thirty Years' War.

7. Ollendorf. The well-known German Grammar.

8. Kotzebue. Dramatist and historian attached to the Prussian Embassy at St. Petersburg. He afterwards entered the Russian service and his Russian sympathies made him unpopular in Germany and led to his assassination in 1819.

9. Secundini. A wealthy family in the district who supplied the Roman army with food.

10. Metternich. The great Austrian statesman was at the height of his power when J.B.S. wrote as above.

11. Bonhote, Elizabeth (1744-1818). Daughter of James Mapes, a prosperous baker and confectioner whose premises were near the King's Head in Earsham Street. She married Daniel Bonhote, a local solicitor. They had two daughters, one of whom, Eliza Dreyer, provided funds for the almshouses in Staithe Road. Mrs Bonhote wrote poetry and published several novels, but her most successful book was *The Parental Monitor*, 1788, a guide to the education of young ladies. In 1792 her husband purchased the castle and Elizabeth's novel *Bungay Castle* was published in two volumes in 1797.

There is a copy in the Bungay Museum. Scott's statement that she built the house between the castle towers is erroneous. Kirby's print, dated 1748, indicates that it was built before she was born. She may, however, have erected a summer house elsewhere on the site.

PART THREE

Fifteen Weeks in Germany, Switzerland and Belgium.

1841

June 12. Saturday At 6½ leave on the "Columbine" for Rotterdam. A cold wet day. Arrive at 11 on Sunday morning and fix at the Bath Hotel.
Evening to the Cathedral service. Organ and singing good. Walk about the promenades and town. Much vice in some of the main streets. Painted girls, dancing, and English sailors.

June 14. Continue my journey and join Alfred at Bonn and together we reach Coblenz on Wednesday at 8½. Establish ourselves at Trierischen Hof. Meet my friends, the Hughes, in the Rheinstrasse at 9 o'clock with a satisfaction which on both sides there is no mistaking and stay with them till 11½.

June 17. Up at 5. Arrange luggage etc. With the Hughes' all the morning and in the afternoon, in their phaeton, go with Alfred and Mrs. Hughes to Netterhof and cross by the Flying Bridge to Neuwied. Walk about the Prince's gardens, which have fine trees and pleasant walks, but are kept most unneatly as to grass and flowers.

June 18. Alfred comes to my rooms to work at algebra etc. (which he continues daily). Look at a moonlight picture by Saal, a friend of Alfred's, and in the evening walk in the gardens at Capellen from 8 to 9. Such lights and such out-door evenings are not to be found in England.

June 22. Up at ¼ to 4. Alfred's studies and breakfast till 9. Then we, with Robert, walk to Plaidt by the ruins of the recently burnt Rutmach.
Dine on "Sauer Milch" at Plaidt at 1 and on our way back, after a walk of 30 miles, eat bread and cheese with "Sauer Wasser", as mine host called his wine, because he had no licence to sell it, and reach Coblenz at 11.

June 28. Mr. and Mrs. Hughes leave Coblenz for Freiburg, after two years residence in this town, taking their family with them, except Alfred, who remains with me.

July 11. Sunday. Alfred, Saal and I to Ems, where we look at the baths and drink the waters. Then to the Kursaal where Rouge et Noir gambling goes on all day. Crowds are walking up and down the Arcade. The Queen of Greece, a kind hearted, sensible and very pretty looking young woman of 26 or 27, with her attendants, were among the promenaders.

July 19. Buy a gun for Alfred and he shoots at a mark in the appointed place in the Fosse.

July 22. Studying steam engines with Alfred; then with Saal. I view Lange's Stadthiche Gallery of Pictures - 200, out of which ten are good. Inspect the hospital managed by the Sisters of Charity which is very neat and clean. They take in about 500 Itch patients yearly.

July 24. Visit the Paulinen and Wein Brunnen Springs - the drinkers and walkers are not looking comfortable. Ascend the very pretty walks and plantations over a bleak hill and down a narrow wooded valley to Schlangenbad. About ten good houses for lodgings, baths, eating, dancing and alas for gaming (just introduced here this year), compose the bath place which is situated in a pretty nook between hills and woods. We bathe: the water is soft but we found no more of the magic effect on the skin which Head[1] describes in his "Bubbles" than we should have found in the waters of the Moselle or the Waveney.
Here we saw a couple of tame snakes, a part of the large family which has given its name to this place.
We then walk towards Rauenthal and lose ourselves in the wood so that we made the walk to Wiesbaden 12 miles instead of six. We had, however, fine wood scenery and grand views of the Rhine. We reach Wiesbaden at 1 1/2. Table d'hôte at the Adler but it was too crowded to allow us to stop there: 200 at least were in the great room. We adjourn to the Nassauer Hof and find my old fellow traveller, Legendecher, there who went with me from Coblenz to London last year.
This is the birthday of the Duke of Nassau. A great festivity is given in the Neroberg. We walk up to it and find several thousands assembled in the woods. Music, wine-tables and dancing. There was much quiet merriment and no disorder. The country people were waltzing, some out of time and ungracefully but on the whole the dancing was far superior to what one would have seen at a popular festival in England.
We then went to the Kursaal which was crowded with people of the

higher classes. Much gambling at Rouge et Noir. A crowded ball in the evening in honour of the Duke, who is, however, at Ems to-day. Only tail-coats admitted and as Alfred was deficient in that article we contented ourselves with viewing the dancers from a side room through a window.

July 25.   Sunda   etc. till 10. Then to the English service at the Evan   , 200 present, preacher, evidently a disciple of Kemble.
At 7 1/2 go to the Railway Station. 300 to 400 people started with us in, I should think about twenty carriages. We reached Cassel in 12 minutes and stayed some time there and in Hattersheim, but reached Frankfurt at 10 o'clock.

July 26.   To the Stadel Museum of Arts. A splendid picture by Overback 2 of Rome added to the list since last year.

July 28.   Leave Frankfurt at 12 by Eilwagen. We keep to the left bank of the Main till the evening. Stop at Hannau, famed for its battle in 1813 between Napoleon and the Allies.
The neighbourhood is quite flat and cultivated for many miles, like a garden. Maize is grown abundantly. Population 8,000.
Hence to Aschaffenburg. It has a castle and pleasant gardens overlooking the Main. The Queen of Bavaria often stays here in summer. Later we enter the forest of Spessart and travel in it for 20 English miles: it is believed to have been a forest in Caesar's time. The trees are now mixed. As we pass through we see now beech, now sycamore, then oak and higher up Scotch firs. It was considered to be dangerous from robbers after the Peace but gens d'armes have now made it safe.
We cross the river by ferry at Wertheim, where the long convent-like castle of the Prince of Lowenstein commands the river.

July 29.   To-day was spent in seeing Wurzburg. The Schloss of the former Prince Bishops (now Kings of Bavaria) is an immense building in the tawdry French style of 200 years ago. It has an enormous square and two odd columns before it. The walks are very spacious, as are the gardens.
Leave at 12 at night with three Jews and a Bavarian peasant; not very sweet society. Our road was constantly ascending and descending, though the hills were not very high. Hops are very extensively cultivated about Neustadt and much tobacco is grown. From thence to Nurnberg which we reach at 12 and fix at the Bayerische Hof.
After dinner we begin to explore this most picturesque and

interesting town. To describe it requires the pencil of the artist rather than the pen of the writer. The architecture of the 14th, 15th and 16th centuries is better preserved here than anywhere else in Germany. The lofty, tapering gables, the richly decorated oriel windows, the projecting ornamented balconies for drawing heavy packages to the top of the houses by means of cranes - many of these abound in this town.

July 31. Still wet and cold. In the morning we looked at the Rathaus[3] and the market and its beautiful fountain and the gallery of paintings of the old German School in the former Chapel of St. Maurice and at the Church of St. Sebald.
In the afternoon to the house of Albrecht Durer and saw his bronze statue, erected in 1840, from a design of Rauch[4] of Berlin. We also saw the Imperial Citadel and the burying ground of St. John, which is a mile north of the town, and the many interesting streets.

August 1. At 9 to the Protestant service in the beautiful Church of St. Lawrence. Candles lighted on the High Altar. Gospel of the day read and printed prayers. An excellent sermon on Abraham's faith in relation to Isaac's birth. A full congregation.
Then view the Frauenkirche, the church on the market place. It has a fine Gothic portal but its interior is spoiled by gaudy paintings. I inspected the Aegidius Kirche after dinner. Italian without and gaudy French within. It has an altar-piece, said to be by Van Dyck and some old carved work, but the most interesting thing in connection with it is the Norman chapel at the north-east, much in the style of those in the Fortress. It is probably 700 years old.
I then attended service at the fine Church of St. Sebald and heard an excellent sermon. We walk to the Eisbahn (railway). It is only five miles long, and then we looked at the canal which is to connect the Danube with the Rhine. This will be navigable for wherries of goods and timber but not for steam vessels. A railway is now planned from Bamburg to Munich.

August 2. Alfred ill with cold. I journalize and read newspapers. Much talk at table d'hôte of canals, railways, art, etc. At 3 by railway and steam to Furth. See an Antiquitathen-Sammlung there. These collections are formed, generally by Jews, they consist of old armour, old ivory or wood carvings, painted glass, old china-ware, ornaments and coins, damasks, tapestry, carved chairs, etc. etc.
Return to Nurnberg by steamer at 4½. Distance five miles English. Time 10 minutes. Price 4d. per head.

A railway is in progress which will go from Munich to Dresden in 24 hours - or even from Berlin to Munich, in the same space of time.

August 3.   Up at 6¹/₂. Leave by Eilwagen with Mr. Bonne, an architect and a young advocate named Preusse. Route hilly after the first ten miles, with fine forest trees. Horses of the peasants active and good. Women at Nurnberg and in many villages south of it have beautiful eyes and are much prettier than those of the north. Cross the canal which is to join the Main and the Danube near Neumarkt. It is called the Ludwig's canal. The soil here is very sandy and the sides must be built of stone. From Kelheim on the Danube above Regenburg. From hence the canal runs to Neumarkt and Nurnberg to Bamberg. Here boats will pass down the Main to the Rhine and thus the Black Sea and the German Ocean will be united by an inland navigation.
The line of our route to-day is much wooded and thinly peopled. The architect and lawyer tell merry stories of Austrians and we rejoin in Irish and English tales.
At 12 at night, after a drive of 65 miles, we cross the Danube by a stone bridge which is 1100 feet long and 700 years old and enter Regensburg, which is on the south of the river.
We lodge at the Krenz Inn.

August 4.   At 9 Messrs. Bonne, Preuss, Alfred and I go to the ancient Rathaus, in the halls of which the Diets of Germany held their meetings from 1663 to 1806. They are very interesting but the dungeons and instruments of torture excite a thrilling of wonder, horror and thankfulness that they are no longer used in Europe.
Of the dungeons, one is a room 5 ft. 5 ins. high in which the prisoner was chained, totally without light or fresh air, another 8 ft. by 6 ins. is a deep hole, aired only by a grate at its top and a third, a similar but narrower den was closed at the top by a heavy stone and the prisoner was left to die of hunger. His remains were afterwards mutilated and dropped into a stone well which communicates, it is said, with the Danube.
We read and examined the descriptions and regulations and plans and drawings in the printed Code of the Empire of the various modes of torture. The book was reprinted in 1736 and the tortures were used to the end of the last century. We afterwards saw the horizontal rack and vertical torturing machine with its stone weights, to break the joints, and the "ladder" and the "Spanish Ass", a sharp edged piece of wood on which the accused sat, with weights attached to his feet and the sharp points of wood on which he was made to

sit, unclothed. All the instruments were still in the lofty dark room in which the tortures were inflicted, and the gate of wood, behind which the judges sat unseen, is still preserved. The whole is well described in Murray's Hand Book for travellers in Southern Germany.

After dinner we cross the Danube in a carriage and go five or six miles on its north bank to Donaustauf and then walk up to the Valhalla. This beautiful pure Grecian temple, 223 feet long by 104 feet wide as measured at its eaves, was begun in 1830. Its object is to serve as a temple for the busts and statues of the illustrious men of Germany of all ages; if their portraits are unknown, their names in letters of gold are affixed to the wall. The present King Ludwig was the designer of this noble work. The architect who has executed it is Klenze. [6] The architectural part alone will have cost two million florins or £166,666. To this must be added the cost of sculpture, road-making etc. The name is that of the Scandinavian Paradise or place of reward for the departed heroes.

The temple stands on four terraces of huge cyclopean work and is placed on the top of a hill which commands a grand view of the Danube and its plains to the south and is backed by lofty blue hills to the north. The exterior is of white Salzburg limestone which will turn yellowish as it grows older. The interior is of beautiful reddish marble, veined with white, peach-blossom and cream colours. The capitals, architraves, etc., are of pure white marble. An attic is supported by caryatides, these figures and the coffers of the ceiling and the volutes and other ornaments are painted and gilded. The effect is beautiful, contrary to my expectation, for until I saw it here, I always thought the Greeks must have half-spoiled their grand and elegant architecture by the plan which they undoubtedly pursued of painting and gilding its ornaments. The outside is still concealed by a case of wood, but the assistant-architect showed us all over the building and allowed us to inspect the drawings. The Prince of Thurn and Taxis and the Princess of Furstenburg, etc. were looking over the building at the same time. It is said that the Tyrolean hills may be seen from the Valhalla front.

August 5. At 2 p.m. Bonne, Preuss (pleasant travelling companions) Alfred and I start in the Eilwagen from Regensburg to Landshut. It was bright moonlight when we crossed the two branches of the Iser "rolling rapidly"[7] at 9 p.m. and we admired the lofty tower of Landshut, 456 feet high. The castle is finely placed on a hill above the town: arcades like those of Bologna and Munster border the principal streets. We sup here, leave at 10½ - travel along the banks of the river Iser and at 4 watch a most beautiful sunrise, one which I have never seen equalled on the north of the Alps.

August 6.   We were astonished this morning to see the snowy summits of the Tyrolean Alps shining in the southern distance, perhaps 80 miles off, but looking not 20.   We enter Munich at 6. The grandeur of the Athenian buildings strikes us as we pass along the Ludwig's Strasse. We lodge badly at the Rôte Hahn. After breakfast receive letters from home which are, on the whole, satisfactory.   We read them under the splendid portico of the Post Office and in the garden of the palace and then stroll through the streets. See the Cathedral - ugly.
p.m. To the King's palace, old and new both inside and out. The new part is beautifully decorated in the interior and painted in the Pompeii style, the only thing of the kind I have ever seen. The subjects in the King's rooms are taken from Grecian authors and those of the Queen's from German. See the King's stables containing 300 horses and 400 mares. Look at the university and other splendid buildings and end the evening with a walk through the fair.

August 9.   Our two companions leave at 6 for Italy. At 10 go to the Glyptothek Repository of Sculpture. The splendour of its halls and their ceilings is wonderful in taste as well as in richness. The Egyptian and Etruscan Halls contain but few works but the Aeginetan Hall is most interesting. I saw these statues at Thorwaldsen's in Rome. They are now fully restored by him and admirably placed. The rooms are fourteen in number and contain much Grecian, Roman and modern sculpture. The gem of the gallery is the torso of one of the sons of Niobe. It is but a fragment but an exquisite one. The building itself of the Glyptothek deserves a long description with its beautiful series of halls and its still more beautiful portico.
Hence walk two miles to the Military Swimming School, a fine piece of clear water, 250 feet long and 10 deep. We revelled in it for 1/2 an hour and returned to dine in the open air in a beer-house garden. We also examine the fresco paintings of the Palace Arcades and in state apartments of the New Palace. The finest I have ever seen, far surpassing those of England and France. The Throne Room, about 56 paces long, is magnificently gilt and is ornamented with fresco paintings of great merit.   After taking ice we lounge down the Ludwig's Strasse, five paces wide and admire its fine buildings. The library is quite Florentine and of the grandest scale and dimensions. We were driven back by a thunder storm.

August 12. To the new library. This is an enormous building containing, when finished, fifty-six rooms, each of three stories of book cases. Staircases are so arranged that every book is accessible to the hand without any ladder. The grand staircase will be very noble. This library will not be finished for books before the end of 1842.

Ludwigskirche also unfinished, will be completed about the same time. It is in Byzantine style with round niches. This is the fourth of King Ludwig's churches. One is the Basilica, two are Byzantine and one Gothic, each admirable in its kind. The enormous painting of the Last Judgement occupying the east end of the Ludwigskirche is by Cornelius.[8] All these pictures of Last Judgements are similar in composition. Christ, with angels above and saints around; the good rising to bliss on the right and the devils torturing and tearing down the damned on the left. To me they are uninteresting, whether by Buonarroti, Rubens, Breughhel or Cornelius. There are some clumsy drawings of arms in this enormous work and the colouring is too rusty-red to please me. I decidedly prefer Hess to Cornelius.

August 13. In the afternoon to Steigelmayer's[9] Bronze Foundry. See his men chiselling many statues which had been cast. See also seven statues of Bavarian Sovereign Heroes, from eight to ten feet high. Splendidly worked and gilded, part of twelve which are to adorn the Throne Room of the Palace - also an enormous swan and the clay model of a statue of Bavaria which is 54 feet high and will be placed on a 30 feet pedestal. It is to stand on a little hill overlooking the Theresien Wiese where the October Festival takes place. It is a grand and beautiful work. The rest of our time was devoted to an examination of the Augsburg railway.

August 15. Sunday. Awakened by the horns and trumpets which every Saturday evening and Sunday morning play half an hour from the balcony which surrounds the Tower of St. Peter's. Letter, etc. and to the English Chapel from 11 to 1.

August 16. To Monsieur Boisserée to see his painted glass. The Ascension of the Virgin after Guido's[10] pictures (of which a copy is in the Pinakothek) and the same subject after Raphael's picture at Dresden, are two most beautiful pieces of glass painting. The flesh, expression and above all the splendid light round the heads, surpass the originals. Monsieur Boisserée shows them to us in a darkened room. One could almost fancy them to be apparitions.

At this time Boisserée was Curator General of Plastic Antiquities in Bavaria.

Try in vain to see Hess's studio but he was out shooting. To the Police Office, etc. A dark evening and the feeling that another summer is gone and the evenings, during which, in consequence of my bad eyesight, I lose so many sources of pleasure and employment, are again approaching. But let the painful thought pass. I have now at least my young friend with me to drive away the feeling.

August 17. Pay a last visit to the Glyptothek and then to the Nymphenburg Chateau. Its gardens are beautifully laid out with a grand mixture of French and English styles. They abound in beautiful streams, waterfalls and fountains. One of the latter in front of the Palace is 80 feet high. The collection of palm and other oriental plants is extensive. We walked the three miles from Nymphenburg to Munich and bathed on our way back.
Theatre in the evening and pack.

August 18. Leave Munich at 7 o'clock by railway to Augsburg. Distance said to be 41 miles. We perform the journey, including several halts, in 2 hours and 13 minutes. The country is swampy and a dead flat. Augsburg has a long and wide street bordered by good but not fine houses. The hotel of the Drei Mohren[11] is excellent and has existed for five hundred years. We looked into the Cathedral which has a high altar and apses at each end. It is ugly and uninteresting. We went through the Rathaus, the large room of which is indeed magnificent and we saw multitudes of models of buildings and machines in wood. View the Schloss and thought of the Conference of Augsburg[12] and looked at the large old brick walls and fosses. The three hours which we employed in seeing Augsburg were quite enough for everything in it, except the collection of old German paintings and the Printing Office of Baron Cotta[13] which is the birthplace of the Allgemeine Zeitung, a political paper, of much interest to Germans. The machinery in his extensive Printing Works is carried on by steam.
After dining at "The Drei Mohren" at an excellent table d'hôte we start by Eilwagen with a Revd. Professor of Philosophy of the Augsburg Lyceum, in which are twenty-two professors and eight hundred students. Till night-fall the country was very uninteresting, it abounded in oats, barley, hemp and flax. After an 86 miles journey we arrive at Lindau on the Lake of Constance, an island connected with the mainland by a long bridge of boats. The view

towards the Alps at the east end of the lake is very fine.

Dine at a lively and good table d'hôte with many travellers from various directions. Tutors with their pupils, officers, artists, bath-goers, but no English besides ourselves.

August 19.   At 2 we embark in a steamer on the lake and cross to Rorschach, which is in Switzerland, after a quarter of an hour's halt we direct to Constance which we reach at 6^1/2. The passage on the lake was delightful, a deep blue sky and a merry breeze so that we could sail as well as steam. The water was blue and green of beautiful rich and varied hues. The expanse so great that in a north west direction we could scarcely perceive the land. The waves are sometimes high (on Sunday, 19th July they were 8 to 10 feet high) so that wooden piles are necessary to protect the stonework of the little harbours on its coasts. The steamers are all built at Constance or Rorschach, the engines come from England.

On the west side of the lake the coast is low and the slopes are uniform, on the south side the hills are lofty and many fruit trees grow on them, also there are vineyards and much corn. We fix at the good Inn of the Adler and from the bridge and the piers of the neat Haven enjoy a glorious sunset. On the lake a few boats with wide sails shone on the blue waters like aerial "things of life" and the bells of the "Ave Maria" conveyed peaceful impressions to the mind quite in harmony with those it had received from the charms of light, shade and colour.

August 20.   Up at 6 full of delightful impressions of yesterday's evening. To the Cathedral, an irregular building with some pretty good tracery, but ugly as a whole and whitewashed inside. To the collection of antiquities in the Concilim Saal. The building itself bears the date of 1388 on the stone on its front. The antiquities are very poor but the prison in which John Huss[14] was confined (he was transferred from the Dominican Convent, now a cotton manufactory) possesses historical interest, as do the memorials of him.

After dinner by steamer down the Unter See and Rhine to Schaffhausen, a distance of about 30 miles through beautiful scenery. The house of Louis Napoleon, Arenenberg, which he lived in with his mother, Hortense[15], before his mad attempt to revolutionize France in 1840, is close on the lower lake.

As soon as we had fixed our luggage we walked and ran by the left bank of the Rhine to the Falls of the Rhine. Surely much rock must have been worn away in places since I saw them twenty-one years ago. They appear to me to be more varied than before and at this time there is so much water which adds to their grandeur. I was altogether far more pleased with them than when I first saw them. The views from a high hill above the castle were fine and those from the terrace and balconies of the castle were all magnificent. The spray, mist and varying outlines and the masses of the water so delighted us that we felt we could never tire of watching them.

August 21.   Saunter on the bridge and on the hills around looking at the clear, green waters of the Rhine until the temptation to plunge into them was irresistible and we had a most delicious swim above the town, whirling round in an eddy about 20 or 30 feet long.

At 12 leave Schaffhausen by diligence for Zurich, a distance of 32 miles and lodge at Storch, in an old Swiss looking hotel which had a most unpromising entrance, but inside was a very comfortable apartment. Here we sit down and remain fixed to our seats for more than an hour, delighting in the view and the lovely evening. Later we enjoy the breeze on the new bridge and we were soothed by the gentle beating of the little waves of the lake as we rested late on its banks.

August 22. Sunday.   Breakfast at 7 and go to the Evangelical church at 8. A venerable old man preached forcibly on the contests between Christian love and self love. "It is sweet and easy to talk of love and virtue but to carry them out is indeed difficult. Each morning is the contest between love and selfishness renewed. Spirit of truth, and love, do thou arm us for the contest, for thou alone can'st prevail" etc.

Banns of marriage were published as in Bavaria, in the only way they can be published decently in a church, namely, they were preceded and followed by prayer that the betrothed might live in happiness as Christians and be united in heaven. The names of recently departed members were then proclaimed with the addition "Blessed are the dead for their works shall follow them" and an admonition to the hearers that we must also soon depart and that our lives may be so lived here that the change may be a commencement of bliss. The service consisted of printed prayers, singing and a sermon. No scripture was read.

At 1 o'clock by steamer to Meilen and then walk a mile to Marienfeld to Mr. Russell's school where are the two sons of Mr. Freeston of South Elmham. The elder boy was out but we saw the younger and gave him their mother's letters and their father's gold. At 4½ cross the lake and then walk to the top of Albis. Again see the snowy range of the Alps in great glory by a most beautiful sunset. The effect on myself is scarcely less than when I beheld them in my younger days. They are the same as they were then and as they were thousands of years ago. "Ewige Alpen"![16] was my involuntary exclamation. Stay on the mountains till dark, then back to Zurich in 2½ hours.

August 23. Up at sunrise and spend the morning reading and shopping. At 5 ascend the Uetliberg which is nearly 200 feet higher than the Albis. There is an hotel at the top, built like a Swiss cottage and here were many visitors this fine morning and amongst them the pupils of the Blind School of Zurich. They actually seemed to enjoy the scene. One came to the edge of the precipice and asked how deep it was, whether one could climb it, etc. They had a guitar with them and sung much in chorus and in parts and alone. We walk home by moonlight but later rain came on and continued all night.

August 24. At dinner talk with four Italians and then go with them under the guidance of one of the partners of the celebrated House of Escher, to inspect their immense machine-making and manufacturing establishments. Their houses of work form quite a little town in and near Zurich and they employ 1200 labourers. The model (wooden) in one of their rooms, alone cost 500,000 guldens (£41,666). We saw the whole process of paper making and were delighted with the machinery by which rags were converted into dry, good writing paper, in a quarter of an hour. The power of the Braham's Press here is 125,000 kilograms - 125 tons, English. In the foundry we saw liquid iron poured like streams of lava into moulds of very varied forms. Coppers of steam engines were being nailed in another room. Woollen carding and spinning occupied another building.
In the flour mills we were raised from the ground to the third floor, as are the sacks of flour. We took four hours in visiting these vast establishments and had then seen only about one third of them.
I put many questions to a director as to the effect of education on the workmen. His answers were most decidedly favourable. He wishes all their workmen to be educated, because those educated are so much better workmen. He has twenty Englishmen and many French and Italians and his observation on the qualities of the different nations as workmen were quite similar to those given by Dr. Kay[17] in the Poor Law Commissioners Report last week. He was not at Zurich at the time of Dr. Kay's visit and his testimony is therefore important as corroborative of what the doctor heard from another partner.

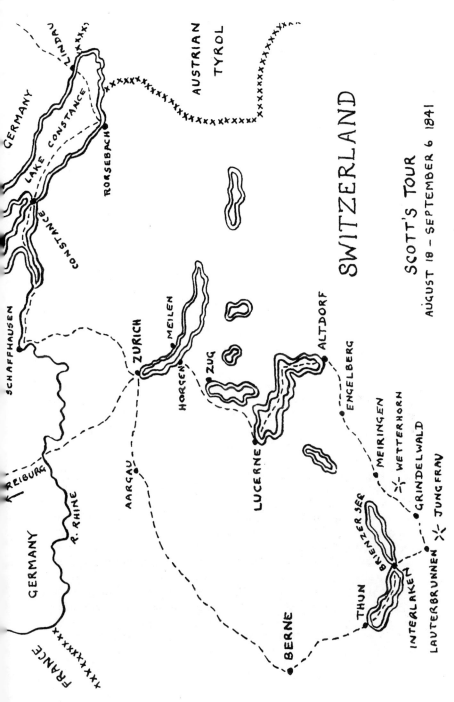

Map of Switzerland

GERMANY

LINDAU

LAKE CONSTANCE

AUSTRIAN TYROL

CONSTANCE

RORSEBACH

SCHAFFHAUSEN

FREIBURG

R. RHINE

GERMANY

FRANCE

AARGAU

ZURICH

MEILEN

HORGEN

ZUG

LUCERNE

ALTDORF

ENGELBERG

MEIRINGEN

WETTERHORN

GRINDELWALD

JUNGFRAU

BRIENZER SEE

INTERLAKEN

LAUTERBRUNNEN

THUN

BERNE

SWITZERLAND

SCOTT'S TOUR

AUGUST 18 – SEPTEMBER 6 1841

Staubbach Falls, Lauterbrunnen

August 25. At 8 leave by steamer, reach Horgen at 10½. Join three Bavarians in a carriage to Zug and to Arth. We walked to the ruined village of Goldau which, as I described in a former journal, was destroyed in September 1806, by a tremendous landslip when 450 persons were killed in it and the adjoining villages: similar catastrophies, though on a less destructive scale, have repeatedly occurred since. Hence we ascend the Rigi with the same companions. The rocks, pine groves and precipices were grand and the waterfalls numerous, lofty and beautiful. We ascend in three hours but were not in the least fatigued, so refreshing is the air. We had a sublime view although it was not the one we hoped for. Clouds intercepted the snowy Alps. We had no grand outlines of the main ridges of rock, ice and snow, but we had clouds rolling far below us and through them, at intervals, we saw the lakes of Lucerne, Zug, Zurich etc., now dark purple and blue; now yellow and golden, as the rays of the sun shone upon them. When the sun gave its magical glory to portions of the rolling masses, leaving others in mysterious deep purples and lighting up the peaks, which in places broke above them, the marvellous beauty was such that we felt as though we were not on earth. No material elements, perhaps, could have so inspired the mind with ideas of the awful grandeur of heavenly power and heavenly regions. But the clouds soon closed around us and we retired to the Rigi Kulm Inn to pass the night and had that delicious sleep which pure air and much exercise always gives me.

August 26. The mountain is still enveloped in clouds and our companions leave in despair at 11 o'clock but we resolve to stay until tomorrow. The clouds remain on Rigi Kulm all day. By supper time our party at the Inn had increased to more than forty travellers, English, French, Spanish but chiefly German and at 9 o'clock, the joyful news was spread that stars and moon were visible.

August 27. At 4 a.m. we got up and saw the stars shining splendidly with a sea of clouds below us. I was nearly ready to quit my room when the sound of the Alpine Horn at our doors aroused all the party to see the finest and most wonderful sight I, perhaps, ever beheld.

An interminable sea of cloud, with grand swelling waves extended to the north which was broken in other directions by the loftier mountains, some of which are as Rossberg etc. rose like islands, while others formed a coast of uncommon grandeur, the higher summits of which were covered with snow. These were gradually lighted up and what with the charms of the rosy tints on the snow and the deep red on the waves of cloud with the sudden burst of blaze from the sun, the scene was one which was indeed deeply felt and will I hope be remembered as long as I live. Words can give so imperfect an idea of the reality that I shall not attempt any further description.

Two hours after sunrise we were called from our breakfast to see a double Iris bow on the clouds below us. It was of small diameter, some ten or twelve degrees. Our own figures were shadowed within the bow and looked about one eighth of its diameter. The red was uppermost.

We had by this time become intimate with five Prussian students and dined with them at 1 o'clock and an hour later we began to descend towards Kussnacht. The dense masses of cloud below remained firm, with glorious sunshine above them. We passed through them, they might be 300 feet thick, and below entered a new world, clear but without sunshine. The chapel and the gorge or "Hollow Lane" where Tell shot Gessler are historically interesting and there is a painting of the event on the outer wall of the chapel.

Hence we walk past the scanty ruins of Gessler's Castle[18] and from Kussnacht to Lucerne, but we passed the entrance to Lucerne in order to visit the Monument of the Dying Lion designed by Thorwaldsen and worked by Ahorn in honour of the Swiss soldiers who fell fighting for Louis XVI at Paris in 1789. It is cut in the face of a high sandstone rock. The Lion is said to be 24 feet long and is admirably designed and worked.

Sleep at the Swan Hotel on the lake, after sitting on the bridges and enjoying the cool evening breeze.

August 28. By steamer to Fluelen; the morning was cloudy, but near Brunnen it cleared. We saw the classical meadow of Grutli, where Arnold, Werner and Walter[19] swore the oath which laid the foundation of Swiss liberty and we passed close by the spot where Tell sprung ashore, which is perhaps more interesting than the chapel. At Altdorf we parted with our student friends, near the place where Tell shot the apple on his son's head, they marching up the valley of the Reuse to the Furca and ascending the steep mountain on the west.

Our route lay by the Waldnacht and the Surenen Alps to Engelberg. The distance was 25 miles and included an ascent of 5865 feet, being 7215 feet above the sea which is itself 1350 feet lower than the lake of Lucerne where we start from. We went two-thirds of the way without a guide but here the pathway ceased and we had to pass slate hills and three fields of old snow, the latter are dangerous to strangers who do not know where the snow is firm, so we asked a young mountain cowherd, whom we luckily met, to accompany us over the ridge. He did so. But three times did Alp on Alp arise, the grandeur of these huge masses of bare rock cannot be described in words. Our descent to Engelberg was equally interesting. Most lovely was the green valley with its convent and scattered Swiss wood houses and how glorious the peaks and snows of Titlis made rosy and pink by the setting sun. We slept as well as wet sheets would allow us.

August 29. Sunday. To the large church of the Convent at 9. The music at the High Mass was good, the people fine, well formed, clean and very picturesquely dressed. The women with white wreaths of braid around their hair and the men, all in their shirt-sleeves and without coats.

We started with a guide from the neat and not expensive Inn of the Engel, to ascend the Joch. This hill is about as high as that we crossed yesterday. The hut on the face of the rock where we drank whey was awfully high and commands most notable views. Two lads live there in summer and make their cheeses.

We had three tiers of mountains to overcome and passed two lakes before we reached the ridge of Titlis with its perpetual snows and glaciers. On our descent we came to a chalet where we drank three pails of milk and ate bread and butter for our dinner at 2 p.m. These alpine herdsmen have 452 cattle, 76 goats and 40 horses under their charge. The pine trees appear of enormous height in our descent, though no tree exceeds 100 feet probably, and many not more than 70 or 80 feet, but as they grow on steep acclivities of 1000 or 2000 feet, towering one above another they look incredibly lofty. A moss called "Fir Tree's Hair" grows abundantly on them. The goats eat it freely. Many waterfalls from the face of a 900 foot rock some 200 feet high, gush in one place seven falls of water. In several places we see ruins of forests of pine, occasioned by the avalanches of last spring which break the lofty trees in pieces and as they cannot be extricated till snow and thaws have rendered them rotten, the stems and trunks lie scattered in majestic ruin. Our walk today was 20 miles, including some 4000 feet of ascent.

The peculiar grandeur of the Surenen and Joch passes, arises from the perpendicularity of its enormous mountains. We reach Meiringen at 7$\frac{1}{2}$ and lodge at the Krone.

August 30. Here the state of our boots rendered a day's rest necessary. After dinner stroll to the Reichenbach Falls and see them thoroughly in every part. They are ten in number, besides rapids and are exceedingly beautiful.

In the evening some of our Strassburg friends arrive.

August 31.   Ascend from Meiringen to the mountain tops of Scheidedeck and through a most beautiful valley of pines, flowers and cattle to the glacier of Rosenlau. The ice here is from 50 to 200 feet thick. The Bath House is in a very beautiful situation. Its waters are sulphurous and cold, but are heated for bathers. We looked here, but in vain, for chamois, but saw three eagles towering above us. In front of a neat wooden chalet, we were quaffing delicious milk and admiring the way the cheesemaker had arranged his many cheeses, when shouts announced that our merry students had overtaken us; we went on together. Now commenced the hissing roar of avalanches, five or six fell in about three hours. On the Faulhorn it thundered and it was sometimes difficult to distinguish the thunder from the roar. The views when ascending the Wetterhorn, Mettenberg, Eiger and the Jungfrau were most sublime.

We saw two more glaciers near Grindelwald - a beautiful and extensive cavern of celestial blue ice in the upper one, with steps cut out to ascend its exterior. I had seen these two before, on the whole they were rather retarded than advanced.

Slept at the Adler at Grindelwald. It was a lovely moonlight night and we persuaded four damsels to sing to us, which they did in good harmony and jodelled very pleasingly. We then strolled along, viewing the light of the moon on the snowy peaks of the mountains and the broken tops of the glaciers. It was a perfect evening.

September 1.   Start, seven of us, with our knapsacks at 7½ and ascend the sides of the Wengern Alp, under a burning sun. The luxury of the occasional cooling beneath the shade and aroma of the pine trees, with the odours of thyme and dianthus in air of surpassing purity, were delightful, they must be felt to be realised. No banquet of turtle, turbot, venison and champagne can equal them.

We found two girls sitting on the brow of the first hill we climbed, whose employment was lace making. At the approach of strangers they began to sing duets most pleasingly, which were accompanied on a stringed instrument. The white teeth, dark eyes and rosy sunburnt complexion of one under her broad straw hat were so beautiful, that I wish much I could have transferred them to a more lasting memorial than mere words. The view of the snow on mountains from the top of the Wengern Alp was grand.

The descent of Lauterbrunnen very steep. Staubbach was all dust and mist. We pursued our walk merrily from Lauterbrunnen (how much enlarged since I last saw it! spacious hotels instead of the

Parsonage in which I lodged), down the grand depth of rock to the still Interlaken. Its meadows are pleasing and its goats descending from the mountain pastures, each to his own house, amused us. The walnut trees are very fine but the place is too wooded and has an oppressive air of dullness. We passed by its many hotels which are said to be very expensive and lodged at the Old Swiss Kauthaus in Untersee.

September 2.   A rainy morning. We all strolled through Interlaken to the Brienzer See. This place looks like a bathing town or village where the people do not know in the least what to do with themselves or their time. The five students who have been our companions, kindly accompany us to the Untersee where we embark. They are lively fellows and we separated with sincere good wishes, one studies Natural History as a Professor and the others are Jurists, which qualifies for all government employments in Prussia as well as for Law.

The mountains were wreathed in mist as we journeyed the length of the Untersee in the steamboat. At Thun we stayed from 1 to 6, bathed in the lake and then by Diligence travelled on to Berne which we reached at 9 and lodged at the "Falcon".

September 3.   Spent 2½ hours in the Assembly of the Swiss Diet, in a room about 50 feet square and 20 high, hung with yellow draperies. Some forty-four Deputies were present, dressed in black coats, waistcoats and pantaloons, with court swords by their side. The President was in an exalted chair on one side and the Secretary at a small table before him, the members at a horse-shoe table with portfolios, inkstands and sprinkling boxes[20] and others at side tables. They do not rise when they speak. They address the Assembly as "Herr President" and "Meine Herren", which they repeat as often as a stammering Englishman repeats "Gentlemen". On one side of the room is a gallery of four rows, to which spectators are admitted. It was quite full, but after a little patience we were able to enter, gratis. Soldiers guard the entrance.

The question was most interesting. Each Deputy gave in a report from his canton as to whether the Canton of Aargau should or should not be compelled to restore the convents it has recently suppressed. Wieland, the Deputy for Aargau spoke very well. The age of the Deputies was, I should think, in no case less than thirty nor more than sixty. No "Hear Hear" or applause or censure were given but the opinion of each member was listened to with silent attention.

Dine at the "Falcon" where years ago I first became acquainted with

Joseph Woods[21], Captain Cook, the two Duncans and the Bishop of Llandaff (Copplestone). Explore the town, picturesquely placed on a peninsular, and view the machinery for raising blocks for building the new bridge. Sultry heat portends a change of weather, I think this is the last day of summer.
We looked at the deer in the trenches, walked to the Enge promenade and saw the grand snow mountains lighted, partially by the setting sun and then "the moon takes up the tale"[22] and we strolled along the streets hearing music, though our pleasure was much marred by the odours from the ill-drained courts and the road-ways.

September 4.   We travelled by Eilwagen from 6 a.m. to 8 p.m. and seemed to go rapidly, but averaged only six miles an hour, exclusive of dinner and other halts, the distance being 72 miles. Alfred was outside and I within. Our companions varied frequently and the Aargau Convent question was much talked about. The district we passed through was generally level, very rich by nature and cultivated with industry, skill and expense.
We dined at Aargau - the gardens of the town are full of beautiful flowers, particularly dahlias, asters, hydrangeas, oleanders and pomegranates. Reach the Hecht Hotel at Zurich at 8½. It has been an entire day of rain and the first of autumn. Summer is gone and the peasants are taking up potatoes in great quantities. Many were ploughing for wheat with four and even five oxen.

September 6.   Leave by Eilwagen at 7. Quit Switzerland and enter Baden. We rise sometimes rapidly, sometimes gradually, to near 2000 feet above the Rhine. The views of the Alps on the south were grand but the Black Forest disappoints me. It is in places much cleared and cultivated but its masses of pines in other parts are very fine, it is very steep and hilly. At dusk we begin to descend into the Hollenthal which is dark and most precipitous and while we were supping, Robert Hughes comes in from Freiburg.

September 7.   Hollenthal[23]. This narrow valley has by no means such horrors as to deserve its title. The woods are not only of fine straight pines but of beech, birch, ash, maple and oak so that the variety of tints is most pleasing. The hills are varied in form, cows and a few goats and some cottages of Swiss-like aspect, but less beautiful, are scattered among them. The rocks of grey and reddish granite near are abrupt in form and at Hirchensprung they are perpendicular and so close together that room is left only for the road and the stream. Moreau[24] led his army through this narrow pass. We arrived at Freiburg at 12 1/2. The town is small but neat, indeed an excellent one, the neighbourhood is pretty but far inferior to the Rhine Valley, which my friends, the Hughes' have left to make their home here. Their house is the best in the town and Alfred takes up his quarters at his father's house and I go to Zahringerhof[25].

September 8.   The Virgin's Birthday. Spend an hour in the Munster, a fine Gothic building. Music good. Costumes of the peasants rich and handsome. Bright reds, greens and blues prevail in the petticoat, corset and aprons respectively, with silver and gold lace headpieces and broad silk lappets attached, female dress very short. Men have long blue velvet coats and red waistcoats. Costumes probably not altered since the time of the potent Dukes of Zahringen (the last died in 1218!)
In the evening accompany the Hughes' to the Rathaus where we meet several of their friends and Herr Von Rech, a member of the second chamber of Baden Deputies, now filling an office at Freiburg like that of Prefect in France. A pleasing man of fifty, full of knowledge and fun and wholly without humbug. Music and dancing were the order of the evening.

September 22.   Prepare to leave Freiburg and my friends, with whom I have spent the greater part of my time since I arrived here on the 7th.

September 23.   Alfred and I start by omnibus and take a slow steamer (which could not get up to Kiel last night for want of water) to Mannheim, where we sleep.

September 24.   Leave by steamer at 6. Mainz at 10 1/2 and Coblenz at 4 p.m. Fix at Trierscher Hof and Saal comes to see us in the evening.

September 26.   We arrive at Cologne to-day at 4 o'clock and fix at the Kolnrischer Hof on the Rhine. Look round and go into the Cathedral, the choir of which appears to me to be more beautiful than ever. The streets very full.

September 27.   Leave Cologne at 8 by the Iron Railway. Crowds go with us. We travel very rapidly on a level surface with little noise or motion and pass under three tunnels: one, I should think, is two miles long. In three hours, that is by 11 o'clock, we were at Aix-la-Chapelle, where we stay till 3. See Charlemagne's Cathedral, spoiled

by the plaster ornaments of two centuries ago and now chiefly interesting for the "Carolo Magno" tomb of that Emperor, a large stone of marble under the dome. We see the Rathaus in which two congresses were held in 1748 and 1818. The shops were well stocked with jewellery, ornaments, saddlery, etc.
By diligence to Liege. Sup and sleep at the Hotel de la Pommelette.

September 28.   Take a general survey of the town. Much appearance of wealth and activity.   Look at the works for the rebuilding of a bridge across the Meuse, which, only erected in 1832, was already giving way and had to be taken down.   The shops are excellent, particularly for fire-arms. From the hill of St. Martin's there is a good general view over the slated roofs and rather pretty country which is partially obscured by the smoke from the factories along the banks of the Ourthe and Meuse.
Leave at 11¹/₂ and go three miles by omnibus to the present railway station and start from it at 1 o'clock.   Much noise and rapid motion but such long stoppages that we took five hours instead of three to go from Liege to Brussels. Pass by Tirlemont, Louvain and Mechlin, the great central station of the Belgian railway, where are ten parallel railways at one point. Reach Brussels at 6. To the Hotel de Suede and take a moonlight view of the park and principal streets after tea.

September 29.   Look at the Hotel de Ville which seems very large but much less handsome than my recollection had drawn it. The market and the Cathedral of St. Gudule are grand and the carved pulpit of wood in the latter is beautiful. A statue of Count Merode by Geefs[26], who was killed in the insurrection of 1830, is well executed. He is recumbent in a blouse, with a pistol in his hand. Then to the Palace given to the Prince of Orange by the town of Brussels. All the pictures have been removed to the Hague so there is nothing to see but a few pieces of malachite and some inlaid wooden floors, which we were obliged to skate over in cloth slippers.Dine at table d'hôte at 4 o'clock in the dining room here - which is a kind of imitation of the English time of dining.   As there was no theatre we went to a café.

September 30.   Intending to get up at daybreak, I dress and being surprised at the non-progress of the dawn, strike a light and find it is only 3 o'clock so go to bed again.
At 6 by diligence to the field of Waterloo and to La Belle Alliance[27], on the Public House of which is inscribed "Belle Alliance, Rencontre des Generaux Wellington et Blucher lors de las

memorable Bataille du XVIII Juin 1815 se saluant mutuellement Vainqueurs".

Then walk to the Prussian Monument at Planchenoit, which is an Iron Cross like those of Waltham or of Godesberg. It is about 20 feet high and is thus inscribed:- "Die gefallene Helden ehrt Dankbarer Koenig und Vaterland Sie ruhen in Frieden. Belle Alliance. Den 18 Juni 1815"[28].

Thence we walked to Frischermont, over the scene of the Prussian attack on the French. Alfred picked up a bullet on a newly harrowed field. From here along the English lines to La Hays Sainte and viewed the two monuments on either side of the road. One to the officers of the Hanoverian Legion and the other to Sir Alexander Gordon, brother to Lord Aberdeen and Aide-de-Camp to the Duke of Wellington, who was killed when he was only 29.

Then to the spot where Wellington longest stood[29] and to the pyramidal mound on which the Lion, cast by Cockerill of Liege, stands on his lofty base. The hill may be from 100 to 150 feet high but I did not estimate it on the spot. The view of the field from here is complete. I surveyed it with a deep feeling of the political consequences of the battle and of the individual suffering of the combatants and their friends and then came that melancholy but elevating feeling of the vanity of human purposes, the instability of earthly things and the mysteries of eternity.

We went on to Hougoumont where the Crucifix of the Virgin, in wood, still stands in the chapel. We then returned to Mont St. Jean and were picked up by a diligence which brought us back to Brussels at 3. By going first to La Belle Alliance, we avoided to a great degree, those pests, the guides and relic sellers.

It seems to me to be rather a reproach to England that whilst Prussia, Hanover and Belgium have erected memorials of the battle to those who fell, there is no English monument on the ground, except the one raised by the brother and sister of Alexander Gordon.

An immense change has taken place in the Forest of Soignies since I was here in 1816. Extensive clearances near the high road have reduced it in this direction to such an extent that one only goes a few hundred yards through forest now instead of two miles. A long street of manufacturing-looking cottages has also united Waterloo with Mont St. Jean. How rapidly do localities change yet we pretend to trace those of Rome and Greece with the most minute detail.

After dinner we go to the theatre where the opera of "William Tell" was disfigured by noisy, false-singing actors and actresses. We came away in disgust before it was over.

October 1.   To the Museum of Natural History in the old Palace of the Spanish and Austrian Regency, very rich in birds. The contents of the Gallery of Pictures were chiefly bad. Four or five venerable Rubens but one excellent portrait by Rembrandt.

October 2.   From 7 to 8 we examine the Monument of the Martyrs of the 1830 Revolution[30] and the excellent Botanical Gardens and then leave the good Hotel de Suede at 10½. and go by railway to Antwerp. Leopold, the King of the Belgians, came in a Royal train just after us. He is still a fine man, but less melancholy-looking than when he was the husband of the Princess Charlotte[31] of England or when he was in Paris in 1822. He came here to-day to visit the "British Queen" steamer, an immense vessel which ran from Liverpool to New York. She has been purchased by the Belgian Government.
Fix at the Hotel de Grand Laboureur on the Place de Meir. All the troops were drawn out to receive the King. Visit the Gallery of Paintings or Musée. It contains 245 pictures. Ten or twelve by Rubens and Vandyck are very good, particularly a Descent from the Cross. A Saviour between two Thieves, Theresa interceding for the Souls in Purgatory by Rubens and a Dead Christ on the knees of the Virgin by Vandyck. There are also some remarkable paintings by Quentin Matsys. We then inspected the docks which are full of vessels from England, the north of Europe and other places. The salutes, as the King disembarked, were grand.

October 3.   At 7 to the Cathedral. The glorious "Descent from the Cross" pleases me more and more and so does the vast area and seven aisles of the church, but the tower never pleased me less. This is my third visit to Antwerp.
In the Church of St. Jacques is Ruben's tomb behind the altar, and in the chapel, at the back of it, is a good altar-piece painted by this artist. There is also a capital portrait by Vandyck in the second chapel on the left.
We had a long hunt for the Church of Augustines to see the altarpiece, also painted by Rubens, which Sir Joshua Reynolds so highly praises, but which we thought must have been much smoked and faded since he saw it and I did not like the composition. We concluded our morning's walk by looking at the outside of the theatre.
Breakfasted at 9½ and at 11 left Antwerp on board the dirty, worn-out old Soho Packet. Thomas Farr and sixty others were passengers. The banks of the Scheldt looked miserably flat and uninteresting. A good breeze. I turned in at 8. and by keeping quiet had no

sickness in spite of some rolling in a cross sea.

October 4.   At 7 o'clock, when I came on deck, I found we were within six miles of Gravesend and had passed through a wonderfully numerous crowd of vessels for twenty-one miles along the Thames. We anchored at the Tower at 11 having performed our passage in exactly 21 hours.

October.

On returning to England after an absence of nearly four months the extracts from his diaries are of no special interest. After inspecting his house and gardens the day following his arrival in Bungay he goes to the National School and notes that a hundred and fifty scholars are present.   Alfred Hughes has been his constant companion abroad and returns with him and continues his studies at Waveney House.
The Distillery at Earsham is often mentioned at this time and was then known as the Norfolk Distillery. Adjoining it was a pleasantly situated house with a large walled-in garden, stables, outhouses and yards and two cottages. It was for sale and was the property of the Butchers of The Grove who had until lately carried on the business for fifty years.

PART III (1841) Fifteen Weeks in Germany, Switzerland and Belgium

References

1. Head, Sir Francis Bond (1793-1875). Author.

2. Overback (1789-1869). Leader of the Nazarene School.

3. The Rathaus. The walls of the great hall are painted by Albrecht Durer and those of the smaller hall contain portraits of Nurnberg worthies and verses by the King of Bavaria.

4. Rauch (1777-1857). Sculptor.

5. Ludwig succeeded to throne in 1825, abdicated in 1848.

6. Von Klenze, Leo (1784-1864). Famous architect.

7. "Iser" Hohenlinden by Thomas Campbell.

8. Cornelius (Lucas). Dutch painter appointed portrait-painter to Henry VIII, died 1552.

9. Steigelmeyer, J.B. (1781-1844). Died before the last mentioned statue was finished. It was completed by his nephew, Ferdinand Miller.

10. Reni, Guido (1575-1642).

11. Still in existence. One room in it, in which Count Fuge, the banker, entertained the Emperor Charles V, is in its original condition.

12. Augsburg. The conference between Charles V and the Lutherans in 1530 to resolve the religious differences of Germany.

13. Baron Cotta (1764-1832). Afterwards Baron Cottendorf, a famous publisher and friend of Goethe and Schiller.

14. Huss, John. Bohemian reformer, born c. 1369 and burned as a heretic by the Council of Constance in 1415.

15. de Beauharnais, Hortense, Daughter of Josephine, married to Louis Bonaparte, King of Holland, and mother of Napoleon III (1783-1837). Louis Napoleon's attempt to subvert Louis Phillippe's Government at Boulogne failed completely and led to his imprisonment in the Castle of Ham.

16. "Eternal Alps"

17. Dr. Kay(1804-1877). Founder of popular English education. Secretary to the Committee of Council on education. Assumed his wife's name of Shuttleworth on his marriage. Afterwards Sir James W. Shuttleworth, Bart.

18. More recent researches prove that this castle did not exist in Gessler's time. Even the existence of Tell himself has been denied.

19. The three patriots who formed the League of Forest Cantons - the nucleus of the Swiss Federation - against the Habsburgs in 1308.

20. Boxes of sand used for drying ink previous to the invention of blotting paper.

21. Woods, J.(1776-1864). Architect and botanist. First President of the London Architectural Society in 1806.

22. From Addison's hymn "The Spacious Firmament on High".

23. Hollenthal - Valley of Hell.

24. Moreau. Executed a masterly retreat before the Archduke Charles in 1796.

25. Zahringerhof is still in existence.

26. Geefs (1806-1860). Belgian sculptor.

27. "Belle Alliance" The meeting place of General Wellington and Blucher at the famous battle of 18th June 1815, greeting each other mutually as victors.

28. "A grateful King and Fatherland honour the fallen heroes. They rest in peace. Belle Alliance, June 18th, 1815."

29. The site has been much altered since viewed by J.B.S.

30.   1830 Revolution. This led to the separation of Belgium from Holland after an unpopular common monarchy of 15 years under the House of Orange. Leopold of Saxe-Coberg (1790-1865) became the first King of the Belgians (see below).

31.   Princess Charlotte; daughter of George IV, died 1817.

PART FOUR

1842-1844

Bungay & London. Paris.

1842

January. *At the beginning of the year the death of Mrs Philpot at Walpole occurs at the age of 93. On the 8th Mrs. Owles of Bungay aged 67 and on the 29th Mrs. Rackham, widow of the surgeon, dies at her house by St. Mary's Churchyard at the age of 70. Another former resident in the neighbourhood, Dr. John Yelloly died at Cavendish Hall, Norfolk, on the 31st. Physician to the London Hospital in 1807 and of the Norwich Hospital in 1820, he retired in 1832 and lived at Woodton Hall, near Bungay which he rented from the Sucklings. Its then owner, the Rev. Inigo Fox Suckling was a reckless, extravagant man and so squandered the family estate that he called on his son to cut off the entail. Soon after, in 1839 to 1840, the Woodton property, which had continued in unbroken succession in the Suckling family since 1348 was sold to Mr. Fellowes of Shotesham. The old Hall was completely demolished, every brick was removed, thus fulfilling the oath taken during a quarrel between Alfred Suckling and Mr. Fellowes when the latter declared that not one stone of the venerable mansion should remain upon another. The Yelloly's were obliged to seek another home and removed to Cavendish Hall early in 1840. In April of the same year the doctor was thrown on his head in a carriage accident and his right side became paralysed. He died at Cavendish, 31st Jan. 1842 and was buried at Woodton. He had ten children - John, the eldest, was rector of Barsham, near Beccles from 1856 to 1868.*
Anna Maria, his eighth child married Robert Alfred, eldest son of Inigo Fox Suckling and it was only through the firmness of Dr. Yelloly about the marriage settlement that the old manor and advowson of Barsham was rescued from the ruin which followed. This Manor and the advowson were purchased by Sir John Suckling, Knt. in 1613. He was the third son of Robert Suckling of Woodton and left his property to his son Sir John, the poet. The latter sold them to his uncle Charles Suckling of Woodton and thus they became part of the estates inherited by succeeding generations of the Woodton branch of the family.

May 12. *Newport.* Arrived here last night with Alfred who is staying with Barber for a time with the idea of taking up engineering.

93

May 19. London. Breakfast with George Thomas of Woodbridge at the Trafalgar Hotel and go to the inspecting of the Guards by Prince Albert, a fine gentlemanly and unaffected young man with a fascinating smile. The Queen's birthday kept today although it was on the 24th. Why?

May 22. Died at Boulogne aged 75 the Rev. Samuel Summers Colman, at one time of Broome Place near Bungay. He was father of my dear friend and schoolfellow, Charles Forster Colman who was killed in action at Secunderabad by the first cannon ball fired in the campaign. He lived about two hours after he was struck, being mortally wounded in the chest and knee and knew from the first he had not long to live. A brother officer was wounded in the arm at the same time. Colman taking off his sash gave it to his comrade to bind round his injured limb saying calmly and cheerfully "I shall not need it again".

June 1. A letter from Isabelle Travers inviting me to her wedding. Hear of Queen Victoria being shot at in the Green Park by John Francis and her noble conduct. The outrage occurred on Monday the 30th but the news did not reach Bungay until this morning.

June 24. Dine at Mrs Kingsbury's with the Cobbs. Mr. and Mrs. Margitson and their son John, just appointed Ensign of the 19th Regt.

June 27. Call on Major Forster and find him ill in bed. Hear from him that Stoddart was again imprisoned at Bokhara on the 19th December last.

June 29. To Sir E.Travers house at 10 and the wedding party leave at 10.30 for the church in twenty carriages. The bride looked very beautiful and all went well. It was very interesting though the full marriage service does seem to me very improper. A gay déjeuner at 11½ with speeches etc. The bride and bridegroom (Charles Smithies) left at 2 for Colchester. Dine at the Travers with some thirty-six mothers at 7 o'clock. A ball at 10 and dance till 3. A very gratifying day on the whole but the parting was bitter from the parents, sisters and brothers.

June 30. Thomas William Coke, Earl of Leicester dies aged 89 and on the 2nd. July, Robert Colmer of Yoxford, late Special Pleader dies, aged 56.

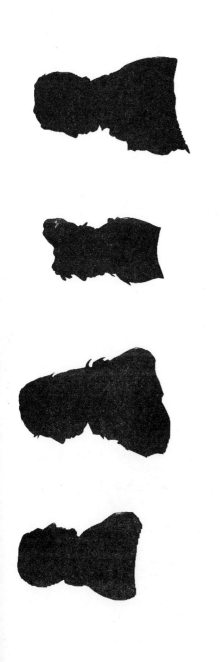

Above: Scott family silhouettes

John Barber Scott   Samuel Scott (1758-1825)   Sarah Scott (1762-1843)   Samuel Scott (1804-1885)

Below: J B Scott's drawing of his family tombstones in St Mary's churchyard

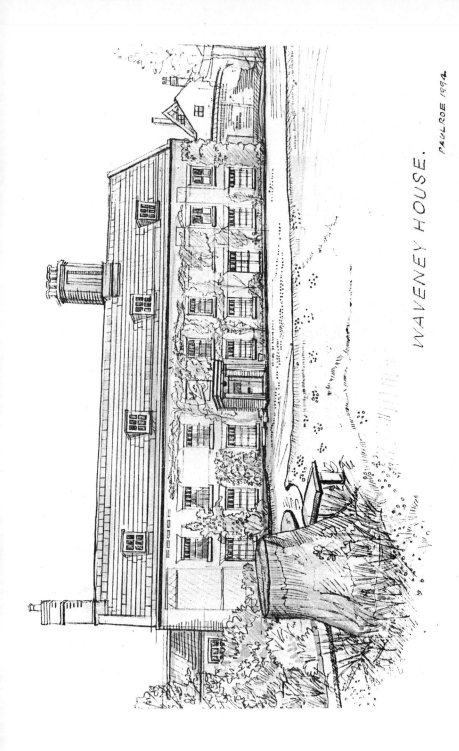

WAVENEY HOUSE.

PAULROE 1994

Waveney House today

1842]

July 6. Alfred Hughes arrives. He has been staying with Barber at Newport and wishes to be bound to him in order to learn engineering. I write to his parents in Freiburg about it and as they offer no objection we make preparations accordingly. Mendham[1], the artist comes from Eye and finishes the portrait he has been painting of him.

July 19. Up at 5 o'clock and breakfast at 7 with Alfred, who leaves by the London coach at 8$1/2$ for London and Newport.

July 20. The Thomas Scotts are making preparations for leaving Shadingfield. I ride over to see them and on the arrival of their son Charles from Norwich, we talk of family matters and approaching changes. Mrs Scott is cheerful at the idea of leaving, her husband much the reverse but has made up his mind to it.

They ultimately took a house in Yarmouth and Charles who was Rector at Shadingfield went to live at the Hall after his marriage.

July 21. My father's and my own old friend, George Barne of Tiverton dies this morning at 5 a.m.

July 29. The Ipswich Assizes. Attend on the Grand Jury from the 29th to August 1st.

July 31. From 7 to 9 walk from Ipswich to Woodbridge, eight miles, to see George Thomas. After breakfasting with him we visit his school of 300 boys and girls and the church which he has greatly improved, laying out about £900 on its repair. Then to the new church, risen about eight feet from the ground, to the building of which he is one of the principal contributors. Call on Mrs Sutton, widow of the late Admiral Sutton of Ditchingham Lodge. She has lost her speech but not her intellect. It was very painful to see her and to remember her past eloquence.

August 1. Leave Thomas early and return to Ipswich. In Court at 10 after breakfasting with Walter Scott. Dine with Judges Alderson[2] and Williams and others.

August 23. Holbrook. Go with Wilkenson to Ipswich and attend an Educational meeting. Bishop Stanley in the Chair. Speeches by Shaw, Sir J.Crewe, Cunningham, Pelham, Long, Hollingsworth etc. Call on Admiral Page, dine at Major Hockley's and then return to Holbrook.

October 4. Bungay. In the evening to a dance at The Grove when it was declared that Hartcup is engaged to Miss Margitson!

October 9. Ride by Flixton to St. Margaret's and go to Adolphus Holmes' church. Hear his new organ and attend the christening of his fourth boy, Edward Adolphus. Archdeacon Overshaw, aged 88 and 4 months, preaches.

October 10. Mr. and Mrs George Sandby and their children leave Bungay.

October 18. To Lowestoft to inspect the Navigation Works just bought for £5000.

October 26. Drive to the Boycotts of Burgh and dine there with Beevor, Salven, Mrs Grey, Miss Copsey and the Miss Carters.

November 13. My neighbour, Mrs Garden, dies at 5 a.m. after fifteen weeks of total insensibility. She was aged about 78 years and had lived in the house at the back of my own ever since I resided at Waveney House i.e. fifteen years. Two days later Richard Smith called Roman Smith, dies at 8¹/2. The tolling of the Minute bell peculiarly solemn.

November 21. Mrs Garden buried at Ringsfield and Richard Smith at the Roman Catholic chapel at Bungay. I excused myself from attending the funeral at Ringsfield on account of shortness of notice and wrote to John Garden and Burncaster to that effect.

I do not find any account of J.B.S. attending anyone's funeral, either friends or relations, up to this date although he did attend a stranger's funeral on a foreign tour.

1843

January 17. Read the report of Colonel Stoddart's assassination and go to the Forester's on the subject. Meet them on my way to Ditchingham Cottage and we hope it is not true.

January 20. Sir Robert Peel's private secretary assassinated by Daniel Macnaughton at 4 p.m. at Whitehall.

January 28. Hear of poor little Studholme Sandby's death this morning and in the afternoon of the certainty of dear Stoddart's.

He was beheaded at Bokhara on the 17th June last year by order of the Ameer.

February 8.   Disturbances at Shipmeadow House. The men refuse to quit the hall without more food, but afterwards retire and brickbat the doors and demolish all the windows looking into the yard so that no part of the glass, lead or iron bars remain. Six of them sent to Beccles gaol.

February 29.   Railway opened for passengers from London to Colchester. The Star coach leaves Bungay for Colchester about 9 o'clock and comes in again at 6, so the journey is reduced from 12 to 8 hours.

April 3.   Drive to Saxmundham and sleep at the rectory, which is occupied by Robert Mann, he being curate to Lancelot Robert Brown, who is incumbent of this parish as well as Kensale and Carlton. Find George Whitaker and Robert Cobbold there. See the schools and visit Thurlow, the sculptor from whom I buy a "Veiled Child".

April 6.   Look over the late Mrs Garden's house and go to the auction in the evening. I bid £1,000, Garneys £1020. It was bought in at £1300.

April 21.   Planting seeds in quiet and enjoyment while Election squabbles are going on at all the polling places in East Suffolk between Rendlesome and Adair. The next day to Beccles with Samuel to vote for Rendlesome.

May 4.   Preparing to leave England for a few weeks in Paris where I have not been for seventeen years. By the little "Star" coach to Colchester and then, for the first time, by railway to Shoreditch. How little does one enjoy the journey by rail. Towns and their interests are avoided, no coaches, carriages, horses or pedestrians are met with - now on a level now on a height - one sees but little of the life of the surrounding country. But the expedition was amusing although the Spital-fields entrance into London is vile. All the shops were closed on account of the Duke of Sussex's funeral[3].

May 10.   After spending a few days in London, Alfred joins me and we go to Southampton, dine at the Pier Hotel and embark on the "Grand Irish" steamer at 6 that evening.

PARIS

May 11. At 7 the following morning we enter the town of Havre. Customs and police were dispatched easily and we fix at the Hotel d'Europe. Alfred and I feeling very happy at being abroad again. I spend an hour or two writing letters and settling up accounts and then explore the quays and streets and mount the hill on the north, from which is a good view of the town and sea.

Dine at $5^{1/2}$ and afterwards to the New Canal and see the ruins of the fine theatre, burnt down a few months ago.

May 12. We leave by steamer this morning and have a very delightful passage along the broad and cheerful waters of the Seine, reaching Rouen at $12^{1/2}$.

The quay is very fine and we lodge at the Hotel de Rouen which stands on it. After a wash, we look at the Pont de Fil de Fer and the stone bridge with its statue of Corneille and that of Boieldieu[4] also on the quay, then to the railway terminus not yet completed and along the promenades near the Seine. I never saw so many parrots collected in one town as there are here, and one hears them in all directions.

To the Cathedral whose iron spire is ugly and not wide enough for its base, a poor substitute for the old wooden one destroyed by fire in 1822. The new roof also is too simple. The church of St. Ouen is much more pleasing, the architecture in the interior is pure and elegant but the facade has never been finished.

May 15. The Paris and Rouen railway was opened to the public only last Tuesday. We go in it to-day and found the carriages very comfortable, the second places (second class) are enclosed with glass windows. The gauge of the rails is not above four feet. Alfred, who is going in for engineering, says they are seven feet on our Great Western, which is of course safer. The rails are not well closed so the motion is rather "rocky". We performed the distance of 85 miles in $3^{3/4}$ hours, passing through Vernon, Mantes and Rosny, crossed the Seine five times and went through several tunnels. Rosny was the home of Sully the celebrated French minister of Henri IV and latterly of the Duchess de Berri. It is here she erected a chapel for the depository of her husband's heart when he was assassinated in 1830.

From the terminus of St. Lazare we walk to the Rue de la Paix and to the Hotel de Hollande, but it was full so we lodge in rooms close by and dine at the hotel with a party of seventeen, amongst whom were no Englishmen but ourselves.

After dinner at 6 I take Alfred down the Rue de la Paix to the Tuileries and Place de la Concorde and we admire the fountains, the Obelisk and the facade of the Madeleine Church, all new since I was here in 1826 - then along the quais, through the Tuileries Palace[5] and look at the new Hotel of the War Department, pass through the Louvre Palace to St. Germain l'Auxerrois and then to the Palace Royal.

Alfred is astonished at so much grandeur of architecture and I am constrained to feel that scarcely any other city presents finer architectural combinations.

May 16. Amongst the places we went to to-day was the Bourse, which is a magnificent building, full of stock-brokers, merchants and speculators (women are not admitted because they gamble too much).

May 21. Sunday. To the English church at 11. In the evening pass the fine new Church of St. Vincent de Paul, not yet finished. Cross the line of the new fortifications which are of enormous extent and see the fort of St. Denis, more likely to annoy the inhabitants than an enemy.

May 22. Inspect the bridge of Les Invalides, a handsome new suspension bridge of 1829. Dine at Hotel de Hollande and see Mlle Rachel in "Judith". A fine actress, apparently about 22[6] with a handsome, oval face and dark eyes. Cheek bones too high and distance from nose to mouth too long for beauty. She has a pretty figure - not grand, and a distinct but not rich voice. She is, I consider, inferior to Miss O'Neill and Duchesnois[7], Talma[8] etc. The tragedy from "L'Enfant trouve" and a merry comedy well performed afterwards.

May 24. It has rained every day since we have been in Paris - today in torrents which quite prevents any intended excursions. I bathe at Les Bains Chinois and dine as usual at the Hotel de Hollande, sitting next to an English clergyman named Errington. During dinner an English artist[9] became furiously mad, hissed like a cat, fixed his eyes horribly and threw the whole party into confusion. I sat with him afterwards for half an hour and he told me he had been travelling in Italy, Greece and Syria with Sir Thomas Phillips[10] of Newport, who is not a man but a demon. That he is appointed to overthrow Christianity and restore the worship of the Deity who was worshipped at Baalbek, he is to be the vehicle of the oracles formerly conveyed through the priests of Delphi and the

Gods and Furies are contending within him, that he knows devils by their wide foreheads and their grin, etc. He gave me such a look that it chilled me from head to foot and he rushed out of the hotel afterwards. We went to the Theatre of Varieties and on our return found he had come back to the hotel and conveyed himself and his luggage away in a fiacre.

May 31. A vain enquiry at the Post Office for letters. Much anxiety at the Hughes' not writing.
We view the Porte de l'Arc de Triomphe de l'Etoile. A noble arch of fine proportions and gigantic size. I think it would have been better without the projecting figures on its east and west faces and with a little more proportion in its cornice. Then examine the fortifications and the spot where the lamented Duc d'Orleans[11] was killed on the 13th of July last by jumping from his carriage when his horses were running away.

June 1. Again no letters, to dear Alfred's great discomfort. We go to the Chamber of Deputies at which 210 members were present. Sanzet, President. Question - the coinage of France. Guizot[12] was there - a thin, grey, sharp-faced man of 55. Intelligent and amiable but not dignified-looking. We heard Messrs. Corne, de Colmont and Delessent speak or read speeches except the second named. There was so much talking that we could not collect the arguments. The President's bell was rung repeatedly but in vain. At about 5 1/2 such heavy clouds came on that one could not see to read in the Chamber and this embarrassed the Speaker and general cries arose for an adjournment. The rain was falling in torrents and deputies and spectators were compelled to wait together near where we were standing in the Hall attached to the Chamber. Very animated discussions arose here on the coinage question.
Two individuals signalised themselves by the loudness and violence of their language and full twenty of the bystanders, ourselves among them, crowded round them. "Vous avez dit une absurdité" exclaimed, in a great passion, a small active man of 35 or 36, to his opponent, a pale, stout and rather square-made dapper-looking man of apparently 47 or 48, with grey hair, wearing a white hat and light fawn pantaloons, the calves of which were evidently padded. This latter little man's face instantly assumed a most irritated snarly expression, which to me seemed the expression of a low kind of malice and an indication of selfish ignoble feeling.
He turned his back upon the younger man and both then strutted about and waited as if anxious and yet afraid to renew the quarrel. Their movements and looks amused us exceedingly and I wished

much for the pencil of a caricaturist to perpetuate their faces. At last the pale-looking elder man left the hall and a gentleman near me said: "Oh M. Thiers[13] est parti". That this paltry, ignoble-looking man could really be the Prime Minister who was near setting the whole European world at war some 30 months ago, certainly surprised me much, but the evidence of my informant who knew the ex-Minister's person leaves me in no doubt of the identity that this individual was M. Thiers. He is a specimen of the worst kind of the modern French school. Evening to a concert at the Salle Vivienne.

June 2. At last a letter for Alfred, but his father had advanced no further than Thun on account of Mary's illness.[14] I write to E.S. Barber (with whom Alfred is studying engineering) for an extra two weeks leave after June 22nd. Incessant rain all day.

June 10. A letter from E.S. Barber giving Alfred an extension to leave of 14 days to the 6th of July.

June 11. Sunday. Leave Paris for Fontainbleau where we stop the night and the next day the Hughes party arrives with the children and their governess.

June 13. A pleasant morning at the Hotel de France with all the Hughes'. At 12. I leave for Paris and see that things are ready for them and move my own quarters to the Hotel de Hollande leaving 5 Rue de la Paix for them, and there Alfred joins his parents.

June 14. To the Hughes' at 10½ they see Dr. Macloughlin for Mary's[15] illness and we all decide to return to England.

June 20. Alfred breakfasts with me and we go to the Chapelle Expiatoire of Louis XVI whose will is sculptured on a pedestal of his statue, and Marie Antoinette's last letter to the Princess Elizabeth (sister to Louis XVI) on that of her own statue. Both these documents contain the most beautiful spirit of benevolence and resignation, self-denial and forgiveness. To read them is a good sermon.

June 23. Packing and leave the Hotel de Hollande at 4½. Dine with Alfred at a restaurant opposite the Bourse and leave in a Coupé de Messageri at 6½, reaching Abbeville at 7½ the following morning.

June 24. Breakfast and continue our journey and arrive at

Boulogne at 2½ p.m. A party of directors and others connected with the Dover railway came here by invitation to a déjeuner with the authorities, but as 35 were expected and 85 turned up, a muddle ensued.

June 25. Sunday. Alfred and I look at the old town and its walls and half-built Cathedral and church. Then to the Napoleon Column[16], finished by Louis Philippe two years ago. It is fine, though its capital is anomalous. Descend over open fields to the beach and return to the Hotel de l'Europe at 5½ and find the Hughes' party had just arrived from Montreuil. After dining we all go out till dark, along the shore and jetty.

June 26. Up at 5 o'clock and leave Boulogne in the "Royal George" steamer at 8¼. Reach Dover at 11½. The T.C. Hughes' start off in their carriage for Canterbury and Alfred and I by coach and railway for London.

BUNGAY

July 10. The bells of St. Mary's announce the marriage of Henry Bellman to Eliza Bewicke.

July 11. Charles Thomas Scott, Rector of Shadingfield, married to Arabella, 2nd daughter of W. D. Thring, Rector of Sutton Veney in Wiltshire.

July 20. Send off the Town Accounts before breakfast and pay off the whole of the Town debt to Fisher and Burtshall. This is the first time in thirty-two years that the town has been free from liabilities.

July 21. Yarmouth. Dine at Sir Eaton Travers' with the Smithies and the next day attend the christening of Isabella's child at the Great Church. Pillew shows us the screen and the sedilia which have lately been discovered.

After clearing off the Town debt Scott employs his energies on the restoration of the Priory and the improvement of the churchyard of St. Mary's.
From the middle of July onwards he was continually in communication with the senior churchwarden about his various plans, and above all he was most anxious to preserve the piece of the old Abbey wall which formed part of the boundary of the Priory

*from the Roman Catholic Chapel along Olland Street, now called
St. Mary's Street.*
*We find him at an early hour in the morning superintending the
work of Rumsby, Nursey and Nunn while they are engaged in
strengthening and restoring the ruins and arranging for the iron
work required for the palisading etc. On Sunday, August 27th he is
up at 5. o'clock on a lovely, still morning and goes along to St.
Mary's churchyard to look at his improvements, but from the first he
is met with great opposition, particularly with regard to the Abbey
wall which the occupiers of the ancient carved house opposite and
several of the smaller tradesmen considered should be removed as it
had no remains of windows, doors or other architectural features
left. On the 9th September, on his way to the churchyard, Scott
found that some malicious person had stripped the old wall of its
covering of ivy and defaced its front with red paint. This and the
continued opposition offered to his plans determined him to
relinquish all work connected with the wall and the church's
boundaries and he wrote to church-warden Mann, accordingly,
adding "I offer no further opposition to the plans of those who think
differently from myself but as manager of the Town purse for the
present year, I cannot consent to pay for changes which I
disapprove". At the same time he undertakes to complete the
palisading and the principal gateway at the N.W. corner of the
churchyard but to desist in the future from taking any steps
whatever regarding the question in dispute. This letter was
dispatched in the morning of the 18th September and in the
afternoon of the same day eight or ten vandals arrived on the scene
and announced their intention of destroying the wall. A crowd
quickly assembled and it was forced over into the churchyard by
means of a battering ram, picks etc. This was the signal for a great
uproar which was put a stop to by the appearance of the magistrate
J. J. Bedingfield and the reading of the Riot Act. No proceedings
were taken against the aggressors.*
*The following verses were written and published in Bungay before
the destruction of the Abbey Wall:*

Inscription for the Old Wall in Olland Street, Bungay.

*Ye passers by who view this wall
With angry eyes regard it not
But let your prayers be - "Do not fall!
But thank the happy taste of Scott.
Destroy not with your ruthless hands
What time has spared - perchance forgot,*

And see! the masons strengthening bands
Display the happy taste of Scott!

Oh' ne'er may battering ram or ball,
Delightful relic be your lot!
But may'st thou stand and brave them all;
And prove the happy taste of Scott!
So ages still to come may gaze
E're yet thine ivied fragments rot,
And thank the hand that would not raze
And bless the happy taste of Scott! "

Avoniensis. Sept. 5th 1843

August 26.   Receive an appeal for Colonel Stoddart and Captain Conolly. A silly thing, for I doubt not that Saleh Mohammed's narrative of their death is true.

September 5.   Read that the unhappy maniac Richard Dadd whom I met in Paris on the 24th May last, has assassinated his own father at Cobden in Kent. *(see diary entry, page 101-102 above)*

October 1.   Drive to Kirby to drink Lord Berners' health on his being this day 81 years old. Lady Berners is 80. Mr. Sheppard 72; the three, 233.

October 10. Sunday.   At the service Abbot Upcher reads and Mr. Hurnard preaches, hand organ, singing pretty good.

October 14.   Dr. Wolff starts from London on his way to Bokhara to search for poor Stoddart and Conolly whom he pretends to be still living.

October 24.   At 10 o'clock leave Bungay by coach for Cambridge with Green of Burgh Castle, Morse of Blundeston and Paget of Yarmouth. At Harleston W. S. Holmes joins us and he and I fix at Emmanuel College. Dine at the University Arms and afterwards look at the preparations for the Queen's arrival tomorrow.

October 25.   At $12\frac{1}{2}$ the men of Emmanuel and Christ's go down in procession to Senate House Square and take order behind the palisades. The sky was glorious and everything festive, flags, garlands, bells and people. I was with Onslow and Wilson of

Emmanuel, at 2 o'clock the Queen and Prince Albert arrived, 1500 horsemen had escorted them to the Triumphal Arch. Scots Greys and Yeomanry escort them to the town. No other horses or carriages were admitted. The applause was immense. We then scoured off to Trinity Quadrangle where the Queen lunched before going to the Hall to receive our address. Two thousand university men in full costume, ranged around while the royal couple read their answer to us very distinctly and feelingly and then proceeded to King's Chapel.

October 26. After breakfasting at Magdalen with Robert Hughes, Miles and Wollie go to the Senate House at 9 o'clock where the undergraduates were enthusiastic but orderly. The Queen and Prince entered at 10 and the Prince was made D.C.L. amidst roars of applause. Dine at Emmanuel Lodge with Dr. and Mrs Archdale and leave the following day for Bungay.

November 15. Called up at 4 o'clock to go to Outney Cottage where Mrs Scott is dying. Send George to Norwich for Samuel and at 10 minutes to 9 the widow of my late uncle dies peacefully and unconsciously, aged 81. A letter arrives the same morning from Alfred telling me of his very painful position with the Barbers, which makes me resolve to go to Newport before the funeral if possible. So after making all arrangements I start off and reach my destination on the 17th. The next morning Alfred comes to breakfast and unfolds his grievances and we consult together. Then to Barber and after hearing his and his wife's statements am convinced of the former's ungovernable irritability and his unjust prejudice against Alfred's friends, the F's. Being quite satisfied with Alfred's conduct I resolve to terminate his apprenticeship. My task was a difficult one, Barber being adverse to cancelling the articles of Agreement. However, at last I succeeded and both parties signed the dissolution, also a testimony of friendly feeling towards each other. Alfred's departure with me being determined, he and I walk about paying bills etc.

November 19. Leave Newport on Sunday, sleep at Bristol, Monday by train to London and then on to Scole arriving there about 1 a.m. on Tuesday morning. Take a gig on to Bungay, turn into my own bed at 6. Rise again at 8½ and Worthington and Samuel Scott breakfast with me and with the servants, we follow the remains of the late Mrs Scott to St. Mary's Church at 11. o'clock. Cookesley takes the service.

The Priory Church of St. Mary with the Scott family tombs palisaded. (19th century)

1843/44]

November 22. Shipmeadow House wilfully set on fire but it was soon extinguished. Damage not exceeding £36 which was made good by the Insurance Office.

December 5. Call on Capt. Dalling R.N. who has succeeded Sir Windham as occupier of Earsham Hall. Much pleased with his wife and her sister Miss Fanshawe. All walk back with me as far as Cautleys, The Rectory, Earsham.

1844

At the beginning of this year there are again riots at Shipmeadow and on the 13th January am summoned with Dr. Owen, Montagu, Bewicke and fourteen policemen to enquire into the cause of the trouble. A policeman had been wounded in the face with a brick, floors were ripped up and a wall broken through. The women had broken every pane of glass in the rooms and burnt the chairs, forms etc. Twelve men were sent to gaol to take trial for riot and a special meeting called to investigate the cause of the disturbance.

February 19. To Shipmeadow at 9 o'clock where Sir J. Waltham, Assistant Commissioner, and thirty guardians attend the meeting. Present the report I had drawn up with the help of the committee appointed. Sir J. W. Waltham and several guardians speak. The examination of the officers turns much against the Governor.
Ten days later the Commissioners report is received and the Governor recommended to resign.

March 6. Hear of the death of Richard Mann which took place soon after 10 o'clock this morning, and am quite awestruck at the unexpected departure of so bustling and active a neighbour. He has only been ill about a week. His death occasions a blank in the town which will long be felt and above all the role of senior churchwarden of St. Mary's will long remain inseparable from his memory. He was buried under the vestry room of that parish on the Tuesday following amidst a storm of a hurricane, lightning, thunder and snow.

April 1. Monday. Bury. Arrived here last evening. To the courts at 11. Lord Abinger[17] in the Crown Court and Justice Patterson[18] in the Nisi Primis. I, on the Grand Jury. Eighty cases of Bills. At half past 7 we go to the Judge's lodgings to dinner. Just as the cloth was about to be removed, Lord Abinger spoke indistinctly, complained of loss of memory, rose suddenly and walked steadily and firmly out of the room. He no sooner reached his bedroom than he became speechless and insensible. While in court he looked well and was clear and vigorous in intellect, ate with great zest at dinner and was very cheerful until the moment of his attack. In spite of bleeding and all medical aid he continued in the same state till the following (Easter) Sunday when he died in the presence of his wife and sons in the 75th year of his age. He was long known as Sir James Scarlett, but had been Lord Chief Baron for ten years before his death.

April 2.   Breakfast at the Angel. Everyone talking of Lord Abinger's sad state. In the Jury room from 10 to 7½. Dine with the High Sheriff Sir Philip Broke and twenty-five others. All very gloomy.

April 3.   Breakfast with Muskett and look over the ruins in the garden. He says if the Duke of Norfolk will authorise him to make Bungay Castle and its yard into ornamental grounds, he will consult me on the subject. In Grand Jury room again till 1. Then dismissed.

April 19. Bungay. Confirmation at St. Mary's Church at 3 o'clock when Alfred is confirmed with two hundred and seventy-two others, by the Bishop of Norwich, Stanley.

April 22.   Samuel Scott leaves Norwich finally after residing there for six years with Foster and Unthank. He is going to London to read conveyancing and chancery business.

April 26.   Am building a rockery in the Bridge House garden from some of the materials of the old Bungay Convent, which is being cleared away. A good deal of the debris was carted to the Staithe and later used in Mr. Walker's garden[19].

April 27. Yarmouth. Go to the terminus of the Norwich and Yarmouth Railway which was opened on the 1st. See the Electro Telegraph.

May 28. London. With George and Mrs. Sandby and Miss Hodson to Conduit Street to see Dr. Elliotson, the celebrated student of Mesmerism, experiment on two young men. They soon fall asleep, one immediately and the other after ten minutes, the doctor merely pointing his finger to their eyes. The muscles of one became rigid at once the other only partially so. The younger sang and talked. Dr. Elliotson gripped them severely but seemed to produce no pain. George has become a believer and has published a paper on the subject - an answer to a silly sermon of MacNeil's ascribing Mesmerism to the Devil.

Mrs Sandby was sent to sleep after seven weeks of restlessness. Dr. Elliotson says he remembers me at Cambridge when he was at Jesus and I at Emmanuel but I forget him.

Dine at the Athenaeum and afterwards to St. James Park to see the King of Hanover, the King of the Belgians, Queen Adelaide, etc., and the Duke of Wellington, go in state to Buckingham Palace to attend the marriage of Princess Augusta of Cambridge to Prince Meckleburgh of Stretiitz.

May 29. Call on the Phillips' and stop an hour with them. Their son Henry has much improved in painting. He showed me his scriptural subject of 'There were women looking afar off'. Afterwards meet Sandby and Lundly and talk again of Mesmerism. Sandby protests that his wife was sent to sleep by Mesmerism as if by magnetic attraction and when in that state was insensible to the pricking of pins and other pain. That she acquired feelings of affection or dislike according as the phrenological organs were magnetised by the operator pointing to them and that she rejected the touch of anyone but the mesmeriser although she willingly responded to his. On our way back visit the National Gallery. It contains one hundred and eighty-eight pictures. Mrs Siddons by Lawrence, the last one, was placed there yesterday.

May 30. To the British Museum to see the Xanthian Sculptures recently imported from Asia Minor by Charles Fellowes, the archaeologist. He first discovered the ruins of Xanthus about five years ago and the marble remains are now on view, which he succeeded in shipping to England last year in seventy-five cases.

July 26. London. Am staying at Morley's Hotel and with Alfred walk to Southampton Row admiring the new streets in progress. To the British Museum and then examine the exterior of the new splendid Royal Exchange and Chantry's statue of Wellington which is exceedingly fine. By water to Westminster to see the new Houses of Parliament.

July 28. To Whitehall Chapel. Sir Robert and Lady Peel and their sailor son William are there. They were saluted by almost everyone when returning home.

July 29.   Final confirmation from Dr. Wolff of the execution of poor Stoddart and Conolly in 1842 at Bokhara.

July 30.   Call on Sir Edward Kerrison at 11½ to introduce Alfred and ask his aid for a commission. Kindly received and request granted. To the National Gallery to see Penrice's Rubens and Guido, lately purchased for £4000 and £900 respectively.

From the beginning of August to the end of September Scott and Alfred are abroad travelling in France, Germany and Belgium.

On September 12 Mrs. Everard, mother of Mrs. Walter Scott, died while staying with her daughter at Ipswich, age 68.

PART IV (1842-1844) Bungay, London and Paris

References

1.   Mendham, Robert of Eye (1792-1875). Artist. Born in Eye, Robert Mendham was apprenticed at the age of fifteen in the family coach- building business. He later studied at the Royal Academy but, on the death of his brother, he inherited the family business which he continued to manage. He exhibited paintings at the British Institution and the Royal Academy. There is a self-portrait in Christchurch Mansion, Ipswich, and a portrait of a young boy in the Manor House Museum, Bury St. Edmunds.

2. Alderson, Sir Edward Hall (1787-1857). Baron of Exchequer 1831.

3.   Duke of Sussex. Son of George III and uncle of Queen Victoria.

4.   Boieldieu (1775-1834). Composer.

5. Tuileries Palace. Destroyed in the Commune of 1871 although the gardens still exist.

6.   Rachel. A good guess - she was actually 23.

7.   Duchesnois, Josephine (1777-1835). A celebrated actress.

8.   Talma (1763-1826). The great tragic actor.

9.   Richard Dadd (1817-1886). English painter, trained at the Royal Academy. His early works were conventional landscapes & literary subjects. When Scott met him in Paris he was clearly suffering from the demonic hallucinations which led him to murder his father (see entry for 5th of September 1843). He fled to France but was caught and returned to England where he was judged insane and sentenced to life imprisonment in the Hospital of St Mary of Bethlehem (Bedlam) at Lambeth and later, in Broadmoor. Encouraged by enlightened doctors, Dadd continued to paint and produced what are now considered to be his masterpieces. They are characterised by remarkable scenes crowded with bizarre, microscopic details and were worked on over very long periods. Some of his work remains with the institutions in which he spent the last 43 years of his life but the Tate Gallery has fine examples, *Oberon and Titania* (1850-54) and *The Fairy Feller's Master Stroke* (1855-64).

10. Phillips, Thomas (1801-1867) Mayor of Newport, lawyer. Knighted for action against the Chartists.

11. Ferdinand, Phillippe Louis. Eldest son of Louis Phillippe (1810-1842).

12. Guizot (1787-1874). Louis Phillippe's chief minister, a celebrated historian.

13. Thiers. French statesman, afterwards first President of the Third Republic. He was 64 at the time of this incident.

14. The allusion is to the anti-Turkish and anti-English policy which he wished Louis Phillippe to pursue by guaranteeing Egypt and Syria to Mehemet Ali, while England wished to maintain the integrity of the Turkish Empire. In 1840 England formed an alliance with Russia, Austria and Prussia and the English blockaded Alexandria. The Egyptians were cleared out of Syria but Mehemet Ali accepted the Viceroyalty of Egypt under Turkish sovereignty.

15. Mary, Alfred's sister.

16. Napoleon Column. Commenced by Napoleon I to commemorate the Camp at Boulogne in 1804-05 when he contemplated the invasion of England.

17. Abinger, Lord (Sir James Scarlett) (1769-1844). Judge. MP for Peterborough, Maldon, Cockermouth and Norwich. Attorney-General 1829.

18. Patterson, Sir John (1790-1861). Judge. MA Cantab. Knighted 1830. Arbitrator in government questions.

19. Walker, Pearse (1785-1859). Town Reeve five times from 1830 to 1858. Landowner who lived somewhere in Flixton Road. St. Mary's churchwarden.

PART FIVE

1844

Five Weeks in France, Germany & Belgium

August 3. After obtaining our passports from the French Ambassador's office and a note of credit from Messrs. Barclay, Broan, Tritton & Co., Alfred and I go to Brighton and fix at the Albion Hotel. A gale is blowing from the south west and we lounge on the Chain Pier (built by Captain Brown in 1824) admiring the 20 feet waves and watch the steamer coming from Dieppe. Then to Shoreham by rail and view the Chain Bridge there, built by the Duke of Norfolk in 1832. Go on board the steamers "Magnet" and "Fame" and walk the six miles back to Brighton where we resolve to stop till Monday, as the Packet is prevented from sailing by the gale.

August 5. Monday At 3 p.m. to Shoreham and dine on board the "Magnet" steamer. Leave Shoreham harbour at 5. Sea still rather swelling and the majority of the passengers ill. I quite well in consequence of lying down on my back before the voyage began and keeping in that position all the time, nine hours, as we entered Dieppe Harbour at 2 a.m.

August 6. Lodge at the Hotel des Bains. Explore the quays, harbour's mouth, bathing establishment and its Reading Room, etc. People bathe along the shore in dresses, and women in jackets and trousers and the men in drawers, and walk from stationary boxes into the sea. Ascend the old castle and the heights beyond it from which are fine views of the sea and of the town and valley of Dieppe.

August 12. To Versailles by the Rive Droite Railway. We spent four hours in the Galleries of the Palace - much increased as to rooms and paintings since last year. The idea of a Palais consecrated to "Toutes les gloires de la France" is good, but the King is overdoing the thing. Many of the recent paintings are very bad - mere daubs - not at all contributing to the "gloire" of French Art, and many of the subjects too are by no means deserving of honourable mention.
Dine at Poissonerie Anglaise at 6, and in the evening to the Opera Comique.

August 15. Assumption of the Virgin. This day is kept as a Sunday in Paris i.e. most of the shops open till 1 or 2 and shut for the rest of the day.
p.m. The Louvre Gallery, to which Alfred has been going daily, and see the Flemish and Dutch Schools from 12 to 3.

August 17. Breakfast in the Tuileries Gardens and finish the first accurate view of the paintings of the gallery and half the statues which I have been going through with Alfred. After dining, examine the progress of the Debarcadere and Paris end of the Northern railway. Much remains to be done, even here. The entrance to Paris will be very bad and through a deep ditch of two or three miles in which one will see nothing. Look also at the yet unfinished Church of St. Vincent de Paul, a fine Roman building, but not without faults.

August 18. Sunday. I to the Madeleine Church and then to the English Church. At 2 o'clock to the Palais des Thermes, most interesting Roman ruins, with the Hotel de Cluny built upon them and now containing two museums of old and carved cabinets, etc. painted glass and armour. Dine near the Jardin des Plants and thence to Vincennes.

August 20. Robert Butcher dies at The Grove, Bungay, this morning, aged 82. Though his death might have been expected at any time for the last six months, we are shocked at the news now it has come and deeply regret our old friend. He was calling at Outney Cottage last Friday morning to enquire if we had been heard of, was taken with a fit on Saturday, continued unconscious until Sunday and died without pain the next morning. (He was Alfred's grandfather).

August 30. Leave our hotel at 3 o'clock in splendid weather. The harvest is almost finished, the stacks very tall and irregular. The farms are more extensive as we go north-east, but not more than one country house was to be seen from Paris for twenty miles and the farmers almost all live in the villages. The roads were straight and along open plains. We pass Nanteuil at 9 and take coffee at Soissons at 1 a.m.

August 31. We reached Rheims soon after 7 and fixed ourselves in a pleasant room at the Lion d'Or directly opposite the Cathedral. This old Roman town of 32,000 inhabitants has little of antiquity in its general appearance, its streets are wide and tolerably neat but the houses modern and unusually low for France, mostly one story only over the ground floor and rarely more than two. It is awfully quiet. There are many hand looms of cloth and thread in the town and suburbs and much commerce in Champagne wine is said to go on here, but there is very little movement in the streets and the prevailing quietness affects even the voices of the inhabitants, who speak in a much lower tone than is usual for Frenchmen. Rheims has no garrison. I did not see a soldier in the place.

The Cathedral did not appear at first so handsome as we expected nor on account of cleanings and restorations does it look so ancient. But it soon gained upon our estimation. The "portail" is really rich and most splendid. The interior is simple and deserves the character which Sir Francis Palgrave the historian (1788-1861) gives it for unity of design in all it parts, even to the richly painted glass. One of its peculiarities is that the Choir enclosure is extended three arches to the west of the transept.

The still more ancient Church of St. Remi is now nearly completely restored. It is of Norman architecture, very large and very grand. This, the Roman Gate and Cathedral are the three great objects of interest in Rheims and occupy a morning to see them well. We spent from 10 to 6 seeing them, looking at the markets, covered-in and open, and in walking over the town with its deep fosses which are now being filled up and the fortifications dismantled. We were surprised here, in Champagne to see no vineyards. One can hardly fancy Rheims the seat of the many coronation splendours which have taken place in it for the space round the Cathedral is very limited for processions and the display of state functions.

September 1. Sunday. A lovely morning. I went at 7 to the Cathedral to see the painted glass illuminated by the bright sun. The Archbishop was gone to perform Mass at another church and the music and service at this were not very interesting. I again inspected the Church of St. Remi and the Roman Gateway and then went to see the remains of a Roman Amphitheatre. This is a mass of concrete, formed of the chalk and gypsom of the country and sand and pebbles. The fragment is about twelve yards long, four thick and fourteen feet high. It was recently of much greater dimensions but the modern barbarians are pushing and hewing it away for road mending and building materials. The whole area of the seats I should think may have been 200 yards by 100. The ground favoured the placing of the basement of the seats, and where hills were wanting, the concrete supplied its place.

At 3 o'clock we leave Rheims for Chalons in a country diligence.

The distance is about 27 miles, which we perform in three hours. Shooting begins this morning and Sunday, which seldom prevents either business or pleasure in France[1], only caused the number of sportsmen to be greater to-day than usual. There are many partridges, some quail and many hares, but pheasants are unknown here.

In the neighbouring woods are roes and boars. We pass through the village of Sillery so famed for its Champagne wine. It is a poor collection of hovels. Though traversing the Province of Champagne, we scarcely see a vineyard within two or three miles of us, but on the slopes of the hills on our south west, between the woods which crown their tops, are very extensive vineyards which produce all the best varieties of this excellent wine. Farmers take their men-servants to lodge and board and hire them for the year at £8 and even £14 a year. After crossing the plains, known as the "Camp of Attila", where countless numbers perished in A.D. 451[2] we enter Chalons at 6.

The Departmental Consul-General is now sitting here and we could, with difficulty, procure beds. Here are two churches worthy of notice besides four or five others. The painted glass in the Cathedral and Notre Dame is very beautiful, both in design and colouring. The devastations committed by the barbarous revolutionists on the sculpture of both, show more deliberate mischief than is often seen, for the figures are worked off by the chisel as well as with the hammer. We finish the day with supper and a bottle of the wine of the country, Champagne, 4 franc.

We had not time to look at the Champagne cellars of Mons. Jackson, the grandson of an Englishman, which are said to contain three millions of bottles and to be cut out of the chalk.

September 2.   At 11½ started in a four horse diligence for Verdun and Metz. The country continues open and treeless till St. Menehould, but here it becomes well wooded. It was dark before we reached Verdun where we stopped for supper and lost the company of three or four lively, good tempered pupils of the Ecole Militaire of St. Cyr who remained here. My thoughts were full of the sad confinement of our countrymen from 1802 to 1814 in this small town[3]. The neighbourhood appears to be pretty.

Of the country from Verdun and Metz I can tell but little as it was faint moonlight and I slept much, but now and then I observed large villages, woods, and hills. A little before 4 o'clock we descended by a zigzag road down the Moselle to the Fortress of Metz.

September 10.   Leave at 6 in a diligence for Thionville and Luxemburg, fortunately we had it to ourselves. The country we passed through was wide and open with its plains, bordered with hills and woods on either side, but having no trees save the perpetual avenues of poplars or elms which border every French Route Royale.

September 12.   At 5¹/2 ascend the banquette⁴ of a diligence and leave Luxemburg by the stupendous road of the Schloss Thor and up again by the Mill Battery. Our route was for long through a high, wide and sloping country, with extensive forests, large tracts of which are being added to the cultivated parts on which oats, barley, hemp and potatoes are grown. When we descend to the banks of the Moselle all becomes pleasing, wide flowing streams, orchards and green meadows, vines in abundance on the slopes and red rocks breaking out from dark green foliage giving a delightful influence to our feelings. The fine Roman monument at Igel, which we admired in April 1840, was the first point which was not new to us on our present journey from Paris to the Rhine.

We reach Trèves under unusual circumstances. Already for some miles we had met or passed many hundreds of men and women, in parties, dressed in their best attire, on their pilgrimages to and from Trèves. An object of extraordinary veneration has been or rather is now being exhibited there. This is alleged to be the very "Coat without Seam" which was worn by our blessed Saviour. To cause a revival of "vital religion" (as the Vicar General Muller, told me when I asked for a ticket to see it) it was resolved to open the wall which had enclosed the chest in which the relic had been placed since it was last exposed in 1810. This was done only three weeks since and the enormous number of 600,000 persons have been to see it in the Cathedral of Trèves during this space of time. I wish I could believe, as many thousands do, that this was the very robe which our Saviour wore, but after reading all the evidence on the subject I am compelled to conclude that the identity, though possible, is in a very great degree improbable. The first objection that a robe of linen (or of whatever other material such as silk and linen or wool and linen mixed) could not have lasted so well for more than eighteen centuries, is of no force at all. We may in most of our leading museums of Europe now daily see pieces of linen which have been preserved from the air in Egyptian tombs for the past twenty-five centuries and are in perfect preservation. As to this alleged Holy Robe, it also, it is affirmed, has been generally kept hermetically sealed from the action of the air. The main argument for the identity of the robe rests upon the tradition - not recorded in history - that Helena, mother of the Emperor Constantine, obtained it in 327 A.D. at Jerusalem, along with the piece of the true Cross and other relics. Having brought them safely to her Palace at Augusta Trevirorum, near where she was born, she presented to certain of her successors, as the most valuable memorial she could bequeath to the city of her earliest regard and associations, this "Coat".

That the Empress did visit Jerusalem out of veneration for the founder of Christianity is, I believe a matter of authentic history but this was nearly three hundred years after the death of Christ. There is no evidence whatever to show what became of the Robe after it fell by lot into the possession of the Roman soldiers on duty at the Crucifixion. Supposing that some devoted follower of the Holy One had purchased it off a Roman soldier out of veneration for the Divine Master, there is nothing to prove that it existed at all in the year 327 of the Christian era, when Helena was at Jerusalem. If she did purchase there a robe said to have been that of Jesus, is it not more probable that some other was falsely sold to her, than that the true one should have really been preserved during three centuries of persecution? I cannot therefore believe that Helena brought the real robe of Christ from Jerusalem to Trèves, but further there is no account during eight hundred years after her death, as to what became of the robe, which she is stated to have brought back with her to her native country.

In 1196 it was remembered that a vesture of some kind, belonging to Christ, was preserved in the Cathedral. The Archbishop, John 1. opened some of the old chests there and in one of them found, what he at once pronounced to be, the Vesture for which lots were cast at the Crucifixion. The history of the robe he discovered may be traced, perhaps from that time downwards until Napoleon sent it from Bavaria (to which place it had been taken in troublous times for safety) back to Trèves in 1810. But the double improbabilities of Helena's coat being the same as Christ's and of the coat found in 1196 being the same as Helena's render further investigation useless. I lament, I cannot believe this as do the thousands around me, but I respect the piety and devotion to the Saviour which leads them to regard it with tears of affection and gratitude and to spend so much time, money and labour to behold, what they believe to have been the coat which enveloped his sacred person during the most important actions of his wonderful life.

We entered Trèves at 11. The hundreds of pilgrims had now become thousands, the streets were impassable and we were obliged to go to our hotel by a back street. A procession was just beginning as I got to the window of my room - crosses and banners, with lines of followers from various distant villages, two to four abreast. They occupied 20 minutes in passing my window. The fervour of these poor people, the lameness, weakness and infirmity which they had defied in order to behold this day, but above all the beautiful harmony with which they sung their hymns, were deeply affecting. Another procession, which we saw and heard, passed under the ancient Roman Gateway of Porta Nigra, singing still more beautifully and made an even more picturesque and deeply moving impression. It was like the processions and chariots which I have heard with rapture in the ruins of the Coliseum. Such a mingling of voices, such an harmonious link to eternity, such serenity and withdrawal from all earthly things.

In the afternoon after dining with 120 persons at table d'hôte we revisited the Roman Baths, etc., and were introduced by the Vicar-General into the Cathedral, where having placed ourselves in the line of processions, we too looked at the Sacred Robe, closely, that is within two yards. It is of the same colour as a piece of cloth taken from an Egyptian mummy case and looks very ancient and unusual. It has wide sleeves which may be 27 inches long, its length perhaps five feet and it has, of course, no seams, it is worked with a kind of pattern and its texture looked to me more like that of fine cambric than of mere linen. It is placed in a handsome mahogany case fronted by plate glass. 25,000 persons have visited it to-day. It was 7 p.m. when we were there and the surroundings were well lighted with wax candles in front and on either side. Two priests were in attendance.

In the evening Alfred finds some old Coblentz acquaintances. I to bed early and leave him to chat with them.

September 13. Up at 4 and leave Trèves in a most crowded steamer with 150 passengers at 5. It is a lovely morning and hay-making is going on. Oxen are drawing long, low carts through the meadows and along the immense expanse of vineyards on the rocky slopes we see white crosses scattered among them. The processions to and from Trèves still contribute to the interest and beauty of the scene. On land they are headed by the priest of the village in full costume as at the altar and preceded by the cross they sing their way to the object of their worship. On the water large boats or wherries, containing from one to two hundred persons were rowed steadily along. Here too was the robed priest, the gilded crosses, the banner of the patron saint and the floating flag of the village.

The various reds, blues and greens of the womens' dresses mingled with the darker clothes of the men formed a rich picture which was still more attractive from its reflection in the still waters of the Moselle. We saw perhaps thirty of such boats during the day. The weather was splendid.

Our passage lasted from 5 a.m. to 7 p.m., it was quite a day of enjoyment and the river, during the whole 96 miles, appeared uninterruptedly beautiful. I loved the scenery even more than before (see April 18th 1840). We closed our delightful day at our old favourite hotel at Coblentz, Zum Trierscher Hof, where we were received cordially as old acquaintances.

September 15. Sunday. To the English Church in the Schloss where Moxon Mann took the service.

September 19. The last few days Alfred has been studying fortifications and as he has not been well we have made but few excursions. Processions are still passing on their way to Trèves. We leave Coblentz at 4 in the afternoon by a Mail carriage of four places - only ourselves in it and stop the night at Hillesheim where we send our luggage forward, all but our knapsacks and walk over the hill towards Gerolstein. The views become very fine - wide swelling country and lofty hills, conical, straight and rounded. We pass over abundance of lava and soon descry the fine ruins of Casselburg Castle.

Its Watch Tower is 120 feet high and from written documents is known to have existed in the 12th century and believed to have been built as a Roman fortress.

Our main object in coming here was to see our friend George Saal, the landscape painter. We left our knapsacks at his lodgings and were soon guided to a spot where we found him with Professor Schirner of Dusseldorf, drawing and painting. He was dressed in a peasant's kirtle and cap. The meeting was a joyous one - no more painting for this day. He is in good health and has improved greatly in his art. He came back to Gerolstein and we spent the rest of the day in viewing, with him, the rocks to the north and in ascending to the Pfaffenkaul and Hagelshaul, two extinct craters of volcanoes and a cavern of a wild and peculiar appearance. We picked up many fossils.

September 21. After breakfasting together, we with Saal, accompany Professor Schirner to the rocks and they sit down and paint on the spot. Saal promises me a painting of the view of Casselburg which he is now sketching. The day was lovely and the air deliciously pure.

I strolled away over immense quantities of fossils to the village of Gees where I excited as much attention as the Duc de Nemours did at Jouy aux Arches. Cries of Jacob, Gretchen, Mannchen etc., drew together half the village to look at the foreigner in an English shooting jacket and a gold chain about his neck. However, the people were civil and kind.

The Lime Tree in Gees churchyard I found to be 23 feet in circumference at 3 feet from the ground. There is a very fine one too at Gerolstein which Saal has painted. From Gees I rambled uphill south over immense quantities of petrifications shells and horns till I came into a magnificent forest of oak and beech through which I strolled in perfect stillness and solitude. It was just such a scene, as probably existed on the same spot, 2000 years ago.

One feels removed in such a situation from all the little cares of life and the mind to be more immediately in communication with the Divine, creating Spirit.

On winding westwards, I at length emerged from the forest to a part which had been cleared by cutting down, burning and the spade and pick and was about to be sown with oats and potatoes. After three hours I return to my friends. Many plants interested me on my way over heath and snow, particularly a creeping, snakelike moss, and abundance of gentians, campanulas, thymes and ericas. Wheat is already up and carted in the valleys but barley and oats still remain unharvested. The Eifel people are very civil and simple-minded but by no means unintelligent. Living is very cheap here, for instance for two beds, four breakfasts and four dinners of great abundance, good quality and cooking, I paid only 8/6. I unwillingly hasten from this retired country but time rolls its ceaseless course and we too must go on. I walk to Budesheim and here Saal and Alfred overtake me in the Wagen and we drive to Prum, which we enter after descending a steep hill through a very fine beech wood. We lodge at the "Goldener Stein", a good inn but filled now with pilgrims journeying on to venerate the "Holy Coat". We had a very merry evening, listening to the jokes and riddles of a party in the Saal. An old soldier whom we met here assured me that he heard Napoleon say near Wagram "Il n'y a q'un Dieu, il ne doit etre qu'un Empereur". He was very positive, on cross examination, that Napoleon had certainly uttered these very words.

September 22. Sunday. After breakfast, Saal leaves us at 8. to return to Gerolstein. He is a good fellow and may he be prosperous and happy.

We were obliged to post from Prum to Aschen, 54 miles and could not even procure carriage horses before 10. Posting is well regulated, all charges are put on to a receipt, which is given before starting. We travelled in a very hilly country, about seven miles an hour and including our voluntary addition to the tariff, "Postillions Frankgeld" it cost us 11¾ per mile. Prum has a spacious church and a cidevant convent, now a school and abounds in tanneries to an extraordinary degree, I should think there were twenty in this little town.

After leaving Prum, we ascend for a long time, the country becoming very wild and desolate and quite destitute of trees. Then comes the district of the Schnee Eifel where, I am told, the snow often lies five feet deep on the roads for many days. It now becomes very cold, with bogs and heaths in turn surrounding us.

We dine at the Post House at Losheim on good food, well cooked and then comes the vast forest of Losheim, partially cleared at intervals. Here wild boars and roes abound, but not near the road.

At Kaltenherberg we descend and come suddenly to hedges of very fine beech, orchards and comfortable-looking whitewashed houses with green shutters. Again we descend further along a capital new macadam road, winding by the face of the rocks to a narrow, clear trout stream. Across the valley are the very imposing ruins of the castle of Montjoie. This little town is curiously placed in a narrow defile. It was Fair Day and its streets were crowded. From this spot to Aschen, the women are particularly handsome compared to any we have seen in our whole tour.

We meet two processions on this rocky road, indeed during the whole day we are constantly meeting pilgrims on their way to Trèves.

September 23. Start by railway from Aachen at 1 o'clock but were detained for an hour and a half in consequence of the single line part of the way and the incoming train being detained at the Custom House. We arrived so late that the Ghent branch had left before we reached Malines so we were obliged to stay at the latter place where we fix and sup at the Hotel de St. Jacques.

September 24. Up at 6 and to the railway to apply for Alfred's hat which he left in the train, and it went on to Brussels last night.

Then to the Cathedral (St. Rumbold) where is the celebrated "Crucifixion" by Vandyck and the carved pulpit which is wonderful for its massive execution. St. Paul fallen from his horse lies under it, at full size. We visited also the churches of St. John, and Notre Dame, the former with the famous altarpiece by Rubens.

Malines is a neat town, the Flemish inscriptions amuse us and are mostly intelligible through German and English but inspire us with no desire to learn the language.

Breakfast, after seeing the town and churches. Leave by railway at 12 arriving at Ghent at 2½. Fix at the Hotel de la Poste on the Place d'Armes. It is clean and well situated. Mount to the top of Beffroi Tower, from which we can see well the plan of the town and the adjacent flat country even to Malines, Antwerp and Brussels. At 6 to the Beguinage Convent, a most singular scene. In this vast enclosure are 600 nuns with black dresses and white hoods with coarse linen veils. They inhabit separate houses in the vast enclosure which is quite a village in itself. The houses of red brick have little courts to them, in whose doors are grates and over them the name of the saint to whom the nun has dedicated her house. They were trudging to their chapel when we entered. Their mode of going in was odd. None came straight towards the middle of the doorway, but close to the wall and side of the door and turned round facing outwards first, before she entered. Inside the chapel they take the folded linen, which till then has laid flat on the top of their heads and spread it over them as a veil. Only a few of them sang the Vespers. Some spread their hands wide and high and kept them in that position while they prayed. On coming out they again kept close to the wall, in single lines, carefully avoiding going out straight in the centre. They are a benevolent body of women, attending to the sick as nurses, both in hospitals and in private houses.

By splendid moonlight wander through the streets of Ghent. There are many handsome houses, both of the old Flemish and the modern European style, and numerous wide streets.

September 25. Clear, bright and cold. We visit the Cathedral and the Church of St. Michael. In the former is a picture by Hubert and John Van Eyck, called the "Adoration of the Lamb". Three large figures above and 300 more below. The latter are stiff and many look like portraits but the figures of the Virgin, the Holy Father and St. John are splendidly coloured, looking as fresh and rich as if done yesterday, though four hundred years old. The Rubens picture of St. Bavonn, the soldier turning monk has the usual peculiarities of this artist, but is finely coloured with some good portraits in it of himself, his father and two wives. It did not equal my expectations.

At St. Michael's Church is a "Crucifixion" by Vandyck. The body of the Saviour is equal to that at Malines, the Virgin is finer in form, attitude and expression, the Magdalene inferior and the horse the same as that on which he placed Charles V.

We walked along the canal, saw the outside of the Maison de Force but had not time to go into it, passed the Citadel erected previous to 1830 by William of Holland just in time to be transferred to Leopold, and returned to our hotel for lunch at 1. See Dr. Forster[5] at 2 at the railway station looking as wild as ever and talking chiefly of clever people who had gone mad. He gave me a book of his on education, asked me to see him at Bruges, where he lives and devotes himself much to astronomy.

We leave Ghent at 2^1/2 pass by Bruges and its beautiful little church, see the wide canal at intervals, exchange the rich soil of Ghent for swamps and marshes and arrive at Ostend at 4. From 4 p.m. till 6 after fixing at the "Cour Imperiale", we walk on the fine terrace and esplanade near the sea. Examine the long jetties and piers and watch the 20 feet high waterfall occasioned by the daily letting off the waters of the Bruges coast into the harbour to scour it. It was a lovely clear moonlight evening.

The town of Ostend is dull and like its vicinity is cheerless looking, except towards the sea whose shore is delightful and causes it to be frequented as a bathing place by many Belgians, Germans, English and French.

September 26. After a pleasant stroll on the sands we start from Ostend at 9^1/2 in the "Widgeon" steamer. The sea was as tranquil as a lake, we coasted along within one to four miles from the shore, passing Nieuport, Furnes, Dunkirk and Gravelines to near Calais before we struck across to Dover.

The whole of this coast consists of dunes or sand hills varying from five to forty feet high, blown up into irregular elevations. There are a few clumps of shrubs (probably Sea Buckthorn) growing on them, but even on this lovely warm day they look very dreary and desolate. Numerous cormorants were fishing off the Belgian shore.

After 8 hours passage we landed at Dover from a boat (the steamer being unable to enter the harbour) at 5^1/2. We ate our dinner at the "Ship" and cleared the Custom House in time to start at ^{1}/2 past 6 by the railway. We flew along smoothly and at ^{1}/4 to 10 were at the Bricklayers Arms in London and before 11 were reading our letters at Morley's Hotel, Trafalgar Square.

We have been eight weeks absent and have had a very pleasant and varied time.

BUNGAY

October 29. At 1^1/2 to the Tuns with Miss Butcher, Alfred and the Mercers to hear Fitzgerald's Imitations[6]. Most amusing.

November 7. Surveying for the proposed railway is being carried out on Bungay Common, but it was not until seventeen years later that a railway was opened here.

November 13. Diss and Yarmouth railway meeting at 1 o'clock.

Capt. Moorsom there to explain his plans to Lord Berners. Muskett, George Durrant, Margitson and other landowners or their representatives, through whose lands the proposed railway may pass. The meeting lasted until 3 o'clock.

November 17. Mrs. Abel comes to tell me her husband, the Master of the National School, was taken seriously ill last night. To see Garneys about him. He continues so very ill that on Thursday I send for Crowfoot, who after seeing him, thinks the case serious but not wholly to be despaired of. However, Abel gets much worse, suffering great pain and dies on Saturday morning, aged 34. Garneys considers that an abcess in the liver must have suddenly burst and caused the distressing symptoms and subsequent exhaustion and death.

November 23. Draw up a petition for the widow of poor Abel and her five children and keep the boys off school morning and afternoon of Friday and also Monday.

November 27. On Tuesday at 2 o'clock see crepe bands tied on the arms of thirty boys who follow their poor schoolmaster to the grave. He was buried at 3 p.m. opposite the porch of Trinity Church.

December 10. Meet the boys at school and give them their savings with my 20% thereon and on the 20th look over the girls' deposits in the Saving Bank and add 20% (*this he seems to have done annually*).

December 17. Mrs Scarfe who would have been 90 years old on the 3rd of next May was knocked down by a cart and runaway horse near the Tuns. On the following Wednesday she died from injuries received.

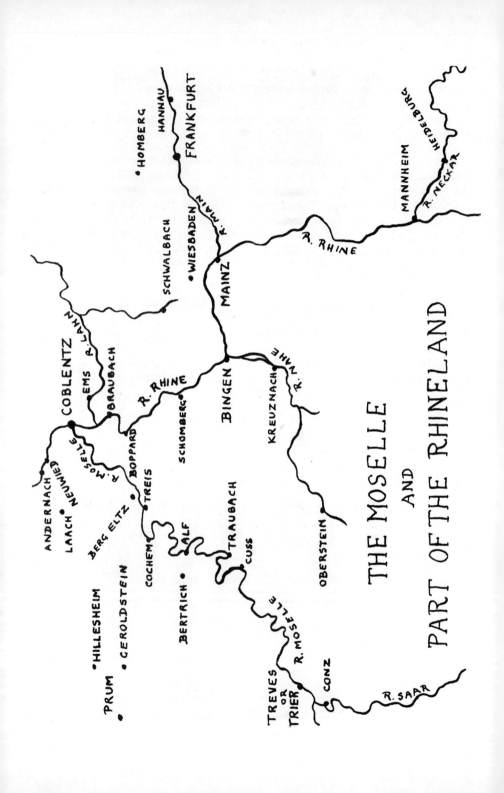

THE MOSELLE AND PART OF THE RHINELAND

Dieppe Harbour

PART V 1844 - Eight weeks in France, Germany and Belgium

References

1. Compare the respectability and calm of the Victorian Sunday.

2. Chalons, Aetius and Theodaic defeated the Huns under their leader, Attila.

3. St. Cyr. Where they were interned by Napoleon.

4. Banquette. Imperial or roof.

5. Forster, Thomas Ignatius Maria (1789-1860). Naturalist and Astronomer. With Spurzheim studied the brain and wrote a sketch on the phrenological system and many other works. Lived at Bruges after 1833 and died at Brussels.

6. Fitzgerald's Imitations. This presumably refers to a recitation by Edward Fitzgerald of some of his free translations of Persian poetry.

PART SIX

1845 - 1851
Bungay, London, Wales and the Isle of Man

1845

January 2. To London and to the National School Society where I engage James Feather on a month's trial as Master of the Bungay National School. The school to be re-opened next Sunday, the 12th, under his tuition.

January 23. Maria, Lady Tuthill dies at Halesworth, the widow of Sir George Tuthill M.D. of Cavendish Square, London.

March 22. John Cooper of Cove Hall dies at 1 p.m. He had lived at Cove since April 1836 and for nearly nine years previously was at Bungay. He was a Fellow Commoner of Caius College, Cambridge, Cornet of the Blues, Captain of the East Norfolk Militia and for a short time a clergyman. Gentlemanly in manner but one of the most useless men I ever knew.

March 27. Dine at the Crowfoots of Beccles with Henchman Crowfoot, Miss Crowfoot and William, Fred and John Farr, Messrs. Bacon, Boycott, Leighton, J. Day, Nicholas of Haddiscoe and Morse. A very merry party all talking of Cooper's will. He left the Farr family £25,000, J.T. Margitson, J. J. Bedingfield, Capt. Sutton, Charles Garneys and Richard Fulcher £5000 each, besides £1000 to J. T. Margitson, William Hartcup, George Sandby, Junr. and C. R. Bewicke as executors. The executors are also residuary Legatees.

April 10. In Chaise to Shadingfield and arrive there at 10 o'clock. Accompany Anna Maria Scott and John Kilner to the church to their wedding. Only members of the family present. After déjeuner at 1 1/2 the bride and bridegroom leave for the Isle of Wight amidst much firing of guns (16 pieces) and cheering from the villagers. Dine at Shadingfield at 6. In the evening music and dancing.

Note on Stoddart and Conolly (see April 11, 1845 below et seq).

Information gleaned from a book by Alistair Maclean, with a chapter on Dr. Wolff, the eccentric missionary, whom Scott met on April 28th 1845. Supplied by Revd. P. A. Skoulding of Flixton,

nephew of Ethel Mann, and related therefore to the Scott family.
(1980)
In 1838 two British officers, Col. Stoddart and Capt. Conolly, were
sent on a diplomatic mission to Bokhara with the aim of securing
British influence in the no-man's land of Central Asia between
Afghanistan and Tsarist Russia. There they fell into the hands of
the Emir of Bokhara, an insanely depraved and tyrannical oriental
despot. He detained them as hostages for four years, inflicting upon
them unspeakable privations and indignities. At one time he
committed them to a dark pit twenty feet deep filled with decayed
human remains and infested with loathsome reptiles and insects,
threatening not to release them unless they renounced Christianity,
became Muslims and entered his service. This they refused to do,
and when he saw they were of no further diplomatic use to him he
brought them out and had them publicly decapitated.
However, the strangest part of this story is that some twenty years
later the sister of one of them received a curious parcel that had
been posted from St. Petersburg. It contained a soiled and battered
copy of the Book of Common Prayer. On the fly leaves she
recognised the hand-writing of her brother. He had recorded the
diary of their imprisonment which included these words: "Thank
God that this book was left to me. Stoddart and I have found it a
great comfort. We did not fully know before this affliction what was
in the Psalms or how beautiful are the prayers of the Church."
A courtier of the Emir who was standing by at the time of their
execution later recalled Conolly's last words: "Stoddart, we shall see
each other in Paradise, near the Lord Jesus."

April 11.   Dr. Wolff reaches Southampton on his return from a
fruitless journey to Bokhara in search of Stoddart and Conolly.

April 22.   In the evening to The Grove with Mrs Butcher, Mrs
and Miss Mercer, Mrs Hughes and Miss Butcher. This is probably
the last time the family will meet together in their old home. All
depressed and making final preparations for leaving it tomorrow.
The next day Mrs. Hughes starts for Andover, I going with her as
far as London.

April 25.   Call on Sandby and find him very depressed and
heartbroken about his daughter Blanche who still lives. His boys are
with him.

April 26.   Begin to read Capt. Grover's "Victims of Bokhara". A
foolish and malicious book which dishonours the writer and

honours Lord Aberdeen, whom it attempts to vituperate.

April 28.　　　Call on Dr. Wolff at 23, Half Moon Street on his arrival from Bokhara and read many of poor Stoddart's letters with him.

April 30.　　　At 2 o'clock to Exeter Hall where more than 2000 persons were congregated to hear Wolff give a history of his journey to and adventures in search of Charles Stoddart and his companion. His narrative took from 2 to 4½. His account of the poor victims' execution and their last words was most interesting. Then George Stoddart spoke and well; but he censured Capt. Grover's just published book severely and Grover took this in great dudgeon. The Chairman, Sir Edward Codrington, called on Stoddart to explain and apologise but he firmly adhered to his statements, repeating his belief in them and regretting his expressions were not agreeable to the meeting. Capt. Randall, Sir Thomas Acland and others spoke but the meeting separated almost before the national testimonial to Dr. Wolff was voted.

May 1.　　　Write a long letter to Miss Stoddart after reading all the reports of yesterday's speeches at Wolff's meeting. In the evening to Lewes to see Joseph Wood[1]. Kindly received by him, his sisters and niece Catherine.

May 2.　　　After breakfast Woods and I examine the ruins of the Priory and walk over the Downs. Dine at 5 and in the evening Mrs B. Abbot and Mr. and Mrs Brown (she a daughter of John Doughty of Brockdish) join the party and talk of Mesmerism.
At 5½ this evening the suspension bridge at Yarmouth fell, owing to defective workmanship in two of the suspending rods and seventy-five persons, chiefly women and children were drowned in the Bure.

May 10.　　　The Rev. Robert Mann of Saxmundham married in Dublin to Harriet, 5th daughter of Sir Edward Sudgen, Lord Chancellor of Ireland. To Fenchurch Street through blocks of waggons and carriages in 1¼ hours. Then by Blackwall Railway and steamer to Woolwich where I go on board the Erebus which is preparing to leave for the North Pole. Talk with Sir John Franklin[2], Capt. Fitzjames and the steward, Hoare. The latter showed me their stores and was a most intelligent and interesting fellow.

Note made by J.B.S. and afterwards inserted in his diary on this date.

1845]

"The Erebus and Terror sailed for the Polar regions on the 19th May this year and fourteen years elapsed before the fate of these ships and their noble crews was known in England. After many fruitless searches it was ascertained by Lieut. Hodson and Captain McClintock, who had been despatched in the steam yacht "Fox" by Lady Franklin, that Sir John died on the 11th July 1847 and that the ships were abandoned in the ice by Captain Crozier and Fitzjames and 103 other of the crew on the 22nd April 1848. Soon after the whole of the survivors died of exhaustion on their way to the Great Fish River."

May 11. Sunday. Attend service at Wellington Barracks from 10 to 12. Dine with Capt. Fisher, then leave him and go to Kensal Green Cemetery. A bright blue sky, birds singing, trees in full leaf, and lilac, almond, etc. flowering gaily. Below, a vast assembly of the dead - still, cold, corrupting. The contrast affecting. The cemetery is very pretty, I like it better than Père la Chaise. Though similar in style it is much better kept and laid out. Two of the most conspicuous of the monuments were those of the quacks, St. John Long and Morrison. Ha! Ha! Poor human nature!

May 15. Walk to Harrow-on-the-Hill and am depressed by its solemn stillness and solitude. Look at Bryon's favourite tomb in the churchyard. The view of London and Windsor was obscured by clouds and the trees and hedgerows were too thick for picturesque beauty. The school is an ugly red brick building and the boys, about 100 playing around, don't look cheerful. A heaviness seems to lie over the whole place.

May 27. After spending nine days in the Channel Isles I arrive in London, and on the 2nd of June, Hughes meets me at Charing Cross and later his son, Alfred, joins us.

BUNGAY

June 8. Hughes is staying with me and in the evening we walk to The Grove where everything is prepared for the auction which is to take place tomorrow. The place looks most beautiful but sad to us who have passed so many days there for the last thirty years.

June 9. Hughes breakfasts with Rix the auctioneer. To the first day of the sale from 12 to 5 when things sold badly. The second day the auction went better. It continued till Friday. The paintings and prints sold on Thursday when I purchased "The

Hours" and some engravings. On the last day of the sale some fifty dozen of sherry, fifty or sixty dozen of port and ninety bottles of liqueurs, cordials and other spirits were auctioned, besides Champagne, Moselle and other wines. In all some 1700 bottles.

There is a small print of The Grove on the first page of the sale catalogue. The house seems to have contained five reception rooms, nine bedrooms and several dressing rooms, besides stables, dairy, brew and slaughter-houses and cellars.
After the death of Robert Butcher the property which included several farms and Laurel Lodge, now Lowlands, was put up for sale. In May 1846 Scott writes to Muskett, the Duke of Norfolk's steward, about a licence to take down the Grove House, which was demolished later. Upland Hall, built by William Hartcup about the year 1854, took its place.

June 14.   Hughes leaves me by the day coach at 9 o'clock. A melancholy departure for us both. On his way to Andover he was upset in the fast train near Slough, which was going at the rate of sixty-nine miles an hour.

June 21.   Hear that the Diss, Bungay and Beccles and Yarmouth Railway bill is withdrawn.

July 11.   News of Blanche Sandby's death and the following day hear that Mrs Chambers of Hedenham is past hope of recovery. She died on the 24th, in her 67th year. Captain and Mrs Dalling call to tell me.

July 25.   Busy assorting memorials of Bungay to forward to Alfred Suckling for his Suffolk History.

July 29.   To Yarmouth. The Regatta takes place today. Four yachts, ten lifeboats and eight yawls are competing. After the matches which last from 12 to 2, two hundred of the lifeboat crews dine together in a tent on the sands. Capt. Jerningham the excellent steward, E. Woodhouse etc., speak.
Two of Nelson's veterans of the Nile and Trafalgar were there and gallant Brock. Leave by train at 8½ and have my pocket picked at the station of a purse containing eight sovereigns.

July 30.   From 11 till 5 give Alfred Suckling[3] details and copies of Bungay history and the next day he arrives to breakfast to receive additional records.

August 15.   John Angell, late Mayor of Norwich, magistrate, dies in Norwich aged 78 and on the 21st. the Rev. John Day, rector of Tuddenham and brother to Mrs Mann of Bungay dies at Brompton aged 61.

At this time the Hughes, Mrs. Butcher and other members of the Butcher family are staying with Scott or in rooms in Bungay, arranging about The Grove estate.

September 11.   Bruce calls, but in vain, to persuade me to act as magistrate as many others have done but it would be too great a discomfort and a tax on my time. Dine at the Kerrich's with lively Lady Morgan, Mr. and Mrs. Jones, he the curate of Geldeston, the Berns, Sandby and Mrs. E. Bacon. The latter plays and Mrs Jones sings delightfully.

September 13.   Call on Sandby at Flixton and walk with him to see the improvements at the Hall. See Mrs Sandby for the first time since Blanche's death.

September 17.   The Norwich Festival, the first day of which disappoints me. Meet many friends and in the evening call on Mrs Borrow the aged mother of George Borrow[4], a kind clever old lady who has continued to live in Willow Lane since her husband's death in 1834.

September 18.   After breakfasting with Edward Fitzgerald[5] at the Royal, go with Brown of Kelsale, the Dallings and Fanshawes to the Festival.   Mozart's Requiem and Sphor's Calvary delightfully grand and pathetic.
Dine with Dr. Archdale in the Close and in the evening to a concert with the Travers and Smithies party. Norwich most gay and picturesque.
Towards the end of September my cousin Charlotte became very ill and continued so until the end of October when she suddenly improved in health.

October 8.   Rose, daughter of J.T. Margitson of Ditchingham, dies at 4 a.m. this morning aged 17.

October 14.   The last surviving maternal relation of my dear mother, her first cousin, Henry Roberts of Dreybridge House, Monmouth, dies suddenly this morning at 6 o'clock without pain or previous illness, aged nearly 74.

October 16. To Ditchingham School to form plans with Scudamore, Collyer and Cookesly for an asylum for the factory girls. Dine at the Smiths of Ellingham and meet Mrs Gillies who is 82, Mrs Nightingale, Mrs. Lawford, the Jones, Cobb, Courtley and his wife, Mr. and Mrs Abbot Upcher and Currie, besides five of their own party.
A splendid display of plate, excellent hock and claret and a capital dinner.

November 7. To Lowestoft and chat with Sarah Worthington. William[6] drives me to Oulton to see George Borrow (the author of "The Bible in Spain" etc.) we found him busy writing his travels without a plan or note of any kind by him.

Borrow and the Worthingtons were friends and I have heard mother say that when she and her brothers and sisters were children, George Borrow often went to see them. He would take up his position in his favourite corner seat beside the large fireplace of their old house in the Lowestoft High Street and tell them weird tales in such a loud and emphatic voice and with such violent gestures that they were spell-bound with terror. The one particularly impressed on her memory was that of Jack and the Beanstalk. Mrs. Worthington could always soothe him when in one of his violent moods but his visits were not enjoyed by the younger members of the family who were all, both boys and girls, afraid of him and were relieved and thankful when he took his departure. My mother's sister, Marion, remembered him as a big, handsome, noisy man who rode a beautiful grey horse and declared that she alone of the children was not afraid of him. He frightened our grandmother very much one day when in one of his furious tempers he rode his horse into the entrance hall of the old house above mentioned. His wife was a tall, gaunt woman and his stepdaughter a regular old maid. The latter, however, married and became Mrs. MacAubrey.

December 3. Planning a monument with Henry Nursey to the memory of John Cooper, late of Cove Hall. *(This was placed over the north entrance of St. Mary's Church, Bungay).*

December 6. Mrs G. Sandby and Miss Savage come and look at my house and the Pompeii pictures *(The Hours).* Miss Savage afterwards wrote a poem on these paintings which was published in the Court Journal in November 1846.

SONNETS ON THE HOURS

Fairest of all the Hours' sweet twilight morn
Steals o'er the earth its beauty to renew,
Distilling lightly from her silver urn,
With shadowy fingers, soft refreshing dew,
Gentle and pure her mien; for her seems meet
The prayer from childish lips that knows no stain,
Or holy dream, where aspirations sweet
Breathe of the Eden man ne'er knows again.
'Neath her mild lustre fade the paling stars,
(Oh they alone her half-veiled beauty guess)
Her smiling sister, day's bright gates unbar,
And on she passes in her loveliness,
Morn's lovely herald, thus oft tears prepare
The path for smiles they do but harbinger.

Where flee the hours? say, in that charmed cell
Sleep they until to earth again they come?
Surely there is some fair, some radiant house
Meet for their resting place, where they may dwell?
They slumber not, recording seraphs wait
While earth on high her faithfull witness bears,
That, clarion-tongued, sounds in archangels' ears,
Through the closed portals of the pyrean gate.
What take they hence? a blotted page, oft rife
With sin's dark shadows; vows by man unheard
And soon forgotten, deeply registered
In once pure tablets of his chequered life -
So sad each annal since their task began -
Well may they weep - if angels weep for man.

What marvel that thy foot-prints fall on flowers
If this thy train, Old Time what devotees
Would raise a shrine to worship to the Hours,
If all the Hours were as fair as these.
For such would men the ruthless tyrant slay,
And such did onward glide when once the sun
Rained his bright couriers on their fiery way
O'er the broad vale of eastern Ajalon.
Time heeds us not; in vain we bid him linger -
He spurs the woven bands of love and song.

Morn smiles upon him and a rosy finger
Gleams in the East and beckons him along.
Chide not his fleetness - let him lightly go -
How sad the hours when his step is slow!

Anna Savage

1846

January 2.   Dine at George Durrant's house, South Elmham Hall, with Mr. and Mrs Bruce, George Sandby[7], and Mr. and Mrs. Alder Rose, Richard and William Mann, Mrs Abel, Mrs Cavell and seven of the family. Home at 12 and find dear Alfred had arrived to my great joy.

January 3.   Alfred's birthday. He is 21. After lunch we drive to Ellingham and call on the Cobbs and then to see Col. Smith's tigers.This was the first meeting between Alfred and Maria Smith (whom he afterwards married).

January 13.   Walk to Flixton and look at the alterations at the Hall. Return by Sandby's house but do not call having heard that her father, General Hodgson is dead.

January 15.   Alfred and I to Gaudy Hall to see Mrs Sancroft Holmes and then to Starston to call on Archdeacon Oldershaw who was out.

January 30.   Call on Mrs. Allsopp, just come to Utting's house in Earsham Street and lately occupied by Mrs Collett. At 2^1/$_2$ the Rev. R. Burgess arrives by the Union Coach from Rendlesham. He and I inspect the schools and churches and in the evening Captain Dalling, Col. Smith and Cookesly dine with us.

Richard Burgess 1796-1881 Biblical scholar, Prebendary of St. Pauls, was a friend of Scott when in Rome in 1826.

February 14.   To Major Forster's and walk for half an hour in the garden with Miss Forster. The Major continues very ill and is not expected to live many days. (He died on the 18th aged 76).

May 5.   To stay at Ousden Hall, and Ireland shows me his house and his five daughters and the next day the gardens and pleasure grounds which are well kept, also the old church, ill kept.

We then ride, I on his bailiff's horse, through the village and over several of his farms to Lidgate, the ancient parish which gave birth to John Lidgate the learned monk of Bury. Here we examined the mounds and the fosses that remain of the old Roman fort. In the evening Mrs John Thorp of Chippenham, Capt. Heigham, Sir Robert and Miss C. Affleck of Dalham, Mr. and Mrs. Jackman of Lidgate, Mr. and Mrs. Fairlie, he is the steward of the Duke of Rutland, and Mrs Macdougal of Kirkheye, dine with us. Pleasant talk and delightful music from Mrs Jackson.

May 7. Sharp and Macdougal, who are staying here, walk with us through the woods in the morning and then we go in a break to Dalham where courteous old Sir Robert Affleck and his good-natured plain daughters show us the old Hall, the old portraits and the ancient avenue and gardens.
After lunching here we proceed to Kirtlings or Catlings where was a splendid old Hall of the Norths and Guildfords.
It was pulled down in 1805 by Dobit, the steward of the Ionian Lord Guildford (Frederick North 15th Earl, one of the founders of the Ionian University at Corfu) except the gallery which the present owner the Marquis of Bute has preserved as an occasional residence. It is of the date of Elizabeth or James 1st time. Dine at 6 o'clock. Much talk with Ireland of times long past when we were at Emmanuel and Dover together.

May 8. Ireland drives me to Newmarket at 12 and after looking over the Union House together, he leaves me and I go on to Ely. Fix at the "Lamb" and at 4 1/2 attend the service at the Cathedral. After exploring the town dine at the "Lamb" and talk to a young waiter, John King Martin, who is well educated but reduced to poverty by the death of his father. He supports his mother and six brothers and sisters by his service.

May 9. Breakfast with Dr. French prebendary of Ely and his family. Go with him to the Cathedral service and afterwards take a complete view of this fine building outside and in. Then to see the fossiled Plesiosaurus at Surgeon Jones' which was found two miles from Ely while cutting the Peterborough railway.

May 13. Beccles. Dine at the Farmer's Club and Labourer's Friendly Society with the Chairman, H. Dowson, Gooch, Sandby, Leighton, Arnold, Crowfoot and about forty others. Much useful talk and some good speeches.

May 20. Ipswich. Stay with Walter Scott in Brook Street. Call on Whiting - too disabled in body and mind to attend to The Grove business for which I desired to see him. Call later on Baldiston recommended by Rodwell for this purpose and afterwards to see Mrs Gee, Miss Colville and Mrs. Reeve.

May 22. Returned to Bungay last evening. Write to Muskett, the Duke of Norfolk's steward about a licence to take down The Grove House.

May 29. At 4 o'clock this morning the House of Lords votes for the second reading of the Abolition of the Corn Laws by a majority of 47. News also of the Waveney Valley Coast lines of the proposed railway being thrown out but those of Stowmarket, Diss and Norwich recommended by the Committee of the House of Commons.

June 4. Bungay. Baldiston and his son come from Ipswich and dine with me at 3¹/₂ and we go up to The Grove to make estimates and measurements of the house etc.
There were several buildings on this estate at the time the Butchers owned the property which included the Stow Fen Farm, Stow Park, Dawsons and Grove farms, Laurel Lodge etc.

June 23. Attempted auction of The Grove estate at the Corn Exchange. Nearly all bought in. The next day the auction again renewed. Hartcup & Cook the auctioneers, come to me to ask what I would give for Lot 1 (Grove). I answer £5000 instead of the £7000 they ask. Not accepted. At the auction in the afternoon buy 10 acres of meadow for £820.

June 25. Call on Mrs Butcher with whom the Hughes and Mercers are staying. Hughes leaves at 5¹/₂ for Cerme and Emily Mercer and Leighton dine with me. Hughes and Mercer have now decided that the unsold property shall be divided between the three sons-in-law, in equal shares - viz: themselves and Saunders.

July 12. London. After breakfasting at the Club, go to St. Mark's College, Stanley Grove, Chelsea, a training institution of the National Society. Many young men were attending the service in the chapel which was performed according to the old Anglo Catholic form. Five clergymen were officiating, chanting etc. From this preparation for future generations I passed to the memorials of those who have gone - the West London and Westminster Cemetery.

July 14. Leave Shoreditch at 11 o'clock and travel for the first time by the railway from Colchester to Ipswich. On arriving go to Walter Scott's and find Mary and Mrs Scott there.

July 21. Bungay. Give rewards to the children of the Infant School. Drive to Henstead and dine and sleep at T. Sheriff's where Ireland, his wife and two daughters are staying, also the Gooches and Mrs Jodrell, the latter is the daughter of Sir Charles Napier.

July 22. Look at Sheriff's very neat premises and gardens. After, drive with Ireland as far as Shipmeadow to attend a Committee meeting on labour at the House with Sir John Waltham and Sandby.

July 27. Ireland, his wife and daughters come to me this morning and look at my prints and gardens, the Bungay churches and castle. The ladies leave for Ousden at 2 1/2, Ireland remaining with me. We go to the Bedingfields, Chambers and Dallings and then to The Grove. At 6 1/2 Captains Dalling and Fanshawe, Col. Smith and Mr. Lockart join us at dinner. A pleasant evening.

July 28. Ireland and I leave by the day coach at 10 1/2 and reach Ipswich at 3 1/4. Fix at Walter Scott's.

July 29. Ipswich Assizes. To the Tower Church, George Sandby preaches well on Capital Punishment and prevention of crime. Baron Alderson in the Criminal Court and Judge Williams in the Nisi prius Court, Sir R. S. Adair, High Sheriff.

August 14. Botwright, carpenter of Bungay dies this night in his 60th year.

August 20. Alfred and I go to Norwich. A meeting of the Medical Association at St. Andrews Hall. Cross in the Chair. Dr. Rankin reads a prosy report. Crowfoot, Worthington, Dr. Wake, Dr. Copeland etc. there.

September 23. Hear, through a note from Col. Smith, of the death of young Marcus Hughes and go to the Coffee Room to see it confirmed by the Indian Mail. Do not tell Alfred of his brother's death until the next morning.

September 24. Alfred extremely unhappy all day. Try to console him quietly. To see Charlotte who is pretty well but her brother is ill in bed. Miss Butcher (*Alfred's aunt*) arrives at 6 o'clock from Norwich and goes directly to bed. Altogether a very sad day.

A letter from Hughes asking us to go at once to Cerme on account of Marcus' death. After ascertaining that Samuel and Miss Butcher are better, Alfred and I start for London and the next day continue our journey to Cerme. Find Mrs. Hughes, Grace and all the family in deep distress.

On Sunday I received a letter from the Horse Guards telling me that no intelligence had arrived at Head Quarters relating to the death of Marcus, but two days later official news comes from Lord Fitzroy Somerset announcing his death. Hitherto some hope had been entertained - now fresh sorrow but Mrs Hughes seems better and all pass a tranquil evening.

All the enquiries concerning their son's death seem to have been made through J.B.Scott. Marcus died of dysentery at Secunderabad on the 29th July.

October 7. After a long talk with Mr. and Mrs Hughes they decide against the army for Alfred and he and I leave them this morning and spend a few days in London on our way back to Bungay.

October 20. To Shadingfield Hall where I join Mr. and Mrs Scott, their son Charles and his wife, Walter Scott and the Kilners. James Kilner, late of the East India Company Sea Service married to Mary Louisa Scott by her brother the Revd. Charles. After the departure of the bride and bridegroom the rest of the party go to Southwold, returning at 6 o'clock to dine. Music in the evening. On the way back to Bungay with Samuel Scott our driver turns into a narrow lane at Barsham and upsets the chaise; this we are unable to extricate so have to walk home and arrive about 2 in the morning.

October 30. Calls from Colonel Smith of Ellingham, Mrs Dashwood of Beccles and Miss Hamilton and Miss Lillistone.

November 19. Meet Scudamore, Cookesly, Collyer and Martin[9] of Bixley at the schoolhouse at Ditchingham about the factory girls home. Martin is part owner of the Silk and Crepe factory.

November 21. Alfred calls on Samuel Hughes C.I. of Duke Street and receives an offer of constant employment at three guineas a week. We write "home" about it and in the evening dine at the Oriental Club with Col. Smith who urges Alfred to accept it. A week later it is decided that he shall go to Hughes and take up engineering as a profession.

November 30. Alfred avows to me his love for Maria Smith and she evidently loves him. The Colonel told me yesterday that he would gladly welcome him as his son-in-law when he has an assured income. Alfred leaves me this evening. I grieve at his departure yet rejoice at his prospects.

December 1. John Whiting, builder, dies at Ipswich aged 70. To him I am chiefly indebted for the improvements of my Waveney and Bridge Houses.

December 13. Flixton Hall burnt down last night. I hear of the fire this morning and walk to Flixton to see the ruins. Nothing is saved but the offices, old and new.
Repairs and improvements have been going on for two years past at the cost of many thousands of pounds and now only the walls remain. Crowds of people there.

December 22. John and Henry Scott of Shadingfield arrive in England after 7½ years absence in Australia.

1847

January. Died at her residence at Brooke Street, Ipswich, my old friend Ann, widow of the Rev. William Gee, whose elder sister Ann Gee married my maternal great uncle Roberts of Dreybridge House, near Monmouth.

January 12. Joseph John Gurney who died at Earlham on the 4th, buried in the Quaker Meeting House, Norwich, with extraordinary respect.

January 29. London. Charles Roberts calls with his nephew, Charles Edward Probyn, who has just returned from the Isle of Man to take a Clerkship in the Treasury. To the first Exhibition of English Artists at the British Institution Gallery with Broadwood and Sully.

February 18. Bungay. Drive early to Shipmeadow House to enquire into a rebellion which has taken place amongst the able bodied men. Three of them have been sent to gaol and the rest are quieter. Thirty weapons have been found on the premises. At 1½ to attend the Eastern Union Railway meeting of which I am appointed Chairman. Capt. Hutton, the Chief Constable for Suffolk, Hartcup, Ransome, Willett, Dalling, Sandby, Denny and Charles Childs address the meeting. Resolution for the Eastern Line unanimously adopted, Sandby comes home with me.

February 25. To Cambridge to vote for Prince Albert's election to the office of Chancellor. Before 5 o'clock 582 had voted for him - 572 for Earl Powis. Dine at Emmanuel and then return as far as Norwich in the evening.

March 24. Fast day on account of the famine in Ireland. At 8$\frac{1}{2}$ leave by coach to Haughley and thence by rail to Bury to the Assizes. Fix at the John Kilner's.
Attend the service at St. Mary's at 4 o'clock with Lord Chief Baron Pollock[10] and Judge Coleridge and the High Sheriff Oakes etc. Eyre reads the Fast Day service and Gould preaches the sermon. No dinner. Coffee at 6$\frac{1}{2}$. The Grand Jury close their labours two days later.

April 21. To Shipmeadow House. A pauper named Jermy found with £200 in her possession. Evening dine at the Chambers with Mr. and Mrs Upcher, Mr. and Mrs Hurnard, Mr. and Mrs Harrison (these ladies were lately the three Miss Days of Earsham Rectory) Mr. and Mrs Bruce and Scudamore.

May 2. To St. Mary's Church in the evening to hear Cookesly's farewell sermon. Nothing in his ministry has graced him like leaving it. Elswood gave a dinner in his honour last Friday to which I was invited.

May 3. Cookesly takes leave of the school children admirably. He has been here eight years and leaves tomorrow. I was very frank with him when parting. He is going to Wimborne in Dorset.

May 6. Hear the decision of the House of Commons Committee against the Eastern Union Extension line to Yarmouth and for the Diss and Reedham line of the Norfolk Company with postponing conditions.

May 7. To a meeting of thirty of the inhabitants, summoned by the Surveyor of Highways to consider the drainage of the town.

May 13. London. Alfred and I in a crush to the Old Opera House from 6 to 7 to hear Jenny Lind[11] in Somnambula. Voice, singing and acting all surpassingly beautiful. The enthusiasm of the immense audience was at its highest pitch.

May 20.   Leave London and go by rail and coach to Tiverton to visit dear Mrs Barne and the Patches.

May 23. Sunday. With Mrs Barne, Catherine and Fanny to St. Peter's or the Old Church, at Tiverton where Mr. Measer preaches. Lunch at the Patches and go to St. Peter's Church again in the afternoon with Catherine, Ellen and Fanny. Measer dines with us at Broomfield at 5½ and gives us an account of his travels in Egypt and Syria. Leave Tiverton on the 25th and return to London.

June 2.   To a General Meeting of the National Society from 12 to 5½. Children examined by Mr. Cook. Report read by Kennedy. Music by Hullah. Present, the Archbishop of Canterbury, Bishops of Bangor, Salisbury, Oxford, St. David's and St. Asaph's, Earl of Powis, Gladstone[12], Acland etc. Most eloquent speeches from Gladstone and Wilberforce, the Bishop of Oxford. Meet Alfred at the Athenaeum and go with him to Greenwich and dine off whitebait.

July 3/4.   Mrs Patch and Measer come to London where I join them at Morley's Hotel. The first evening we go to Covent Garden Opera and the next day to Harrow to see Drury at his school house. Return home on the 6th.

July 17. Yarmouth. Call on several friends and with Sir Eaton Travers and Mackenzie inspect the alterations at St. Nicholas Church. Dine at the Dawson Turners with Dr. Planchon, the French botanist, Miss Jane Clowes and Turner.

July 26.   Susannah, wife of Archdeacon Glover, born Bonhote of Bungay, dies at Southrepps, widow of Dr. Reeve and Dr. Jefferson.

July 29.   Lord A. Lennox and Mr. Coope elected M.P.s. for Yarmouth. The Marquis of Douro and Mr. Peto for Norwich, Chevallier Cobbold and Hugh Adair for Ipswich.

July 30.   The Archaeological Institute holding its meetings in and near Norwich from the 29th July to the 5th August. Attend a sectional meeting and hear Lee Warner lecture on Brancaster as the Brannodunum (Roman Fortress) etc. and Professor Wallis on

Norwich Cathedral, its architecture and history. Spend two hours in the Cathedral and palace and an hour at the public library with Lady Hooker and Mrs Gunn, Dawson Turner's daughters.
Then to the Castle and afterwards preside at dinner at the Royal. Twenty-two members present. At 9 to the Bishop's Palace to a crowded conversazione, Bancroft the American Minister, Lord Braybrooke, Mrs Hamilton Grey, Mrs. Opie[13], the Dean of Westminster and the Marquis of Northampton amongst the guests. The cellars and kitchens of the Palace of Herbert de Losinga were lighted up and beautiful madrigals performed by the Cathedral choir. The next two days spent in Yarmouth.

August 2. With Charles Palmer and others go by steamer to Burgh Castle where we join the Norwich division of the Archaeological Society again. Hartshorne lectures in the castle to two hundred of us. Return in two steamers by Breydon to Yarmouth and repair to the church where Professor Willis describes its architecture and history; at 5 the Institute dine at the Town Hall, one hundred and twenty members present. Mayor Burroughs in the Chair. Good speeches from the Marquis of Northampton, the Bishop of Norwich, the American Ambassador, Henry Mackenzie, Sir John Boileau and others.

August 3. To Norwich where John Archdale gives a lecture at the Guild Hall on Gateways and especially those of the city. To the library at 2. Dine at the Swan with one hundred and thirty. The Bishop in the Chair. Capital lectures from Sedgwick, Buckland and J. M. Kemble and good singing from the Norwich Choir.

August 4. Breakfast at the Archaeological room at the Royal and then by special train to Wymondham where one hundred and fifty of us explore the church superficially; then on to Ely, where we are received by Dean Peacock. Willis lectures in and on the beautiful Cathedral. Lunch at the Deanery and return to Norwich at 6.
The morning of the last day of the meeting of the Institute is spent at the Guildhall, where discussions at the Council Room and a general meeting and speeches take place after which we disperse on our various ways.

August 8. Walk by the Common and Bath Hills to Ditchingham Church and spend two hours there inspecting Scudamore's improvements which will cost £250 and for which he has collected only £50.

Old paintings of the time of Henry VI have been discovered. One of the Last Judgement with an inscription over it "Discedite a me maledicti in oeternum" in an arch between the chancel and the nave. Also three curious figures crowned and in ermine - one bearing a falcon, one an axe and all have labels not legible to me, together with three figures also crowned and in armour along trees and stars.

August 11. Bungay. Examination of the Boys by the school Committee from 9 to 12. At 2 o'clock all the scholars meet and go in procession to The Grove where they have tea, cake and fruit in front of the house. They dance till 7. Many ladies and gentlemen, tradespeople and others look on and Alder, Curate of St. Mary's is very active in promoting the fete. Weather lovely. Send the infants to and from it in a wagon with Philip Bear in attendance.

Died after nine days illness, Henry Reynolds, corn merchant and clerk of the Bungay Savings Bank. A good, conscientious and honourable man. Quiet, yet firm and independent, of little pretence but of great and real religion and charity.

August 14. To another meeting about the drainage of Bungay. After two hours discussion it ended in a refusal to do anything.

August 15. Mrs Richard Mann's father, Mr. Waters of Arminghall dies at Wainford, Bungay, after six days illness.

August 18. Shipmeadow. Salary of the schoolmaster raised from £20 to £30.

August 23. Have lumbago but dress and go in a barouche to Norwich, taking Grace and Alfred Hughes with me to St. Andrews Hall to hear Jenny Lind. She sings superlatively well and with Gardonie and Mr. and Mrs Lablanche and a good orchestra gives a delightful concert to an audience of two thousand.

August 29. Drive Grace to the re-opening of Ditchingham Church. A large party of clergy, ladies and some laymen present. The old pews have been done away with and open benches substituted by the Rector, Mr. W.E. Scudamore. Bouverie preaches an excellent sermon. £65 collected.

August 31. Inspect the St. Olaves temporary wooden bridge and the old one about to be taken down which was built in 1768.

November 14. Sunday Schools. A hundred and forty-two present.

Mr. and Mrs. Alder and the two Miss Alders, two Miss Reynolds, two Miss Bewicks and E.Bellman, Miss Butcher and young Butcher from the Staithe, Ambrose Botwright, William Fenn, Robert Clarke and Walter Bull there. The above- mentioned are always in attendance as teachers. In the evening W. Fenn comes to see me.

In October Willie Worthington was staying at Waveney House during which time Henry Davey painted his portrait and now his mother is at Outney Cottage and is having her portrait painted by the same artist. It seems to have been finished towards the end of November when she returned to Lowestoft.

December 2.   My friend William Fisher promoted to the rank of Rear Admiral. Write to him with congratulations. This week the deaths occur of Mrs. Schults of Gillingham, aged 88, Henry Burtsal of Bungay aged 67, William Dalrymple late surgeon in Norwich, aged 76 and Charles Smithies, D.C.L. and clerk aged 34, the latter the husband of Isabella, daughter of Sir Eaton Travers.

December 7.   Town meeting at 3½.

J.B. Scott re-elected Town Reeve and presides over sixty guests at the dinner at the Tuns.

December 15.   By coach to Haughley and thence by rail to Ipswich to the opening of the Museum. Speeches therein and afterwards to look over Ransome's Iron Works with the Bishop of Norwich, Berners, Henslow, Long of Saxmundham, etc. At 5 o'clock dine at the Town Hall. J.C. Cobbold M.P. presides. Speeches from the Bishop of Norwich, Dr.Buckland, Dean of Westminster, Professor Henslow, Allan Ransome, Yarrell, Hugh Adair and others. Later the Bishop and twenty of us take coffee at George Ransome's.

1848

January 3.   Dear Alfred is 23 today. Beside the present I had already given him which was lying on the dining room table were these lines in reference to his birthday:-

> Thy hand, O God with worldly bliss
> Hath made my cup run o'er
> And in a true and faithful friend,
> Hath doubled all my store.

> Ten thousand, thousand precious gifts,
> My daily thanks employ
> And not the least, a cheerful heart,
> That takes these gifts with joy.'

We dine at Ellingham at 4 o'clock and spend the evening there.

January 4.   Dinner party at the Sandby's of Denton and meet Captain John Meade, the Chambers, Forsters and Mr. Lathbury. The following night to a dance at the Forsters.

January 15.   This afternoon spoke to R. J. Margitson just as he was quitting his lower office at the Bank. He was then in good health and spirits. Two days later I heard of his sudden death. He went out shooting on the morning of the 17th with Henry Wilson of Kirby and Kerrich and fell down lifeless near Leys Wood at 10 a.m. aged 65. He was a solicitor, a member of the firm of Kingsbury and Margitson, now Margitson and Hartcup. He resided at Ditchingham and was buried on the 22nd.

January 22.   Tumultous assemblages now collecting in Paris which so far are kept in check by the soldiers. During the next few days the papers are full of sad news. On the 24th Louis Philippe abdicates the throne and a Republic is proclaimed. On March 3rd the French King and his Queen Amelie land at Newhaven, Sussex after a week's concealment in Normandy.

March.   This month Mr. and Mrs Hughes come to stay in Bungay. Most of their time was spent with their son Alfred and J.B. Scott. Mrs. Smith of Ellingham comes to call on the Hughes at Waveney House. Their first meeting and all seem pleased with each other. Daily meetings take place between the young people but Colonel Smith definitely declares that without a permanent income from some profession he cannot allow his daughter to marry Alfred. The engineering work with Samuel Hughes came to an end last October.

March 14.   Sir William and Miss Delaney are at dinner at Mrs Goudry of Drayton.

March 25.   Pope Pio Nono flies from Rome in the disguise of a servant of the Bavarian Ambassador.

March 28.   At 8 o'clock this evening Isaac Jermy, late Preston, recorder of Norwich and his son Jermy were murdered at Stansfield

Hall by James Bloomfield Rush. The news fills us with horror.

April 4.   Bishop Stanley confirms four hundred and nine candidates at St. Mary's Church, Bungay.

April 10.   A memorable day in London. It was announced that as many as two hundred thousand Chartists or Republicans would over-run London, strike terror into Parliament and plunder and destroy the city. This threat was met by immense precautions on the part of the Government, the police and the inhabitants of all classes. From the latter one hundred and seventy thousand were sworn in as Special Constables, all determined to put down outrage and revolution. We arrived on Saturday, Alfred went with Hopkins to Bedford Square and Tottenham Court Road and I, after breakfasting at my Club, to St. Paul's Churchyard at 11 o'clock and entered Earl de Grey's Regiment, Lord Sydney's division. Amongst those sworn in were Prince Louis Napoleon, Comte D'Orsay, the Duke of Buckingham and crowds of officers. The Chartists had a signal moral defeat which (God grant) may preserve England.

April 18.   Alfred and I to Ramsgate. Explore the pier and harbour, Captain Martin R.N. the harbour master shows us the new steam dredging machine built by Sir John Rennie at the cost of nine thousand pounds. We also see the new Roman Catholic church with house attached, built by Pugin [14] and Christ Church, the Protestant one lately erected at the cost of nine thousand pounds.

April 19.   Walk to Deal. Look at the boats along the shore and at the vessels in the Downs for two hours - pass on to Walmer and see the interior of the castle and the rooms once occupied by William Pitt and Lord Liverpool and now by the Duke of Wellington. The Duke sleeps on an iron bedstead, with a plain mattress and without curtains. He rises at $5^{1/2}$ and walks for two hours before breakfast. Queen Victoria and her suite visited him here for six weeks in 1843. Return to London on the 25th.

May 1.   Set out for Chester and on arriving call on Dr. Thackeray, and was most kindly received by his daughter Jane, his good old father-in-law and my friends John and Maurice Jones.
At 2 p.m. we start by the railway opened this day from Chester to Bangor. Flags were flying and crowds watching along the whole line for our arrival. At $4^{1/2}$ fix at the beautifully situated Penrhyn Arms which I visited when I was nineteen.

May 2. A glorious morning. Walk by the shore and hills overlooking the lovely Anglesea banks to the Menai Suspension Bridge and a mile further on to the still greater wonder, the Menai Britannia Bridge about to be constructed of iron tubes to be erected on five grand Anglesea Piers. Two thousand men are now at work on it. We spend two hours admiring and investigating it and then walk over the beautiful Suspension Bridge and return by rail to Conway.

May 3. Up at six and look at the old house Plas Mawr, inscribed

'AVEXS ANEXS Sustue Abstu 1576'.

Then at the Tubular Bridge 360 feet long. We watched it in the centre from the adjacent Suspension Bridge whilst an engine, tender and five carriages passed over it and could perceive no vibration whatever. After inspecting the massive ruined castle leave Conway by the wonderful Tubular Bridge and reach Chester again at 11 1/2 where immense crowds were assembled. Dine at Dr. Thackeray's with his brother, a well known physician at Chester, grandfather of Thackeray the novelist, daughter Jane, William Jones and his two daughters and son and Mr. Lovell.
To the race course where great numbers of people were picturesquely grouped. Alfred and I see the Chester Cup run for by thirty-four horses - a splendid sight. Peep of Day beats War Eagle and the rest. In the evening get with some difficulty to the railway station and proceed by train of twenty-three carriages to Crewe. Sleep at the Crewe Arms. After spending a few days in Liverpool, leave on the 8th for the Isle of Man, arriving at Douglas in the afternoon at 5.30. Here we are met by Cholomley and Captain Probyn and the three girls. Stay at Castle Mona Hotel prettily situated, with gardens and hills behind it. Dine at 7 and coffee at 9 with my cousins. Margaret (Mrs. Probyn) has lately broken a blood vessel.

May 11. Walk by Frogmore to Castle Ward, a fortified hill with mounds but no walls remaining. Then to see a farmer's wife who is a friend of Margaret's. The husband had been cutting many crosses of little green boughs which are to be placed in secret places about the farm and before the doors to keep off the fairies who used to come on this May eve. For the same purpose fires were burning on the hills around. I counted ten, produced by burning the furze and gorse and 'Horns' were being sounded all over the island. Though by most these ancient May ceremonies are now regarded as mere fun, yet I believe some of the old Manx people and our farmer's wife among the number still believe in fairies and the potency of these charms.

May 15.   After various excursions with the Probyns we leave Castle Mona, a good and beautifully situated house, late the Duke of Athol's, but now an hotel at 6 1/2. Embark on board the steamer at 7 1/2, Henry Probyn sees us off. About a hundred people on board for a pleasure trip to Whitehaven. The wind soon rose and the waves too. We were but four hours performing the 45 mile journey but most of the passengers were very sea sick for the first two hours. Pass St. Bees steep head, enter Whitehaven harbour and land on the pier amid twelve to thirteen hundred spectators.

June 2.   Arrive at Northampton this morning having visited the principal towns and places of interest on our return from the island. Breakfast together at the George Hotel and then Alfred departs for Peterborough, Ely, Trowse and Bungay and I for London.

June 4. Sunday.   Service and Sacrament at Westminster Abbey. Bishop Mount of Gloucester and Bristol takes part in it. The transepts are now thrown into the choir for the sermon and the Abbey altogether greatly improved in the last two years. To Dulwich and dine there with Charles Cholomley, May and Susan Roberts and Caroline Probyn. Walk back, they coming part of the way with me.

June 7.   To the annual meeting of the National Society. Examination by Allen from 12 to 2. The new Archbishop, Sumner, in the Chair, a debate from 2 to 6 1/2 on the management clauses proposed by the Committee of Council on Education. Great bigotry, intolerance and ambition shown by a large crowd of the clergy; Sugden, Denison and others leading the cry, but it had been excited in the first instance by Kay Shuttleworth's proud, overbearing manner as Secretary of the Council. The Bishop of Oxford, Wilberforce, made a most powerful and eloquent speech which caused Denison to withdraw his motion. Dine at the Athenaeum.

June 16.   Returned home yesterday after an absence of ten weeks. Accounts from 6 to 8. Sandby and Kate come to see me from 1 to 2 o'clock. Drive to the Chambers and then call on Scudamore whom I find laid up with a sprained ankle. In the evening to see Mrs Dreyer's new Almhouses called 'The Bungay

Homes'. Go through Hannah Butcher's accounts which she has kept for me while I have been away.

Miss Butcher appears to have managed his house and servants and also to have paid all expenses relating to the schools and farm in his absence.

June 23. By Jordan's coach to Yarmouth and then by rail to Lowestoft to see the Worthingtons. Much talk about a murderous attack on Capt. Cook at Corton yesterday by two vagrants.

June 24. The Worthingtons have Mr. Loring, a minister of the Church of England, staying with them to learn medical treatment and the use of drugs. He is from Wurtemburg and is going out to Guiana.
Dreadful news towards the end of this month of the insurrection in Paris and of the battles there on the 23rd, 24th and 25th.

July 3. At 7 a.m. Mrs Butcher the widow of Robert Butcher of The Grove dies at Cuddon's lodgings in Trinity Street, aged 86 years. She was baptised at St. Mary's Ilketshall, 28th February 1762 - entered in the register as 'Anna Maria, daughter of Grigsen Hayhoe and Ann, his wife.'

July 4. From today, Tuesday, to Friday the 7th. inclusive, my cousin William Worthington was examined six hours per day at Somerset House for matriculation into the London University. He is now 18½ years old.

July 12. At 12½ Mrs Butcher's funeral procession starts from Cuddon's lodgings - the hearse and first mourning coach with Mr. and Mrs. Mercer, Miss Butcher and myself and the 2nd. with Alder (curate) and Webb (doctor). W. G. Courtley reads the service and the body is interred in the family vault at Earsham. Hughes had written to me previously stating he could not attend on account of his wife's illness and Mrs Saunders left the day after her mother's death.

July 14 and 15. With Hughes, Mercer and Hartcup about The Grove affairs. The two sons-in-law leave hoping things are arranged in a fair train to settlement.

July 19. A cricket match between the Beccles and Bungay Clubs on Bungay Common. Charles Scott, T. Sheriffe, Joddrell etc., play for Beccles. Currie[15], the Collyers, Wilson, Garneys etc., for Bungay:

```
Beccles 1st Innings   84
Bungay   "     "     115
Beccles 2nd    "     138
Bungay   "     "      55 with only 3 wickets down
```

The match was stopped by nightfall. A thousand to twelve hundred spectators present.

July 24.   To the re-opening of Yarmouth church. The old galleries and pews have been removed. The service was beautifully performed by the Norwich choir and the Bishop of Norwich preached. Mackenzie the late, and Hill the future minister took part in the service. Lunch at the Town Hall when Mackenzie, the Bishop of Norwich, the Bishop of Oxford, Baron Alderson, Hill and Guizot (late of Rome and now Minister of France) speak admirably. The service resumed at the church at 4 o'clock. Four thousand present. The Bishop of Oxford preaches well. £233 collected. A thunder storm and heavy rain succeed a splendid day.

July 29.   At Lowestoft again with the Worthingtons. In the evening to Borrows and "Don Gorgeio" goes with us to read the Irish News at the Bath House.

News of an incipient rebellion in Ireland was causing some excitement at this time.

July 30. Sunday.   No sea bathing this morning on account of not wishing to shock Worthington or to induce his boys to rebel against his puritanical scruples.
To St. Peter's Chapel. Randall reads - Cunningham preaches and we go to sleep.

July 31.   Leave Lowestoft by the Blue Coach loaded with twenty-eight passengers all going to the Ipswich Assizes. Hear the trial of Gower and Balls for assault on Captain Cook at Corton on the 22nd June last. The former sentenced to fourteen years transportation and the latter acquitted.

September 10.   Alfred leaves me to pass a year at Wingfield to learn farming. The next day go to Lowestoft and arrange with Worthington about Willie's education at King's College and talk with the latter about his expenses there.

October 28. Call on Sir William Dalling at Earsham who is living in the Distillery house which until lately belonged to the Butchers of The Grove.

November 13. Hear that W. H. Crowfoot is dying and shortly after George Sandby calls to tell me of his death. He died at Beccles after only four days illness aged 68, of typhus fever caught from a patient.

December 18. Mrs Ann Anderson, daughter of the late Thomas Rede of Beccles and widow of Lieut. Colonel Anderson, once of the Dragoon Guards and of Laurel Lodge, Bungay, dies aged 80. She was brought from London to be buried here on the 26th. Call on Archdeacon Ormerod in his newly built house at Redenhall.

December 26. After a good deal of dodging between the lawyers Hartcup and Elswood it is decided that Alfred shall take possession of Stow Park farm.

From now onward there are frequent references to his work there although he does not inhabit the house until October 1849.

1849

January 8. Dine at Kingsbury's with Miss, Mr. and Mrs. Crabtree, Mrs Cross, late Maria Crabtree, Major Mann, Mr. and Mrs Mosse, Charles Woodhouse, Mr. and Mrs Hartcup, Miss Margitson, Thomas Brettingham, the Cobbs and Alfred. Afterwards go to Childs' musical party at the Corn Hall which was excellent.

January 10. Shipmeadow. A most important change takes place here, viz: outdoor relief to the able-bodied men. The House is too full and oakum is to be given them to pick at home. 4 lbs per man. Alfred to dine with Colonel Smith and his tenants. Charles Woodhouse stays with me.

January 17. The election takes place at Bury for a surgeon for the hospital there. Hearne 77. Newham 87. J. Kilner 272, until Mr. Creamer paid 400 guineas for Mr. Hearne and gave 200 votes for him as an annual subscriber!

January 23. Alfred and I to Norwich to hear Jenny Lind sing delightfully in St. Andrews Hall for the benefit of the Norwich churches.

March 12.   Woodward, Dissenting Minister at Wortwell, gives a lecture at the Corn Hall, Bungay, on the Geology of Suffolk and Norfolk. Two hundred there.

March 17.   Drive to Ellingham and meet Mr. and Mrs Jessop, newly married and lately come to Topcroft Rectory.

March 29.   The trial taking place of James Blomfield Rush for the murder of Mr. Jermy[16] of Stansfield. Attended the court at Norwich the first day. He was condemned to death after six days trial. He defended himself.

May 12.   From 11 1/2 to 1 1/2 at a Sanitary Committee at St. Mary's vestry when I again make vain efforts to induce Surveyor Gower to join in a scheme for draining the town. (*See August 14th 1847.*)

May 15. Lowestoft. Find Worthington at home and walk with him to the end of the North Pier to see the new terrace and houses and the hotel just completed and being furnished. Dine at Worthington's with his pupils, Ray and Umpheley. Afterwards go to Corton to see the exterior only of Mrs. Birkett's new house as she was out. Then to the Fowlers where I meet Miss Day and Millicent Leathes. Return to Lowestoft and inspect the plans for the drainage of the town.

June 6.   To the annual meeting of the National Society. About seven hundred schoolmasters there. The Archbishop in the Chair, fifteen bishops, the Duke of Buccleugh. Lords Harrowby, Nelson, Colchester, Kenyon, Castlereagh, Fielding etc. Denison moves and Charles Wordsworth seconds, in speeches lasting two and a half hours, resolutions hostile to all agreement with the Privy Council Committee on Education. An obstinate and tumultuous debate thereon which lasts till 8p.m. Archdeacon Manning's amendment, which is rather less violent, carried.

   The conduct of the young clergy most violent, irreverent and disgraceful. Dine at Verrys with Samuel Scott and to the opera afterwards.

June 8.   Samuel Scott called to the Bar by the Society of Lincoln's Inn.

June 11. Sir John Waltham calls and talks long with me about the Shipmeadow building loan. With George Hopkins to the Academy and to Etty's exhibition for the second time. Hear Bright speak for a few minutes on 'Arbitration versus War' to an immense assemblage at Exeter Hall.

June 13. Breakfast at U.U. Club. By rail to Dachet - walk across the Home Park to Windsor where I meet Ireland with his wife and daughters on the terrace. He offers to nominate me for High Sheriff for Suffolk but I refuse. Ascend to the top of the Round Tower from whence a fine view and see the works of the Western and Southern Railways approaching completion. Dine at the White Hart and in evening to the service at St. George's Chapel.

June 29. Alfred and I make out a list of all my property to him as to his marriage settlement and Stow Park and examine the proposed mortgage thereto to me.

June 30. Willie Worthington comes to stay with me. George Cleveland having driven him over from Lowestoft.

July 5. Alfred and I attend at Elswood and Hartcup's office and the conveyance of Stow Park from the co-heiresses of Robert Butcher to Alfred Hughes is completed. At 4½ we drive with Willie to Denton Lodge where Mr. and Miss Sandby give a most pleasant party. At 6 o'clock tea and strawberries. Look at the roses and the beautiful view and their garden and then dancing on the turf by the light of the setting sun and a full moon till 9. All very happy. Mr. and Mrs Hughes, Grace, Susan, Alfred and Richard, Mr. and Mrs Bouverie, the Smiths, five of them, Capt. and Mrs Dalling, Mr. and Mrs Chambers, the Bedingfields, Wilson, Mrs and Miss E. Forster, the Bruces, Letitia, Mercer and Messrs. Rose, Tuffnell and Cautley were the party.

July 9. Mrs Bewicke, widow of the Rev. Thomas Bewicke dies at Trinity House and on the 16th. Catherine, daughter of the late Thomas Paddon dies after a few weeks illness, aged probably about 74. A person of extraordinary vivacity and activity, generally cheerful and kind but trifling and vain. She will be missed in the streets of Bungay. Another name connected with the town long before my birth has passed away.

July 18-19. The Royal Agricultural Society Meeting in Norwich. Attend both days and in the evening of the 19th to the grand dinner at St. Andrews Hall when eight hundred were present. The Earl of Chichester in the Chair. E. Woodhouse breaks down as usual. The Duke of Richmond was the best speaker as he is the most popular man of the day. At 8 to a concert at the Corn Exchange.

July 24.   To a ball at the Kerrich's at Geldeston. One hundred and twenty there. Howlet's band from Norwich in attendance and a splendid supper provided. Among the guests were the officers of the 16th Lancers, the Gardens, Schultz's, Bedingfield, Forsters, Hughes, Smiths and all Beccles.

August 4.   Mrs Eliza Leach, born Hood, dies of cholera in South Lambeth after fifteen hours illness. She was a cousin of Samuel and Charlotte Scott.

August 7.   From 3 to 5 attend the sale of The Grove property by W. Butcher of Norwich. The Grove and fifty-eight acres sold to Robert Burtsal and Fisher for £2680, the latter giving seven hundred for the house. Laurel Lodge with forty acres of land bought by T. C. Hughes for £2180.
In the evening dine at George Sandby's with Colonel Hodgson, Miss Western, Miss Cartwright of Bury and Mr. and Mrs Robert Cobb.

August 10.   A meeting of the Feoffees about taking up the pavement in the Bungay Market Place carriage road and macadamising it.

August 16. Lowestoft. Bathe from the end of the North pier with Willie Ray, Cleveland, Joachim, Watson and young Norton. Willie breakfasts with me in the coffee room of the Royal. Lunch with Norris and Miss Hart who is now residing with him as companion to his daughters. Walk with them and Montgomery Norris to Kessingland Church and then to Robinson Crusoe's (John Davy) to see his fossils and other curiosities. The latter speak of the beauty of my mother.

August 20.   After breakfasting at the Royal, escort the Kerrich's and Bessie, Charlotte, Hester and Willie Worthington to the North Pier where with the Leathes and others watch the yachts, yawls, punts and rowing boats contending in the Lowestoft Regatta. Eight thousand persons added to the population of the town for this day. Dine at the Worthingtons at 6. Music till 8 and then walk to the station to see the trains depart.

1849/50]

August 21. Escort my nieces to the pier head whence we see the second day of the Regatta. Evening to view the fireworks on the Battery Green.

August 22. Bathe with the boys as usual and later to Mutford with Alfred to see my colt 'Hotspur' and the bullocks on the Burgh marshes. See Borrow at the edge of the lake on our return. Walk back from Mutford to Lowestoft.

August 31. An outbreak of cholera has been announced at Beccles and today discussions take place with the doctors about a Cholera Address to the inhabitants of Bungay. To see Alder (curate) and Drs. Garneys, Currie and Webb and Fisher[17] thereon.

September 6. Edward John Stanley, Bishop of Norwich dies at Braham Castle, Dingwall in Ross-shire where he had gone with his wife and daughters. His body was brought back by sea to Yarmouth and buried in the nave of Norwich Cathedral.

September 23. Died at Deptford, Commander James Wolfe Roberts, R.N. aged 90 years, of which he had been blind nearly seventy. My venerable old relative was one of the finest specimens of cheerfulness, activity and resignation under so great a calamity I have ever seen.

November 5. The Rev. J. D. Hustler formerly tutor of Trinity College, Cambridge and Rector of Euston dies suddenly of apoplexy. He was brother to my friend and tutor William Hustler. The following day Mrs Elizabeth Dreyer, widow of the Rev. Dreyer of Bungay dies aged 77.

November 8. Lowestoft. Arrived here by omnibus last evening and am staying with the Worthingtons. This morning saw the "Enterprise" and "Investigation", Lieut. James Rose's ships sailing by on their return from Prince Regent's Inlet after their vain search for Sir John Franklin.

1850

January 4. At 5½ to a tea party at the Corn Hall given by Mr. Childs where twelve instruments and sixty voices perform most excellent music under his leading. The concert lasts till 11 o'clock. Two hundred and eighty persons of various classes pleasantly assembled.

1850]

January 25. This night four hundred and thirteen paupers slept at Shipmeadow House, a greater number than at any period since 1837. Forty beds were made up in the large board room and some in the library.

January 28. Charles Arnold of Rugby lunches with me on his way to Aldeburgh and is coming again tomorrow on his return journey. Take him to hear the boys sing at the school and then to see Childs to talk about music for the people.

February 1. Charles and Walter Scott come unexpectedly and lunch with me. Walter has agreed to enter into a partnership at Newcastle-under-Lyme, having given up his practice in Ipswich.

February 5. Capt. John Sutton calls to tell me of his brother's death after much suffering. Major Samuel Sutton, son of Admiral Sutton of Ditchingham Lodge, died at Kenilworth on the 3rd. aged 43. He is to be buried at Ditchingham tomorrow.

In 1853 the window in the east end of the chancel was given by his widow to his memory. It was put in by Messrs. O'Connor of 4, Berners Street, London, at the cost of £90.

March 27. Assizes. The court opens at 11. Lord Chief Baron Pollock charges the Grand Jury. Waddington foreman. Twenty-two present. J. J. Tuck as great a bore as ever. Dinner with Judges Pollock and Wightman and renew acquaintance with the latter after an interval of thirty-two years. (*See journal of October 1814.*) He most cordially invites me to his house. Delightful recollections of my first continental tour in 1814.

April 5. John James Bedingfield, formerly of Ditchingham Hall from whence he removed to Aldeburgh, returns to the neighbourhood and takes the late Mrs Dreyer's house in Bungay, Trinity Hall. The bells ring in his honour.

May 29. Attend the annual meeting of the National Society. Rather less violent and much less crowded than in 1849. Present the Archbishops of Canterbury and York, Bishops of Exeter, Gloucester, Landaff, Winchester, Colchester, etc. Denison makes his usual sneering venomous speech, (he was a great opponent of secular education), Page Woods speaks admirably. I went with Samuel Scott, Bouverie, Mackenzie and George Hill.

June 6. To a meeting of the Labourers' Friendly Society at St. Martin's New Hall, Long Acre, Lord John Russell in the Chair. Earl Harrowby, Lord Ashley and others speak. A Mr. Reynolds and thirty Chartists interrupt and one man was taken out by the police. Earl Harrowby collars Mr. Reynolds and hands him out also. Dine at the Athenaeum with Bouverie.

June 9. The Rev. Joseph Badely, Rector of Halesworth dies aged 48.

June 11. With Charles Roberts and Samuel to see the ancient pictures in the British Gallery. Then by the park to Westminster Chapter House to see the remains of some fresco paintings and architecture of the 14th century which had been previously concealed there by piles of dusty records and their cases.

During this visit to London J.B. Scott has a dispute with Willie about "that vile habit of smoking and tells him he must give it up or I him". Apparently they did not meet again until the 14th.

June 14. Willie comes by appointment to my lodging to explain his conduct of Saturday the 8th but is sullen, obstinate and shows much ingratitude and absence of right feeling. Our parting less friendly than before, much to my sorrow and his probable disadvantage.

June 19. Bungay. Mrs Edwards, wife of W.C. Edwards[18] the engraver, dies aged 80. A sufferer for three and a half years from paralysis.

June 30. To the schools. Alder there for the last time. In the evening to St. Mary's to hear his farewell sermon. Sir Robert Peel thrown from his horse on Constitution Hill.

July 1. R.E. Hughes appointed curate of St. Mary's Bungay under Archdeacon Glover.

July 2. At 11 p.m. after three days of great suffering Sir Robert Peel dies in the dining room of his house in Whitehall Gardens.
On the 3rd the House of Commons rise without transacting any business in consequence of grief for his death. He was buried the following Wednesday at Drayton church in the village in which he had his country residence.

1850]

July 8. The Duke of Cambridge dies at 10.20 p.m. aged 76.

August 1. Inspection of the schools by Mitchel. After examining the masters and pupil teachers he reports well of the former and fairly as to the latter and gives us all valuable suggestions.

August 8. Dine at Priest's house, Flixton with the Misses Hodgsons, Humphrey and Miss Dalling and three baronets - Sir John Waltham, Sir Windham Dalling and Sir Shafto Adair. Sir Windham tells many anecdotes of the Peninsular War and Wellington, and Kate (Mrs Sandby) and Miss Dalling sing.

August 11. Sunday. Yarmouth. St. Nicholas Church at 10. Immense congregation as usual and the service beautifully performed, Hill preaching.

August 12. After breakfasting with the Scotts inspect the new South National Schools, 180 boys, 170 infants and 160 girls.
Call on Dawson Turner and return to Bungay in the evening.

August 28. The Submarine Telegraph laid down from Dover to Cape Grisnez, in France, and message sent by it.
T.E. Webb, for twenty years surgeon in Bungay, leaves with his family on account of his wife's health. Succeeded by E.B. Adams.[19]

August 30. Dine at Earsham Hall with the Dallings: Captain and Mrs. Fanshawe, Capt. E.J. Bird of Arctic and Antarctic fame, Cautley and Miss Chambers. Capt. Bird considers that Franklin and his vessels were lost in 1845, their first year.

September 6. Races on Bungay Common. Look at them for a short time. Perhaps two thousand persons including crowds of harvest-men and country people, but I don't subscribe on account of the drunkeness, gambling and quarrelling which follow.

September 14. Auction of colts etc. at Flixton Grange belonging to Sir Shafto Adair.[20] They fetched more than a thousand pounds.

September 18. At a vestry meeting at St. Mary's a resolution carried that cottage property should be rated to owners instead of occupiers and on the 20th at Trinity vestry, where I attend as Chairman, the rating of owners as tenants under £6 instead of occupiers was carried.

1850]

October 12. Samuel Scott breakfasts with me. He returned from Lowestoft last night and tells me that Bessie Worthington is engaged to Lawrence Till, lately an engineer but now of Oxford also that Willie has made an offer to the daughter of Dr. Wallich, the botanist of Calcutta which was accepted, but the matter damped by both their parents.

November 10. To Brooke Hall to stay till Monday with the Holmes'. Lady Miller and her daughters Mary and Fanny, George Holmes and his wife and the Beales' dine with us.

November 11. To Brooke Church in the morning and afternoon. It has recently been restored, unpewed and benched by John Holmes. Later with John and George to see the former's bullocks, cows and horses and his yards, stalls etc. Agreeable and religious talk in the evening.

November 13. Mrs Dreyer[21] buried at Thwaite. A scene of disappointment about her Will.

November 19. William Martin of Bixley Hall, joint proprietor of Ditchingham Factory, taken ill with a sore throat and dies after a few hours illness aged 47.

November 28. Her Majesty's Inspector of Schools, the Rev. M. Mitchell, comes to stay with me and in the evening Bouverie, Capt. Dalling, Bruce, George Sandby, Scudamore and Alfred join us at dinner.
The next day the examination of the National Schoolchildren takes place in the morning from $9\frac{1}{2}$ to $1\frac{1}{2}$ in the presence of the ministers of St. Mary's and Trinity, Bouverie and several ladies. Result "Fair", Master Feather and the pupil teachers written exam is held in my library from $2\frac{1}{2}$ to 6 o'clock. Alder, Collyer, Campbell, Charles Garneys, W.G. Gwyn and Alfred dine with us. Much discussion on schools.

December 4. Dine at the Kerrich's of Geldeston and meet Count des Aubiers, a very pleasing, quiet Frenchman who married Miss Fowler of Gunton. The next evening to a ball at the Kerrich's. Sixty present.

Bridge House (now Scott House) from the garden

PAUL REE 1994

PAUL KER 1994

1851

January 11.   Grace Hughes accepts the Rev. George Tufnell as her betrothed.

January 22.   Robert Meade, eldest son of General the Hon. Robert Meade, formerly of Earsham Hall dies suddenly of heart disease, aged 42. He was staying with his sister, Mrs Ricado. Drive to Mrs Dowson's at Ditchingham where I hear that my old schoolfellow, Preston, died suddenly in Norwich.

January 24.   Alfred discovers bones, pottery, Roman tiles, a foreign horseshoe etc., in black earth at Stow Park, two feet underground.

Scott seems to have made a thorough examination of the spot where these Roman remains were found with the result that large quantities of pottery, some capitals of wrought freestone of a Norman character and other fragments were unearthed. These were all dug up some four feet south-west of the Stow Park house and several pieces of the pottery and a spearhead and bones are in my possession at the present time. (E.M. 1943.)

April 6.   Hartley, Fellow of Magdalen College, Cambridge takes the duty for Collyer at Trinity Church having been appointed to succeed him as curate.

March 30. London.   After breakfasting at the Club, call on Charles Roberts and with him look at the front of Buckingham Palace and walk round the Exhibition Crystal Palace admiring the exterior. Cross Hyde Park and see the Marble Arch removed from Buckingham Palace to Cumberland Gate. Effect good.

March 31.   The vaults of a new cellar at Cuddon's brew house at Ditchingham fall in and kill four boys and break brewer Gosling's leg. The accident was caused by loading the sides of the vault with wet silt before the mortar was dry.

May 1.   Opening of the Great Exhibition of all nations. A grand day. See letters written thereon. Breakfast with Mrs and Miss Wilmot at 7.30 and walk by the Parks to the Crystal Palace. Enter at 8.30. At 10.30 Wellington arrives. The Queen, with Prince Albert and all her royal train arrive at 12 o'clock. Meet Sir E. Travers and Frank Lysley etc. Twenty thousand inside, perhaps a million visible outside. Perfect order and good feeling everywhere. God be praised.

May 3. Crystal Palace from 12 to 6. The more I see of it the greater is my astonishment. Eye, mind and heart are filled with delightful objects and the excitement of the last few days make early rest and sleep indispensable. After dining with friends am so over-powered by sleep that I am disinclined for theatre or other amusements. Return to Suffolk on the 10th.

May 17. Bungay. Give directions to Botwright to take down the Octagon barn on the Drift Road, which was built in 1804. Joseph Cattermole makes a drawing of it yesterday and today.

May 21. The Rev. W.P. Cooksley married at Bungay to Eleanor Bewicke. Grace and Alfred Hughes drive from Stow Park and help the wedding party in giving cakes and wine to the boys and girls from the school. Much singing and cheering.

May 25. Sunday. Alfred Hartley takes the duty at Trinity Church for the first time as curate to Mr. Collyer who has removed to Gislingham. He preaches exceedingly well.

May 26. Plan wall and a small plantation with paling on the site of the Octagon barn.

June 22. Very hot. Hartley calls. The congregation has already nearly doubled since he came to Trinity Church.

July 8. Dine at 4 and go to Childs' musical party at 5.30. A pleasant evening and good music. Eighty singers and thirty instrumentalists. Three hundred in audience.

July 30. Walter Scott, now of Newcastle-on-Lyme marries Maria Furnistone as his second wife.

Their grand-daughter was Mary Webb nee Meredith, the authoress of "Precious Bane" etc., b. 1881 d. 1927.

Alfred exceedingly happy at the prospect of his marriage to Maria Smith in September. God grant him the realisation of his best hopes.

September 3. Alfred comes to me at 11. He and I execute deeds connected with his approaching marriage, with Elswood and Hartcup as solicitors. Charles Woodhouse arrives from Bury in the evening and we talk of tomorrow's wedding and his duties as one of Alfred's trustees.

September 4.   Charles Woodhouse and I go to Stow Park in a carriage and pair and take dear Alfred and his brother Robert to Ellingham Hall. At 11 o'clock to the church where Alfred Hughes and Maria Smith are married by the Rev. Robert Cobb. They went through the service admirably and look thoroughly well and happy. I went with Alfred and returned with Colonel and Mrs Smith and Lucy. Fifty-six breakfasted in a marquee in front of the house. Alfred spoke excellently. At 2½ Mr. and Mrs Alfred Hughes start for Trowse Station in a carriage and four, passing through Bungay and were greatly cheered by the crowd. R.E. Hughes goes back with me to Waveney House and dines. Spend the evening with Charlotte and Miss Hannah Butcher.

September 5.   Note from dear Alfred from Trowse. Colonel Smith calls at 12½. Charlotte ill from yesterday's exertion of meeting the bride and bridegroom on Earsham Dam on their way to the station at Harleston.

September 9.   Letters from Alfred and Maria full of right feeling in every respect and as much happiness as mortals can feel. It makes me shed tears of joy at the time when once on this day I shed tears of bitter misery and despair.

The anniversary of his mother's death which Scott never forgets and always mentions in his diaries on this date. She died of scarlet fever in 1809.

September 18. Lowestoft.   Arrived here by rail yesterday and am staying at the Royal. Call on General and Mrs. Meade and Caroline in the afternoon about 3.30 when they were all well and lively. At 5 o'clock Mrs. Meade was taken ill on the pier with a paralytic stroke and the doctor, Worthington, was sent for and remained with her all night.

September 19.   Mrs. Meade rather better and the next day the doctors think she will recover.

October 3.   A vestry meeting of Trinity Parish when it was resolved: "It is very expedient to re-pew the church but that no part

of the expense is to be taken from the church rates." Subscriptions
put down at the time were -

The Town Reeve Elect £50
J. J. Bedingfield   £20
J.B.S.   £25

Rev. A.C. Hartley
and Elswood   £10 each
Burtsal, Fisher
and W. Mann   £5 each.

*The following week is spent in London, and on the 9th Scott notes
the extraordinary darkness from 8.30 to 9.30 a.m. followed by
heavy rain from 10 to 4 o'clock. Consequently only 90,813 at the
Exhibition. On the previous Monday and Tuesday the attendance
had been 107,815 and 109,915 respectively. From London he goes
to Paris for a week, returning to Bungay on October 22nd.*

THE WEEK IN PARIS

*Folkestone to Boulogne: Train to Paris: Hotel superior to any in
London: Spends four hours looking at pictures in the Louvre: Goes
to the theatre: Notes on many improvements to the streets, markets,
quays and public buildings, works being carried out by Louis
Napoleon: Attends church services twice on Sunday: 14-hour
journey back to London.*

BUNGAY

November 5. Hear of Dawson Turner's deplorable marriage and
his leaving his house on the Quay at Yarmouth.

November 20. Dine at Chambers and meet Rev. W.F. Wilkinson
and his wife who have come to Hedenham Hall from Saxlingham.
Recognise him as of Corpus College, Cambridge whom I knew at
Archdales in 1815.

December 14. Sunday. After attending the schools and Trinity
church call at Glover's on Dr. Wolff who is staying with the
Archdeacon. In the evening to St. Mary's where he preaches for the
third time today on the subject of the Jews, past, present and future.

December 15.   From 2 to 4 to Wolff's lecture on his missionary travels for the Jews, and afterwards he dines with me at 5.30 with Glover, Hartley, Cobb, Adolphus Holmes and Alfred. He is most amusing. At 8 p.m. to the Corn Hall where I was called to the Chair and spoke for half an hour eulogising the conduct and character of Charles Stoddart. Wolff then described his travels in Bokhara in search of Stoddart and Connolly until 11 o'clock.

December 16.   Charles Costerton, surgeon at Yarmouth, dies suddenly aged 64.

December 18.   Sir Thomas Sherlock Gooch M.P. for Suffolk till 1820, dies at Benacre Hall, aged 85.

PART VI

1845-1851 - Bungay, London, Wales and the Isle of Man

References

1. Wood, Joseph (1776-1864). Architect and botanist.

2. Franklin, Sir John (1786-1847). Arctic explorer. Died on third expedition. Knighted 1829.

3. Suckling, the Rev. Alfred. Rector of Barsham and author of "The History of Suffolk". Barsham Rectory was the home of Catherine Suckling, Nelson's mother. Other branches of the family descended from the 17th century poet, Sir John Suckling.

4. Borrow, George (1803-1881). Author. He was born at East Dereham, son of an army captain. After working as a literary hack in London he adopted a wandering life, associating for some years with gipsies. His experiences are recounted in his two most celebrated works, "Lavengro", 1851, and "Romany Rye", 1857.

5. Fitzgerald, Edward (1809-1883). Poet and translator. He was born and spent most of his life in Suffolk, chiefly in Woodbridge. He studied at Trinity College, Cambridge, and was a friend of Tennyson, Thackeray and Carlyle. His sister Eleanor married John Kerrich of Geldeston Hall, near Bungay, and Fitzgerald frequently visited her there. He often walked over to Bungay where he became friendly with John and Charles Childs who ran the printing business. It was Charles Childs who first published Fitzgerald's most celebrated work, "The Rubaiyat of Omar Khayyam" in 1859 in a small limited edition of 250 copies.

6. Worthington, William C. Lowestoft surgeon, married Sarah, sister of Samuel Scott who was cousin of J.B.S. Ethel Mann's grandfather.

7. Sandby, George. There were two George Sandby's. The father lived at Denton Lodge and the son was rector of Flixton and lived presumably at the Priest's House which was then the Rectory. The son was later one of the executors of Scott's will.

8. Smith, Col. John of Ellingham Hall. Known as "Tiger Smith", he shot

99 tigers, some of them man-eating, while serving in India. His diary is still with his descendant, Col. Henry Smith who also has the last remaining stuffed tiger in the Hall. There were six until recently as well as numerous tiger-skin rugs.

9. Martin William (1803-1850). The silk and crepe factory at Ditchingham had been established by Mr Grout of Norwich, who had previously established a silk factory at Yarmouth. In a letter from Samuel Scott to his brother John, written in October 1824 (see "An Englishman at Home and Abroad" Vol. 1, p. 197) it is stated that Grout planned to erect the factory on a meadow in Lizard Lane, Ditchingham. The factory prospered under the successive managers until 1896. The site was later used for Ditchingham Maltings.

10. Pollock, Sir Jonathan Frederick (1783-1870). Judge. Tory MP for Huntingdon. Attorney-General 1834. Chief Baron of Exchequer.

11. Lind, Jenny (1820-1887). Swedish singer, naturalised British 1855. Travelled extensively in Europe and America.

12. Gladstone, William Ewart(1809-1898).Statesman and author. Liberal MP and Prime Minister four times.

13. Opie, Mrs Amelia (1769-1853). Novelist and poet. Married John Opie, painter. Street in Norwich named after them.

14. Pugin, Augustus Welby Northmore (1812-1852). Architect and Ecclesiologist. Writer. Specialist in gothic and provided drawings for Houses of Parliament.

15. Currie, John Legge. Surgeon. Practised in Bungay for over 30 years and latterly lived in Trinity Hall. Retired by 1900 but his date of death unknown.

16. Jermy, Isaac Preston (1788-1848). A Recorder of Norwich and well-known public figure, he was owner of Stansfield Hall near Wymondham in Norfolk. He had been in prolonged dispute with his tenant, James Blomfield Rush over the ownership of nearby Potash Farm. On November 28th, 1848, Rush entered Stansfield Hall and shot Jermy and his son with a blunderbuss, killing both of them. Young Mrs Jermy and her maid were also injured. Rush was executed on Castle Hill, Norwich, on Saturday, April 21st, before a crowd of several thousand spectators. A wax model of him was exhibited at Madame Tussaud's Chamber of Horrors later in the same year. Mementoes of the event

are displayed in Moyse's Hall Museum, Bury St. Edmunds, and Thetford Museum.

17. Fisher, N.B. Successor to Dr. John Brettel. Died 1853, aged 43.

18. Edwards, William Camden (1777-1855). Engraver of portraits and illustrations for the printing works owned by Brightly and Childs.

19. Adams, Edward Burnam. Surgeon, practised 1851-1879.

20. Adair, Sir Robert Shafto, later Lord Waveney, was son of Sir Alexander Adair, from whom he inherited the Flixton Hall estate. His extensive alterations to the house were interrupted in 1846, when a disasterous fire destroyed the major part of the buildings. The Hall was later entirely restored by his son, Sir Hugh Adair.

21. Dreyer, Eliza (1773-1849). The daughter of Daniel Bonhote, the Bungay attorney, and Elizabeth née Mapes, the authoress. Eliza married the Reverend Richard Dreyer, Rector of Thwaite, and a former curate of Bungay St. Mary's. In later life she lived at Trinity Hall and in 1848 founded and endowed Homes for five women over the age of sixty, the widows of poor Bungay tradesmen. In her will, published the following year, she also left sums of money to be invested to provide an income for buying clothing and other necessities for the poor. The Almhouses named after her are in Staithe Road, and were visited by Scott on June 16th, 1848.

Ellingham Hall in 1852

Bungay Castle with Mrs Bonhote's cottage. c. 1817

PART SEVEN

1852 - 1862

The Last Ten Years

1852

January. Commence the year with resolutions and prayers for future usefulness to my fellow creatures and call on various friends with New Year's greetings. Sign a paper with Bedingfield and Elswood which guarantees that in the event of an adequate gift from the Society for Building Churches being made and accepted by the churchwardens of Trinity towards benching the same, I jointly with them will be responsible that the sum of £300 be forthcoming.

January 4. The West Indian Mail steamer 'Amazon' burnt and lost S.W. of the Scilly Isles and one hundred and thirty-five persons burnt or drowned at 4 o'clock this morning.

January 29. The Rev. R. L. Page, tutor of my boyhood, dies at Panfield Rectory, aged 80. He had long been feeble in mind and body.

> "When I remember all my friends so linked together
> I've seen around me fall like leaves in wintry weather,
> I feel like one who treads alone some banquet hall deserted
> Whose lights are fled whose garlands dead
> And all but he departed."

February 10. Col. Smith very ill with heart disease and must go to London at once and place himself under the care of Dr. Latham, by order of Dr. W.E. Crowfoot. Alfred is to go with him.

February 18. Smith very much worse. On receiving this bad news from Alfred go immediately to Ellingham and escort Mrs Smith and her maid to London. The rest of the family and Cobb arrive the next day.

February 21. Colonel John Smith dies at 3 a.m. in the 61st year of his age. Formerly Lt. Colonel in the 2nd Madras Infantry he has been owner of Ellingham Hall since 1846 when he succeeded his uncle Henry Smith, who for twenty-nine years was solicitor to the East India Company and Clerk to the Draper's Company. The funeral took place on the 27th at Ellingham. Besides relatives and friends, many Bungay tradespeople and others assembled in the church and churchyard. A fine rainbow stretched over the grave while the body was being lowered into its resting place.

April 12. Charlotte, widow of Admiral Sutton dies at Aldeborough, aged 73. She was buried at Woodbridge in the church of St. Mary's beside her husband.

Their tomb is in the north porch in the entrance to the Seckford Chapel, adjoining the chancel. The Suttons lived at Woodbridge after the sale of Ditchingham Lodge in 1831 and the Admiral died in June of the following year.

Fanny Kemble[1], alias Butler, reads Shakespeare's Henry VIII at the Bungay Corn Hall. A good audience. The reading excellent though rather exaggerated. Many people from Beccles there.

April 24. The Earl of Albermarle quotes the opinions and words of myself and George Sandby in the House of Lords on the state of Labour under Free Trade.

June. Go with Hartley to Trinity Church and with Bedingfield settle about the restoration of the tower windows, the plan of which I had discovered at the beginning of the month. Nursey to be employed.

July 12. In the afternoon, on my return from home from driving to the farm and to Ellingham, find the first letter ever delivered at Bungay by a second post. It was a sad one from F.O. Patch, announcing the death of his second daughter, Annie. She died at Broomfield, Tiverton of rapid consumption after only fourteen days severe illness.

July 20. Sarah Freestone of St. Margaret's, South Elmham married to James Pomeroy of Sussex Place, Regents Park.

July 26. Up at 5 o'clock and at 7 Mrs Pulford comes to inform me that her master and my neighbour Mr. Elswood is dangerously ill. He went up to London on the 19th last and at 2 a.m. this morning an electric telegram arrived desiring his clerk, Butcher to hasten to him immediately. Butcher accompanied with Barkway, the doctor left at 4 a.m. The next day, Tuesday, Elswood, who for thirty-six years has been a solicitor in Bungay, died at Covent

Garden New Hummun's Hotel after an operation for hernia. He was born at Chard, Somersetshire and was probably about 74.

July 28. Lowestoft. Fix at the Royal. To see the Worthingtons new unfurnished house in Harbour Road *(now London Road)* and dine with them in their old house in the High Street.

July 29. The Cove estate, the property of T.C.Scott of Shadingfield, sold in London to Sir Thomas Gooch with four hundred and twenty acres of land for £16,750.

August 2. Drive to Thwaite, retired as a place can be with its ignorant peasantry, its church with Norman tower and thatched roof and stillness, sending the memory back to past ages and with its tombs and inscriptions to Gambles, Bonhotes, Dreyers and Sayers reviving in my mind the thoughts of boyhood and youth.

August 6. Drive to Earsham Hall and sit with Mrs Dalling for half an hour. Then to Denton to see Archdeacon Bouverie's clerestory windows now being put in by Nursey of Bungay.

August 26. Colonel William Sutton of the Cape Mounted Rifles, a mighty hunter though a very small man, comes to see me in the evening from 8 to 9. He is the youngest son of the late Admiral Sutton of Ditchingham. Ask him to dine tomorrow evening with some other guests.

August 28. Capt. Dalling, Cobb, Greville, the Chesters, Charles Woodhouse, William Mann and Alfred. Sutton very loquacious about Africa.
The same night at 10.30 Frederick Farlway and his son Edgar call to show me a letter received from Elswood's executors declaring his bankruptcy in 1815 for £12,768 still unsettled, and that officials will come and take possession of all his effects under a fiat of bankruptcy. Thus the Bungay tradesmen will lose all he owes them.

September 14. Arthur Wellesley, the great Duke of Wellington dies at Walmer Castle at 3.15 p.m. after a few hours illness, aged 83 years and four months.

October 5. At 12 o'clock go to Trinity Church where all the old pews have been removed, except Mrs. Barlee's[2] which is a large one in the centre of the nave. During the alterations a piscina has been discovered which contained a skull, also a brass plate to the memory of Lionel Throckmorton with two coats of arms, besides many coarsely painted figures on the S.E. wall.

October 7. To Yarmouth in connection with the National Schools. Fix at the Royal and go to the service at the church at 11. The Bishop of Norwich preaches on "Despising one of these little ones". Cold collation in the newly restored Priory Hall at 2 o'clock. Speakers, George Hill, the Bishop of Norwich (Hinds), Baron Aldersom, Capt. Pearson, Dr. Hook, myself and Charles Palmer. To church again in the afternoon, a large congregation and an admirable sermon from Dr. Hook of Leeds. Dine at George Hill's with twenty-four others. The three points impressed on the assembly by this day's sermons and speeches are :-

1. Persuade more to come to Schools.
2. Send more books home with the children.
3. Provide good lending libraries for former as well as present scholars.

October 12. Meet Hartley, Bedingfield and three carpenters (Botwright, Darby and Foulger) at Trinity Church to decide about the reading desk and pulpit. The new window in the tower was finished in July last and the old ones restored about the same time.

November 9. Meet engineer Bruff and Messrs. Hartcup, Bedingfield, Walker, Mann, Burtsal, Childs and Burton at the King's Head about the railway from Tivetshall to Bungay.

December. At the beginning of the month Mr. Bedingfield was taken ill with a fainting fit in Trinity Church, succeeded two days later by a paralytic stroke and loss of speech. The doctor (Adams) considers him in great danger.

December 7. Town Reeve meeting. No bells and no flags hoisted in consequence of Bedingfield's illness. Am appointed Town Reeve for 1853. Eighty-two dine with me at the King's Head. Captains Dalling and Margitson, the Revs. Holmes, Cautley and Hartley, William and Richard Mann, Walker, Burtsal, Fisher, Adams, the Catholic priest etc. etc.

December 26. Trinity Church re-opened and benched and on the whole much improved. Among the friends and neighbours who died this year are:
Sandby, the Rev. George, of Denton died February 9th, aged 84.

Smith, Colonel John, of Ellingham Hall, February 21st aged 61.
Sutton, Charlotte, widow of Admiral Sutton, aged 73 April 12th.
Bacon, Sir Edmund of Raveningham, the only son of Sir Edmund
Bacon, April 14th. at Bryanstone Square.
Meade, General the Hon. Robert, July 11th aged 80. Formerly of
Earsham Hall.
Elswood, Azariah, solicitor of Bungay, July 26th.
Palgrave, Lady Elizabeth, late of Yarmouth aged 83.
Clissold, Charlotte Matilda, wife of the Rev. S. Clissold of Wrentham
aged 54.
Mann, Mrs. widow of Richard Mann of Bungay, September 16th.
Fisher, Admiral, dies in London aged 72, September 30th.
D'Eve, The Rev. Edgar Rust, aged 58 at Abbots Hall, Stowmarket,
November 27th (At Bungay Grammar School)

1853

January 1. Bedingfield, John James dies at Trinity Hall aged 80.
He had been insensible for twenty-nine days.

January 10. Alfred and Maria Hughes have a son born, their first
child, a healthy boy. Christened Harry Scott Hughes.

January 11. To a large meeting at Beccles of landowners and
occupiers, to consider the means of carrying off the floods of the
Waveney at the bay at Mutford Bridge. Kerrich in the chair. Biddar
expounds his plan. Speakers: The Mayor of Beccles, The Town
Reeve of Bungay, Dowson, Farr, Alfred Suckling, Captain Dalling,
Safford etc.

March 6. The highest flood I have seen for years. At Waveney
House the water was over the gravel path and into the arch of the
stable yard.

March 9. Kerrison. General Sir Edward Bt. K.C.B. dies in
Stanhope St. London aged 77. Born at the Staithe House, Bungay in
1776.

March 17. Mary the wife of Thomas Charles Scott and late of
Shadingfield, dies of apoplexy two hours after the seizure. Born the
17th Sept. 1781 at Shadingfield Hall as Mary Ingate, married the
18th September 1806, was aged 71½ at her death. She was a woman
who was always desirous of adding to the comfort and pleasure of
all within her reach - rich and poor, high and low, and she was

humble-minded. Notwithstanding a degree of deafness which for the last few years prevented her hearing and joining in general conversation, she was wonderfully patient and cheerful. Attend her funeral at Shadingfield Church in cold and rain on Wednesday 23rd. The Rev. George Lemon takes the service which was attended by her husband and family, including the Kilners, two of whom had married her daughters, and the Boydons.

March 18. Dyball, William dies of apoplexy. He had been Town Clerk of Bungay for many years. He was honest and plodding in the execution of his duties. Very selfish in his feelings and limited in his ideas and never gave to any public or charitable institution, but he was sociable and popular among the tradesmen of the town.

March 30. Meade, Anne Louisa, relict of the late General the Hon. Robert Meade dies aged 68, sister of Sir William W. Dalling of Earsham House, Norfolk.

April 26. Another very high flood, the highest I have ever seen since I lived in Waveney House. The next day the water goes down very quickly.

May 27. Thomas, George, J.P. of Woodbridge formerly undergraduate of Emmanuel College, where in October of 1811 he set the college on fire accidentally, dies aged 63. Garneys, Mary, 5th daughter of Charles Garneys of Bungay dies May 31st aged 16.

June 16. To Lowestoft for Bessie's wedding, arriving at the Worthington's at 10 o'clock. The party goes in seven carriages to the church where the Rev. M. Beaumont marries Bessie Worthington to Lawrence Till. The procession returns through the town to the Royal Hotel among some thousand people, where a splendid déjeuner was provided. Present six Mrs Worthingtons, the bridesmaids, who were three Miss Worthingtons, Miss Magney and Miss Till; besides were Mr. and Miss Fred Till and Ernest, Mr. and Mrs Harrison, Mrs Trimby and Mr. Beaumont. A very pleasant party. The bride and bridegroom drive to Somerleyton and take the train there to Cambridge where they stop till Saturday.

June 18. Meet Samuel Scott and Frank Worthington at Blackwall Station and see the latter off on board the *Wellesley*.

July 10. Fisher, W.B., surgeon (successor to the late J. Brettel) was found dead in his bed. He had died of apoplexy three hours

previously. He had no previous illness and was aged 43½ years.
To Trinity Church this morning. Charles Hartley takes leave of his
congregation after being here for two years and two months.
During his curacy the church has been benched and improved and
the congregation increased. Though too "High Church" in his views
he is much a Christian. He is going to Beccles as Master of the
Falconberge School.

July 25.   Leach, surgeon of Vauxhall and widower of Eliza née
Hood, cousin of the Samuel Scotts, commits suicide having been in
a deranged and gloomy state of mind for several months.

July 31.   Abel, Fanny Maria, widow of Matthias Abel, schoolmaster
and postmaster, dies after a long decline, aged 41, born Cotman of
Diss.

August 2.   To Trinity Church from 10 to 12 with Nursey, fixing
the Throckmorton's coat of arms on his tomb, found during the
alterations last autumn.

August 13.   Childs, John dies in his 70th year at his house in Broad
Street, Bungay[3]. An energetic printer, a man of obstinacy, prejudice
and forbidding manners. He was buried in the Independent Chapel
ground on the 18th.

August 18.   Cooper, Bransby, surgeon (nephew of Sir Astley
Cooper) dies suddenly at the Athenaeum this afternoon, aged 61.
At Bungay Grammar School in 1805 and 6. At Edinburgh 1815-
1816 he was my fellow student.

August 20.   To Outney Cottage and meet Dr. Hood, a cousin of
Samuel Scott, who tells us the history of his life.

*Frequent meetings take place between Hood and J.B. Scott who
drives him to Flixton and to Shipmeadow House and gets his advice
about some of the school children. His son,Charles Hood of
Bethlem Hospital and Lord Chancellor's visitor in Lunacy, also
stays for a few days at Outney Cottage during his father's visit. Scott
had previously written to him about poor Richard Dadd.(See page)
During the Hoods visit, Hannah Butcher, who had lived with
Charlotte Scott ever since the death of her mother-in-law in 1843,
leaves her and goes into lodgings at Wright's on the Flixton road
'from very right motives'. Apparently she did not get on with Dr.
Hood but her friendship with the rest of the family continued.*

September 1. Lady Adair dies this day in London. She was buried at Flixton on the 10th.

September 28. Mr. and Mrs Mortlock take possession of Laurel Lodge, Bungay, which the T.C. Hughes' have lately vacated.

October 10. Between 3.30 and 4.30 Capt. Dalling calls with Capt. Fanshawe and the former talks most clearly and cheerfully about the North West passage, Franklin, Bird, Russia and the Dardanelles. When leaving he looked quite well and walked away in his usual manner. Just before reaching home he stumbled and would have fallen but Fanshawe supported him to Earsham Hall. Garneys and Crowfoot were sent for but he never spoke again and died soon after 7 o'clock. Garneys came to tell me of this awful event at 8.30. Poor dear Captain Dalling's sudden death affects me deeply. For many years he has been my uniformly kind, considerate and courteous friend. He had Wellingtonian ideas of DUTY which made him appear sometimes stern and harsh but his heart was kind and tender, and he was thoroughly just. He had an extensive knowledge of foreign countries and acquaintance with the leading men of the world during the last forty years, so his anecdotes were always very interesting. Amongst those who visited him were many naval men of distinction. As Baronet and owner of the Earsham estate he would have been useful and active. Much good which I had anticipated for this neighbourhood is lost by his sudden passing. He was buried at Earsham on the 18th at 11 o'clock. His wife, Sir Windham Dalling, John Meade and the Fanshawes attended his funeral.

Captain John Windham Dalling was the youngest son of Sir John Dalling, Governor of Jamaica and a native of Bungay. He entered the Navy in 1808, was present as a midshipman at the battle of Trafalgar and saw much service throughout his life. Obtained Command in 1817 and 18 and after 1826 commanded the Nimrod and Relief Sloops in Leath and the Mediterranean stations. Took Post rank in 1828 and from November 1830 to May 1842 commanded Daphne, first Class C off Lisbon and in the Mediterranean. Married in 1844 Frances Ann, daughter of Colonel Fanshawe R.E. and died 10th October 1853 aged 64.
The death of Captain Dalling was a great blow to J.B. Scott and it was not until the end of the month that he seemed equal to resuming his ordinary activities. From numerous entries which occur in these diaries and the many interests they shared in common, one realised the friendship which existed between them.

1854

The year opens with very cold weather, snow and a tremendous gale from the east. The roads almost impassable. On the 5th no coaches in or out of Bungay. The mail due at 6 a.m. not in till 5.15 p.m. A deputation consisting of Dr. Adams, Dyball and W. Darby formed for calling a meeting for the relief of the poor.

January 12.   Griggs, Thomas, of Bungay and Earsham dies.

January 16.   Bohun, Eleanor, daughter of the Rev. J.F. Browne Bohun, formerly of Bungay, dies at Blackheath after a long illness and much suffering.

February 17.   The Inspector of burial grounds attends at Trinity Church and gives notice that a notice from the Secretary of the Home Department will be issued for closing our burial ground on January 1st 1855.

March 5.   A Vestry meeting at St. Mary's to consider on what terms that parish should unite with Trinity in providing a common burial ground. Hartcup, Gower, Childs, Hughes and I speak in favour; Smith, Hudson and Mortlock against. Glover also against; he is a most disorderly chairman! Resolved by 28 to 9 that no expense be incurred by St. Mary's and that the present ground is sufficient.

March 20.   Charlotte Affleck aged 47 married not to W.N. Glover, Curate of St. Mary's, but to his father the Venerable Archdeacon Glover of Norwich who is 77.

March 29.   War declared against Russia by England and France.

July 11.   At 4 o'clock join the baptismal party from Stow Park at St. Mary's, Bungay. Harry Scott Hughes received into the Church. His sponsors, myself, Henry Smith, and Mrs Smith as proxy for Grace Hughes. Alfred Collingwood Hughes also baptised - his sponsors - Robert E. Hughes, George Tuffnall and Lucy Smith. Glover officiates. Present besides Mrs and Miss Forster, John Hughes, the Rev. E.P. Postle, Cobb and Mrs Abbot Upcher. Afterwards we have a pleasant tea-dinner with Alfred and Maria at Stow Park.

July 22.   Barber, E.S.B. my second cousin dies of fever aged 42.

185

He went out to Borneo and Lebuan as civil engineer to the Eastern Archipelago Co. in April 1853.

July 24.   Camel, Mrs of Ditchingham, widow of Dr. Camel dies in consequence of an accident which occurred at the foot of the hill near Ashmans, Beccles. She was in a phaeton driven by her nephew Mr. Wales and seized hold of the reins causing the vehicle to overturn. She died at Ashmans Lodge at 10 p.m.

August 4. Lowestoft. Meet Marion Worthington and Mr. Leathes and his daughter Mary and see them off at the station at 6.30 on their way to Germany. The former is going to school near Stuttgart for three years.

August 31.   Sworde, the Rev. Thomas formerly curate of Bungay St. Mary, dies at Thetford.

October 21.   Yelloly, Mrs, dies aged 70 at Cavendish Hall, Suffolk. Widow of Dr. Yelloly, formerly of Woodton Hall.

October 31.   Barlee, Mrs Frances of Dukes Bridge, Bungay, dies after a few hours illness, aged 74.

November 6.   Katherine, the beautiful daughter of the late General Meade dies at Brighton aged 37.

December 4.   The Halesworth, Beccles and Haddiscoe Railway opened.

December 7. & 9. Committee meetings were held for the distributing of coals and £100 was collected and 410 tickets issued.

December 11.   Mrs Dalling finally leaves Earsham Hall.

December 12.   At 3 p.m. a telegram dispatch was received from London announcing the death of Thomas Griggs. General surprise and sorrow. He had been a draper in Bungay for many years but latterly lived in his pleasant house *(now The Elms)* at Earsham, which he built. He died after a few days illness at Croydon where he was staying with Mr. Parrington who had been associated with him in his business at Bungay. Grigg was beloved and respected by all classes for his steady, judicious kindness and was one of the best of the guardians of the Wangford Union. He was buried at Earsham on the 18th.

December 20.   Hartcup gives a feast to one hundred workmen on the roof-raising of his new house *(Upland Hall).*

December 22.   The large family pew belonging to the late Mrs Barlee who died on the 31st October last, and which stood in the centre of Trinity Church, has now been removed and new seats have taken its place. The first service after its clearance is to take place on Sunday next, the 24th.

December 30. Saturday. John Garden of Redisham Hall dies this evening of acute inflammation of the lungs, and the following Wednesday at a meeting at Shipmeadow House, Sandby and others having in vain tried to speak of his death, I propose amongst the tears of almost all present a resolution of our sorrow and condolence with his family. Ten days later his widow Amelia S. Garden dies of the same complaint, and after four days illness. She was the daughter of the Rev. John Lewis of Gillingham

1855

January 28.   The Misses Owles[4] and their fourteen pupils attend Trinity Church. Show them into the seats allotted to them. The house late Elswoods' is now used as a school and the Misses Owles moved into it on the 19th instant.

February 6.   Read, Harry of Beccles dies, aged 76. He was Usher at the Bungay Grammar School about 1792 and afterwards a land agent.
Farr, Thomas also at Bungay Grammar School, son of Thomas Farr of Beccles dies. He was with De Lacy Evan's army in Spain in 1835.

February 20.   Kate Sandby married at St. Georges, Hanover Square, to Henry George Bowyer, son of Sir George Bowyer and Inspector of Workhouse Schools.

March 5.   Thomas Charles Scott, late of Shadingfield Hall dies this morning at his house in King Street, Yarmouth. Reported to be 72 but really, I believe, 76. He is to be buried at Shadingfield.

March 9.   Skippen, J. a notorious character called 'Blood Skippen[5] died at the Cherry Tree Inn.

March 10. John Scott Worthington, who for nearly twelve months has been a pupil of Mr. J.G. Johnson of Norwich, *(Surgeon)*, absconds without notice to parents, Master, or fellow pupils under a pretence of a visit to me. His departure was not known till several days afterwards.

March 13. Arrive at Shadingfield at 2.45. George Lemon precedes the funeral procession, reading part of the service, and T.C. Scott's body is borne from the Hall to the vault at the east end of the church by his former labourers. Followed by Charles, John, Henry and Anna (Kilner) his children, and James and John Kilner, James Boyden and Edward Sharpin. The sons descend into the vault to take a last look at their parents' coffins. All of us with the exception of George Lemon return to the Hall and dine. Home at 7 o'clock.

March 26. The Rev. W.G. Courtley, formerly Fellow of Clare Hall, Rector of Earsham dies at 10.30 a.m.: he had been a chaplain in the army, galloped away from Waterloo and officiated in Madeira when General Meade was there. He was a strange compound of malevolence and kindness, a good classic but never giving real information to his hearers.

April and May. *At this time Archdeacon Bouverie was making several additions to Denton church, improving the west end and the steeple. Flixton church also was undergoing thorough repair.*

June 1. The Bungay Trinity churchyard and the Independent yard closed for burials. This morning a licence received from the Bishop to bury in the new cemetery.

June 5. Tiverton. Arrived here from London this afternoon. The town is gay with decorations for the Agricultural Show, etc. Call and see Mrs Barne (who is now 78) and her daughters Katherine and Fanny. Fix at Broomfield and talk with Patch and Mary and Miss Roe till 11.30.

June 6. Visit New Place early this morning and am received by Mrs Barne and her daughters. Lady Carew and Mrs Fortescue, Lady Duntze (Miss Ryers) Mrs Lucas etc., come to breakfast at 11 and the bazaar opens at 12 in a field adjoining. Explore old St. Peters Church lately restored and the newly built St. Paul's Church in West Exeter. Call on John Barne's widow and then to the bazaar. Dine at 7 and walk about the town amongst crowds of merry people. At 10 to a ball held at Blundell's School.

June 7. To New Place and meet Mrs Heathfield's three daughters and her son Henry. After escorting the Misses Barnes to the bazaar, to the agricultural show. Evening dine with Patch and Captain Lucas at the agricultural dinner presided over by Lord Fortescue who speaks in a hesitating manner but the matter is good. Other speakers Sir Thomas Acland, Lord Ebrington, Amery etc. Spend the evening at New Place and Broomfield, walk by the park to the cemetery. No chapels built yet, but the licence has been granted. Dine at New Place at 1.30 and tea at Broomfield. Leave by the 7.25 train after much enjoyment.

July 16. Bungay. At 3 o'clock a confirmation at St. Mary's. Three hundred and thirty-eight candidates. At 6.30 Bishop Carr, late of Bombay, assisted by Arnold and Archdeacon Ormerod, consecrate our Trinity Cemetery amidst thunder and rain. The procession was headed by boys singing the 17th and 90th Psalms.

July 22. Bedingfield, Mrs. the widow of J. J. Bedingfield Esq., dies at Trinity Hall, aged 88. She was buried at Bedingfield.

July 30. Fonnereau, William Charles, of Christ Church, Ipswich, dies, aged 50.
Drive to Beccles and then on by rail to Lowestoft having heard from Samuel and Worthington that Sarah is in great danger and is suffering from an enlarged heart.

August 5. Sarah, daughter of my uncle Samuel Scott and wife of William Collins Worthington, dies at Lowestoft at 10 p.m. this Sunday evening. She was born on the 28th February 1802, and had more than half a century of varied enjoyments and sufferings. Gifted with a lively perception of the beautiful in nature, in art and in sentiment, she derived from those sources her best pleasures, but her sensitive mind and heart were not sufficiently under control, her feelings were misunderstood and too rudely crossed, thence came much suffering, disappointment, irritation, and at the last almost indifference. I trust now all is peace and happiness with her, and for ever. She was married on the 1st August 1826 and had thirteen children of whom ten are living.

August 7. Letters from Samuel Scott about the death of his sister and from Grace Hughes on her marriage to George Tuffnell at Runwell, lately curate to Archdeacon Bouverie of Denton,

Norfolk. What a contrast! "Telle est la vie".
To see Hannah Butcher and then poor Edwards who appears to be dying. I am much cast down but seek relief in employment about school projects.

August 10.　To Lowestoft. At 1.30 hearse moves from Worthington's on the Pakefield Road to St. Margaret's Church. It is followed by one mourning coach containing Worthington and his son John, Henry Wetton, Samuel Scott and myself. Sarah was buried by the side of her daughter Ann, near the wall to the S.E. of the churchyard. Francis Cunningham reads the service feelingly. Few persons present. After our return, walk for a long time in the shade of the garden with poor Hester and Bessie (Mrs Till). The next day talk with Charlotte and Hester in the room in which their mother died and return to Bungay about 11.

August 22.　William Camden Edwards, born in Monmouthshire, died this morning at 2 a.m. He was a good engraver and possessed much poetic genius and artistic taste. He admired nature fervently: a glorious sunset or a simple flower made him thankful, happy and devout. He was thoroughly simpleminded, sincere, kind and liberal, walking humbly with his God though he attended no public worship in temples made with hands. My father loved him, so did I and the Dawson Turners and the very few friends who knew him. He came to Bungay to engrave portraits for the Bible, Pilgrim's Progress and the other works published by Brightly at the Printing Works here. In 1821 he left Bungay for a time but returned later and settled in rooms on the Flixton Road where he died. He was interred in the Cemetery on the 27th, the first adult to be buried there. Mr and Mrs Wright, Dyball, Parrington and myself followed his remains to the grave in this, to him, land of strangers.

August 29.　In the afternoon with Mrs Wright and Dyball, look over his engravings, letters and drawings and later spend two days sorting and arranging them. Finally I left his papers with Miss Turner at Yarmouth.

September 2.　Adams, for thirty-five years Clerk of the Parish of Bungay, dies this night of dropsy, aged 70. He was buried the Wednesday following and a beautiful muffled peal was rung after the funeral.

September 8.& 9.　Battle of Sebastopol and the storming of the Malakoff Tower and the Redan. On Sunday Sebastopol evacuated.

The news reached Bungay Post Office on the 11th. Walk to Stow Park to tell Alfred and his wife and then return home. Bells ringing, processions starting, flags flying and in the evening bonfires with tar barrels and a concert given by the Hungarian Band at the Corn Hall from 8 to 10.

September 16. Great sale at Butley Abbey of Suffolk horses bred by the late Thomas Catlin. More than five thousand persons present. One hundred and forty-five horses sold, including colts, and fetching £6,700.

October 2. Charlotte Scott returns from Yarmouth after ten weeks absence, her brother Samuel comes with her.

December 27. Dine at Flixton Hall at 7.30 with Sir Shafto and Lady Adair, Sir D and Lady and the two Miss Cunninghams, Mrs Harry and Lucy Smith, Miss Jones, Alfred and Maria Hughes, George Sandby, Mr. and Mrs Bowyer, Miss Sandby and Mr. and Mrs Schreiber; and the next evening to a Juvenile Ball, dissolving views and a Christmas tree at the Meades. Eighty-four present from the age of three to eighty-three. Home at 3 o'clock. Amongst others was Harry Scott Hughes, born 11th January 1853!

Deaths in 1855 *(listed by JBS)*

Garden, Amelia S; widow of John Garden of Redisham Hall dies the 10th of January after four days illness. Daughter of the Rev. John Lewis of Gillingham.
Baker, Benjamin; hairdresser and tax gatherer dies 2nd of February, in his 86th year.
Read, Harry; of Beccles dies 6th of February. He was usher at the Grammar School about 1792 and afterwards a land agent.
Farr, Thomas; also at Bungay Grammar School, son of Thomas Farr of Beccles. Dies 8th of February. He was with De Lacy Evan's army in Spain in 1835.
Brock; the widow, dies in the almshouse, 9th of February, aged 84.
Scott, Thomas Charles; dies 5th of March.
Butcher, Henry; dies at St James South Elmham, 7th of March. Brother to Miss Hannah Butcher.
Skipper, J; a notorious character called "Blood Skippen" died at the Cherry Tree Inn, 9th of March. Had suffered punishment in the Bungay town stocks. *(at the Butter Cross)*
Cautley, Rev. W.G. of Earsham , dies 26th of March.
Bedingfield, Mrs; wife of J. J. Bedingfield Esq; dies 22nd of July at

Trinity Hall, aged 88. She was buried at Bedingfield.
Fonnereau, William Charles of Christ Church, Ipswich; dies 30th of July, aged 50.
Worthington, Sarah nee Scott; wife of W. C. Worthington of Lowestoft dies 5th of August, aged 53.
Edwards, William Camden; engraver, dies at Bungay, 22nd of August.
Adams, for thirty-five years parish clerk of St Mary's dies 2nd of September, aged 70.
Haward, Charles, dies at Wharton Street, aged 67, late of Flixton Abbey, 24th of November.

1856

January.   The year commences with various dinner parties and a Union Ball was given at the Corn Hall from 9.30 to 3 o'clock. Two hundred present. Good music, dancing and good fellowship.

March 28. Lowestoft. Fix at the Worthington's house to settle divers business with Seago the lawyer and the Worthingtons, relating to matters arising from Sarah's death.

April 1.   On this bright, sunny morning read of the confirmation of the signing of Peace with Russia and France on the 30th after two years war. Just such a morning as that on which forty-two years ago, I heard at Cambridge of the signing of Peace, also at Paris.

April 7.   James Kilner elected Chaplain of Chester Castle and preparing to leave Stafford.

The family of Kilner were the owners of the Shadingfield Hall estate before it was purchased by T.C. Scott at the beginning of the nineteenth century. Both James and John Kilner married daughters of Mr. Scott.

July 21.   Thomas Jeckell, architect from Norwich to lunch. He and I measure and plan in Trinity Church from 2 to 7.

At this time J.B. Scott was contemplating the restoration of the ruined chancel.

August 6.   Miss Sandby's Garden Fête at Denton. Go with young Gould. The Hughes go with the Forsters from Yarmouth with whom they are staying. Meades, Holmes, Kerrichs, Bedingfields,

Col. Humphry Sneyds, Upchers, Bouveries, Ormerods, etc., there. Altogether over eighty. Gardens lovely, and weather celestial. Howlett's band and good singing. Dancing later. A very pleasant party from 3 to 9. o'clock. Alfred returns with me and stops the night.

August 16.　　Visit poor Margaret Hart and her sister Eliza. I had not seen the former since 1854 and during the whole of that time she has been suffering from dropsy and been operated upon thirteen times. She is cheerful, thin in the face but of enormous size otherwise. She was lying in bed. I stopped with her from 1 to 3 o'clock and then returned by rail and coach to Bungay. Evening spend an hour with Hannah Butcher.

Miss Butcher is now in failing health and Scott seldom passes a day without going to see her.

August 18.　　Call on Mrs Hartcup in the new Grove House.

September 4.　　Frank, Charlotte and Marion Worthington and Cholomley Roberts staying with me. Drive by Earsham Hall, Denton and Flixton to Stow Park and find the Meade children there, Rosa, Ada, Aubrey and Constance, also the Smiths from Ellingham. Tea in gipsy fashion under a sailcloth in the woods. Much play with the children and the little Harry Scott Hughes.

September 22.　　The tower of Flixton church falls while George Sandby is taking his holiday in Normandy and Brittany.

A church is mentioned in Flixton Domesday Book and the ruins of the ancient building, which were being re-erected at this time, certainly appear from their description in old histories to be of Saxon origin. In 1796 the chancel was in ruins, the bare walls containing the window openings being the only part remaining. The Anglo-Saxon tower was the most ancient portion of the building and consisted of uncut flints, laid in rough horizontal courses, and together with the walls of the south aisle was leaning dangerously to the south-west. In spite of the dilapidated state of the church, services seem to have been conducted within its walls until a short time before the commencement of its restoration in 1855 when George Sandby, then the vicar, held services for the parish in the adjoining village of Homersfield. Meanwhile the square Saxon tower was becoming more and more ruinous in consequence of the subsidence of its foundations and finally

collapsed altogether. By November seats were erected in the body of the church and the Sacrament administered by the vicar in the new chancel on the following Christmas Day.
The Vicarage was built in 1849. Up to that time Mr. Sandby lived in the 'Priests House' at Flixton. The present church was entirely rebuilt by Sir Shafto Adair in 1861 after the design of the older edifice. It was seated with oak benches from oak grown on the Flixton estate. The architect was Mr. Slavin.

October 30. Miss Margaret Hart dies at her lodgings at Diss after three years severe illness. Her amazing piety, patience and cheerful resignation and active benevolence were delightful to witness and were of much content to herself here and, I trust, forerunners of great joy. She was for a long time my neighbour when living with Mrs Garden, Senr. She had reached her 43rd year and was buried at Reydon. Her sisters Eliza and Mary and Emily Gurdon attended her funeral.

November 9. Sir Edward Gooch M.P. for East Suffolk dies at Benacre Hall aged 54.

December 2. Am elected Town Reeve for the seventh time. Preside over eighty guests at the Town Dinner. Fenton sings a new version of 'Old Bungay'.

NOTE
The original version of this song was first sung by the actor, David Fisher, at the Bungay Theatre in 1816. It has continued to be sung, with some modern verses, at the Town Dinner annually up to the present day.

OLD BUNGAY (1856)

Tune: "The Roast Beef of Old England"

Of Beccles, and Harleston, and fifty more such,
With their Railways and Stations we've heard overmuch;
But as for their traffic, 'tis moonshine and boast!
Old Bungay laughs at 'em and beats the whole host;
For of all places, Bungay's the place of renown;
O what a place is Old Bungay!
Old Bungay's a wonderful town!

That our trade is a brisk one, there's none can deny,
Who have been in our Markets to sell or to buy;
And sure at our Shops you may get what you wish,
From a gold wedding ring to a brown earthen dish;
    For of all places, &c.

We've merchants of all sorts, malt, timber, and corn,
Coal, paper, rag, liquor, and dealers in horn;
And we've Millers and Bakers, all honest no doubt,
And so we'll believe till we've found the rogues out;
    For of all places, &c.

We've Bankers, a host, who have money galore,
And a Factory, where they turn out by the score;
We've gas in our streets, not so bright as the day!
But we must not find fault till we're called on to pay;
    For of all places, &c.

We've a foundry for type, we have printing by steam;
Of charities too, we've a full-flowing stream;
We have homes for the widow, we've schools for the
mass,
And reading rooms too for the working man's class;
    For of all places, &c.

Our Lawyers, tho' strange as the case may appear,
Can keep a good practice with consciences clear;
And if health on the number of Doctors depends,
Old Jenkins's all we shall die my good friends!
    For of all places, &c.

At our Inns you are certain to meet with good fare;
And for Pumps there's the town one, that stands in the
square,
'Tis a wonderful Pump! so the good people say,
Once it drained the town funds every fraction away;
    For of all places, &c.

Our stately Church Steeple most Steeples excels;
But low are our whispers in praise of its Bells;
We've a handsome old Cross, and a modern Corn Hall,
And a noble old Castle, that overlooks all;
    For of all places, &c.

> *Then let us all rise, and unite heart and hands,*
> *And like Bungay of yore on our own bottom stand;*
> *Thus our old Town shall flourish, nor crumble nor fall,*
> *And the sun of prosperity shine over all;-*
> > *Then, of all places, Bungay retains its renown;*
> > *O! what a place is old Bungay!*
> > *Old Bungay's a wonderful Town!*

1857

January 3. On this his 32nd. birthday, Alfred is with me from 12 to 2.30 giving me full details of his deplorable financial position. I am very unhappy about his affairs.

January 27. Sir Edward H. Alderson dies in his 70th year. He spent some of his early years in the Trinity Vicarage, Bungay.

April. *This month Scott has an attack of bronchial pneumonia. Crowfoot attending him. By the 22nd. he is well enough to go to the Corn Hall and preside at a lecture given by B.B. Woodward on 'Old Bungay'. Two hundred present. A second lecture on the 24th when three hundred attend. Scott had assisted Woodward by supplying him with many details relating to the town and continued collecting further notes for him. Woodward was at the time contemplating a history of Bungay but I cannot find that it ever matured.*

April 24. Harry Smith marries Amy H. Green, daughter of Colonel Green of Twickenham.

May 16. Chester. Am staying with the James Kilners till Monday.

May 17. With James and Mary Kilner (née Scott) to the castle gaol chapel. James is the chaplain. One hundred very attentive convicts at the service who sing with much fine harmony and feeling. Afterwards inspect the solitary cells. *p.m.* Service at the Cathedral from 4 to 5. The anthem beautiful, the bishop very ugly. Call on Miss Jane Thackeray from 5.30 to 6.15.

September 8. Charles Edward Probyn, Assistant Deputy Commissioner General, son of Thomas and Margaret Probyn (my cousin) dies of fever, at St. Lucien, the West Indies.

September 15. Bungay. Mrs, Miss and John Patch arrived from Tiverton yesterday to stay with me. All in a 'Fly' to Norwich where Alfred and Maria join us at St. Andrews Hall for the Norwich festival. The next day again to the festival. Beethoven's Mount of Olives and Haydn's Seasons. Former exquisitely grand but the latter wearisome and poor. To the museum and home at 7.

October 14. The Rev. R. H. Hughes married at Newton, Cambs., to Frances E. Pemberton daughter of C.R. Pemberton Esq.

October 26. Francis Edward John Kelso, son of General Kelso of Bungay and late Captain of the 72nd Regt. Highlanders, knocked down by a runaway horse near his new house at Slough nr. Windsor, and died immediately, aged 48.

November 9. Write to the Lord Lieutenant of Suffolk requesting to be omitted from serving as a Commissioner of the Peace.

J.B.S. always resists any suggestion that he should serve as a magistrate.

November 18. With Richard Cattermole from 9.30 to 12.30 about fixing up the names of the streets and houses in Bungay.

November 24. Mr. Henry Finch, surgeon comes to live at Trinity Hall.

1858

January 1. Dine at Aldolphus Holmes' with Gervais Holmes of Emmanuel and John Holmes of Trinity and with Clarkson and his wife and Mr. Holmes of Gaudy Hall.

In his spare time Scott is now looking through the Trinity Churchwardens books and transcribing the earlier ones which date from 1537.

January 26. The Rev. W.H. Glover, Incumbent of St. Mary's Bungay, married to Frances Caroline Bridges. The ceremony was performed by her father-in-law Dr. Molesworth at Rochdale, Lancashire.

February 12. Goat Skippen[5], a somewhat notorious character and the last person who was punished in the town stocks, where he sat for two hours, dies in Chapel Lane, Bungay in his 90th year.

February 18.   Glover and his bride arrive at Bungay at 8 p.m. and are greeted by large crowds and friends. Bells ringing and much cheering.

March 2.   Isabella, daughter of Sir Eaton Travers and widow of Charles Smithies marries the Rev. George Alston of Swannage and on the 4th her father dies at Yarmouth aged 76. Rear Admiral, Sir Eaton Travers' funeral takes place at Ditchingham on the 10th. Bedingfield and I await it at Scudamore's. The hearse and procession arrive from Yarmouth at 12.45 drawn by twenty-six horses. The Rev. George Hill and Dr. Dunn precede. Lady Travers and her four sons - Duncan, Eaton, Frank and William, and her two daughters Mary Fisher and Isabella Alston and their husbands, follow, also Mr. and Mrs Tom Steward, Frank Steward, four Scotts. The upper bearers were Macdonald, Isaac, Preston, myself, Steward and J. Bedingfield. Hill reads the service. Sir Eaton was buried beside his daughter Anne who died in 1835. William Travers, wounded in India, returned home only last Monday ignorant of his father's death. Scudamore explains to us his project for a new church near Ditchingham Factory.

March 15. Schools. A nearly annular eclipse of the sun. Give a lecture on it to the school boys and see it with them from 12 to 2. Dark twilight at 1 o'clock. The cows come up from the Common and birds flutter home to their nests.

April 8.   Alfred comes to consult me about moving to Thorness in the Isle of Wight to a farm of 460 acres. After further talks with him and with Maria, he decides to take it from Michaelmas next.

April 15.   Frank, Edward and James Worthington come to see me. Aged respectively twenty-two, eighteen and seventeen. We all walk to Stow Park and talk about Thorness. They return to Lowestoft on the 17th. Frank, I hope, is fixed in the right path (he has given up the sea and is studying medicine) the other two are agreeable and rather clever but wanting in self control.

April 26.   The schools most flourishing. 244 present this morning. Alfred with me three hours arranging about the Thorness agreement.

May 8. London. Meet Mitchell at 11. o'clock and go with him to the Crystal Palace. Meet the queens of Portugal and England in the garden at the entrance. They were accompanied by Prince Albert and were quite close to us. To the Choral Festival of 5000 National Schoolmasters, teachers and children. An immense audience. The next day meet Alfred on his way back from Thorness and we see Petre about the lease of the farm.

June 3. Bungay. J.T. Pelham, Bishop of Norwich gives his first Visitation Charge, an admirable one. Lunch at the King's Head. A pleasant gathering of many old friends: oppositions abated and a kind forbearing feeling prevails. Leighton, Sandby, Holmes, Charles Scott etc., present. A conference takes place in which the Bishop, Archdeacon Ormerod, George Allsop, Upjohn etc., take part.

June 20. Died at Lee Cottage, Brompton, Dawson Turner aged 82, the once energetic and talented friend and guide of my youth. Formerly of Yarmouth.

July 11. Major John Mann arrived from India last night after eight years absence and was at Trinity Church this morning and again in the evening.

July 12. Confirmation of three hundred and three persons at Bungay by the Bishop of Norwich. Charge good but interminably long.

August 3. From Southampton to Cowes. Alfred Hughes who had been at the Isle of Wight since the 18th of last month, meets me on the pier and drives me to Thorness. We look at the house and farm and dine at Porchfield Cottage at 7.30. Spend the next two days examining the place and making plans for the ground round it. Discuss improvements to the farm buildings with Mr. Joliffe a builder and walk over the marshes on the west side of the farm. Am full of hope for Alfred's success in this enterprise. Leave for Cowes on the afternoon of the 5th. Dear Alfred and I part with full hearts and eyes at 5 o'clock.

August 20. In the afternoon J.B. Wilkinson and his wife arrive at Mrs Kingsbury's and Cobb comes for me. Spend a pleasant hour together. He, amiable, clever and as eccentric as ever.

September 6. Inspect the intended Penitentiary at Ditchingham now being erected. To see Miss Sandby, probably the last call on her at Denton.

October 18.　　To Stow Park. Alfred has returned from the Isle of Wight and with Maria is in the midst of packing, valuing and selecting. 'What a break up' said dear Maria sadly and I return unhappily with 'Perhaps it's all for the best'. Cheer up afterwards, resolving to find new employments of usefulness and to follow up old 'ones more vigorously for the rest of my life.

October 21.　　All leave Stow Park and stay with me, Alfred going back during the day to complete arrangements with Captain Moore who is taking on the farm and house. After a very pleasant eight days visit they depart for Ellingham.

November 8.　　Alfred leaves again for Thorness where I join him on the 15th for two or three days and we make plans for the garden, roads etc. and look over the house and magnificent farm buildings. We also cut down trees and fences and make other improvements. Both leave for London on the 19th.

December 2.　　Alfred and Maria and their five dear children leave Ellingham and Bungay for the Isle of Wight, I going with them to London where we all stay at 22, Suffolk Street. Alfred, Maria and I to the Princess Theatre in the evening to see 'King John' admirably performed by Charles Kean.
The next day accompany them to Waterloo Station and see them off to their Island. Afterwards with Charles Roberts to Hampton Court where I dine with him and his wife who talks of 'bad servants' as usual. Stop the night there.

December 11.　　Return to Bungay after spending a few days in London with Maria and Alfred. The latter accompanies me home and then goes to Ellingham.

1859

January.　　The usual dinner parties take place at the beginning of the year at the Meades, Bouveries, Kingsbury's, Cobbs etc., and a concert and Christmas tree at the Corn Hall got up by the Childs' when Cramer, grandson of Francois, plays delightfully on the violincello.

January 27.　　Dine at the Mortlocks at Denton Lodge who have lately succeeded Miss Sandby, now living at her new house at Starston.

March 3. To see Miss Sandby and her house at Starston and lunch with her.

(She died the following July on the 2nd, and was buried at Denton on the 8th.)

March 27. James Feathers' last day at Bungay National School and Trinity Church. He takes a tearful leave of me this evening. He is leaving for London and Oswestry tomorrow.

May 10. My cousin Henry Gee Roberts gazetted K.C.B.

May 20. London. Attend the first day of the sale of Dawson Turner's library at Puttock and Simpsons, also the following day when the Norfolk and Suffolk collections were sold and included Fox's St. Lawrence, Ipswich and Suffolk portraits and parochial surveys.

June 1. Bungay. The Beccles, Woodbridge and Ipswich Railway opened and Warnes' coach ceases running from Bungay to Harleston.

June 8. Sunday. Wingfield's Charity. The Bishop of Norwich preaches at St. Mary's Church in the evening to an overflowing congregation. Probably 1000 present.

June 9. Drive to Halesworth and travel for the first time by the newly opened Suffolk Railway by Saxmundham and Woodbridge to Ipswich and London 4.19 to 9.

June 10. The second day's sale at Puttock and Simpsons of Dawson Turner's Autographs and Bloomfield's Norfolk etc. The last named bought by the British Museum for £400.

July 19. John James Raven comes to Bungay as Master of the Grammar School. He dines with me at 1.30 and stops till after tea.

July 31. Sunday. An organ and choir first installed in Trinity Church. Organ good but not powerful. Walesby, organist - poor. Eight men and ten boys sing well.

August 3. Alfred arrived last night. Talk from 7 to 8 this morning about Mr. Robert Harrison, son of the surgeon at Braintree and lately returned from New Zealand. He calls at 9 o'clock to arrange about taking Stow Park, and at 10 we all go and look over the farm which Captain Moore is giving up.

September 14.   Sarah Garneys married to her cousin, Frederick Freeman. On the 20th the son and daughter of the late N.B. Fisher, surgeon of Bungay marry Miss Orpen and Mr. Williamson of London.

October 14.   Mrs Parkinson and her three daughters move from Ditchingham Lodge to my Bridge House. In the evening drive to Ellingham Hall where twenty-one dine in the newly arranged dining room, and the drawing-room was opened for the first time. Dance till 12.

October 15-25.   London and then on to Cowes and Thorness to the Hughes'. The week spent at Thorness has been a singularly happy one but has seemed very short. On leaving the Isle of Wight on Saturday I felt much depressed and had a sad foreboding that we should not all meet again in happiness. I record this feeling here but hope that it may prove an erroneous one produced solely by the suspension of much beloved society and not in any way prophetic! Perhaps caused by the cold, cheerless weather.

December.   *The Christmas of this year was spent at Broomfield, Tiverton, with the Patches. He mentions two delightful conversations with old Mrs Barne at New Place 'my true friend of fifty years'*

Though not strong she is cheerful and her memory as correct as ever. We talked of 1809 and of varied recent events. Her kindness to me is very genuine as it always has been.

1860

The first fortnight of this year is spent at Thorness.

January 28.   Saunders, Robert (husband of Anna Butcher of The Grove, Bungay) dies at Henley-on-Thames in his 77th year. James Worthington, who with Mr. Raven of the Grammar School, dines with me and receives a lecture for his indolence and frivolity. He becomes cool and sullen and leaves abruptly as did his brother William nine years ago.
Fortunately for himself he goes to his elderly cousin and apologises on the following Sunday and is forgiven.

February 28. A tremendous hurricane from the west and north-west. Trees, walls, slates and tiles blown in all directions. Smith's mill at Ellingham lost its head and its brick tower crashed. Farrow's wall at Bungay, two hundred feet long, and Webb's Music room at Rose Hall smashed by falling trees. Hartcup at The Grove loses 200 trees. Adair 100, Bedingfield 50, Earsham Hall 50 and Worlingham Hall 600 at least. The gale lasted from 1 to 4.30 a.m.

March 15. Evening, dine at George Sandby's with Mrs Bowyer and Mrs Brocas, Mortlock and his wife, Mrs and Miss Smith, Mr. and Mrs Tarver and C. Evans. Excellent music and much enjoyment.

March 21. Mr. and Mrs Harrison of Stow Park dine with me and also C. Evans (now engaged to Miss Ormerod). We go at 7 o'clock to Kirby School room to Lucy Smith's Ellingham choir concert, which was very good. Evans sleeps at my house.

March 28. Drive to Shipmeadow House, the first time for four months. Sandby also there for the first time for twelve months, he having broken his thigh last March and been laid up until lately. First drill on the Grammar School ground.

About this date there was a great revival of the Volunteer movement and Scott was one of its most strenuous supporters in Bungay and the neighbouring towns. He was a regular attendant of the drills and did everything he could to promote the efficiency of the Bungay Company.

April 19. Scott, Walter, son of T.C. Scott of Shadingfield, dies near Stafford.
In the afternoon the Bungay Rifles assemble for drill in uniform on the Common for the first time. Crowds of people to see them.

June 16. B.B. Woodward appointed Librarian to the Queen.

June 17. A stone wall found two feet beneath St. Mary's churchyard. It was twenty-six inches wide and four feet deep and is between the steeple and the Roman Catholic church.

June 21. Bungay. Go with Tarver, the Prince of Wales' tutor, to St. John's Ilketshall to see the church now re-opened and benched.

July 3. Tuesday. Edward Worthington sails from Gravesend in the

'Evening Star' for New Zealand. Frank, Charlotte and Hester, his brother and sisters come to me at 5.30 and I take them to Childs' musical party at the Corn Hall. They stop with me till Thursday.

July 12. Hester Worthington married to Edmund Norton[6] at Haverstock Hill by Lawrence Till.

August 6. The restoration of the stone work to the S.W. of Trinity Church began preparatory to putting in the new window, the work to be carried out by Nursey.

October 3. Drive to Beccles and then go on to Lowestoft to the Royal Hotel where I meet Michel, just returned from Spain. The *Tonnig* steamer's boiler blew up and thirteen men killed and wounded off Yarmouth. The next day the steamer was towed into Lowestoft harbour. A dreadful sight of killed, dying and maimed victims and desolation.

October 8. Review and inspection of the Bungay, Beccles, Halesworth and Harleston Rifle Volunteers at Flixton Park by Colonel Shafto Adair. Colonel George Wilson commands. Ten thousand spectators estimated to have been present.

November 2. The railway opened from Bungay to Harleston. Travel from the temporary station on the common[7] from 12.40 to 1 o'clock and back from 1.40 to 2.10. Agreeable line and view. Later to a meeting to promote the Volunteer movement. Margitson, Raven, Childs, Adams and myself speakers. Thirty recruits join.

December 25. Christmas Day. The thermometer down to 1 Fahrenheit in Bungay. It was 22 below freezing in my bedroom. The schools should have been re-opened on the 31st. Monday, but continue closed in consequence of the severity of the weather.

1861

January 1. Weather unprecedently severe. A general distribution of coals, tea and sugar in the two parishes causes me to defer Smith's, Wingfield's and Dreyer's Charities for the present.

January 6 and 7. An attempt at re-opening the schools but had to close them in consequence of snow and frost. It was not until the 14th that the children were able to attend again regularly. About this time Scott began to suffer from some skin trouble which caused him much discomfort. However it soon passed off but was succeeded by swollen ankles, shortness of breath and the various symptoms of a failing heart. The severe cold continued and early in February he went to Thorness and stayed with the Hughes. While there he seems to have been very weak and ill and on the 27th returned to 'town' and consulted Dr. George Burrows of Cavendish Square who told him his circulation was feeble and his heart not regularly powerful. He returned to Bungay on the 10th of March and struggled on with his work at the schools and visited them almost daily.

April 2.   Not up till 1 o'clock. Very ill! Samuel Scott arrives from London and is with me from 2.30 to 4. Mrs Smith and Lucy come for an hour. All most kind. Am re-elected honorary churchwarden of Trinity, Bungay with very kind testimonials.
Frank Worthington comes from Beccles and Alfred arrives from the Isle of Wight. Alfred and Frank sleep at my house and Samuel stays with his sister. Rejoiced and contented to see them all. Alfred left again on the 10th.

April 13.   Alfred comes to Waveney House on the 13th and Samuel returns to London on the 16th having been in Bungay for six weeks chiefly from the kind desire to attend to my comfort and to help me with my work during my severe illness.

June 12.   The following received from Cambridge: "The Vice Chancellor gives notice that the Presentation of the Perpetual Curacy of St.Mary's Bungay, now vacant, has lapsed to the University in consequence of the Patron being a Roman Catholic. The Vice Chancellor also gives notice that the election of a Clerk to be presented to the Perpetual Curacy of St. Mary's will take place on Tuesday, October the 22nd."

June 15.   William Worthington who has been away for ten years, and Edward who went out last year to New Zealand, arrive at their father's house at Lowestoft.

July 19.   Drive to Denton and see the nice new bridge over the Wash begun six weeks ago.

July 23.   Tarver as Diocesan Inspector inspects the Bungay National Schools. Several persons present. I there from 11 o'clock to 1.30.

July 25.   Married at St. George's Hanover Square, Charles

Henry the eldest son of Charles Roberts to Mary Crompton only daughter of the late Roger Crompton of Sunnyside, Avenue Road, Regents Park.

July 28.   The Rev. Charles Bowen first does Duty at Bungay St. Mary.

August.   Although in very bad health, Scott drives out daily to see his friends and continues his interest and work at the National Schools. His most frequent visitors at this time seem to have been Tarver, Raven, the Cobbs, and Smiths of Ellingham, and Bouverie. With the consent of his doctors it is decided that he shall go to Thorness again and early in August he leaves Bungay accompanied by Alfred Hughes. He stood the journey fairly well but a few days after his arrival there became very ill and Dr. Hoffmeister, surgeon to the Queen at Osborne, was called in.

October 3. Sunday. At 9 p.m. died peacefully my dear friend Hannah Butcher. Patience, humility and charity were the characteristics of her whole life. She was buried on the 9th at St. Margarets, South Elmham. Think of "Saturday night will come at last" a saying of old Colonel Capper's so often quoted by Hannah Butcher, whose Saturday night has now come.

December 14. At 10.50 p.m. Prince Albert, Consort to the Queen, dies aged 42 after a few days illness from typhoid fever. At the beginning of the month Samuel Scott comes for three days to help me with various Bungay business.

December 23. Rather stronger. Many thoughts of the Queen and of the Prince who is now being interred.

Deaths 1861 *(listed by JBS)*

Churchyard, William, chemist & druggist in Bungay, dies suddenly aged 61. January 4th.
Worthington, Charlotte, sister of W.C. Worthington, dies at Dover after six days illness, aged 66. January 9th.
Procter, Admiral Sir Wm. Beauchamp Bt. dies at Langley aged 79. March 13th.
Carthew, Laura Wade, last surviving daughter of the Rev. Thomas Carthew of Woodbridge Abbey dies aged 82. May 21st.
Carthew, George, Solicitor at Harleston the last of the Carthews of

Woodbridge, aged 84, May 31st.
Rackham, Willoughby, née Mary Padden of Bungay, dies in London aged about 83. June 2nd.
Bewick, Calverly Richard, formerly of Bungay dies at Ripple House near Walmer, aged 63. June 7th.
Suckling, died at Paignton, Devon, Catherine widow of the Rev. Horace Suckling, Rector of Beccles aged 88. July 7th.
Gaussen, died at Montagu Place, Russell Square, William Gaussen, Esq., the youngest brother of the late T.R.Gaussen of Brookmans Park, Herts., July 9th.
Pearson, George, Pensioner at Emmanuel with me, dies at his rectory at Castle Camps, in Cambridge, aged 67, after a few hours illness and his third daughter aged 21 the same afternoon. May 13th.
Anna, Isabella, Baroness Noel Byron, widow of the Lord Byron aged 66 dies at St. George's Terrace, Regents Park, May 16th.
Harvey, General Sir R.J. C.B. dies at Thorpe near Norwich in his 75th year. June 18th.
Spall, Harriet (Burgess) the wife of William Spall, coach- maker, Bungay on July 18th.
Hughes, Anna Maria dies of decline at Southsea, aged 21, July 26th.
Boyden, Susanne (Ingate) the wife of James Boyden and sister of Mrs Charles Scott dies at Beccles aged 69. August 10th.
Rabett, Reginald late of Bramfield Hall dies in Northamptonshire, aged 64. September 10th. *(Schoolfellow of J.B.S.)*
Brettingham, Thomas Clarke dies of an apoplectic fit at his house, Higham Lodge near Manningtree aged 71. September 20th. *(also a school fellow).*
Roberts, General Sir Henry Gee K.C.B., dies at his house in Herefordshire, aged 60. *(maternal cousin).*
Alder, Rev. E.T. dies at St. Matthew's, Islington. Formerly Incumbent of Metfield and later curate of St. Mary's Bungay, aged 61. December 2nd.

1862

January. Towards the middle of the month Scott left Thorness and went to the Avis Hotel at Cowes. Here his servant, George Catchpole, goes to him from Bungay. His health was getting decidedly worse and on the 11th January is this entry:-

Preparation for a consultation with Dr. Jenner, who sees me with Dr. Hoffmeister and pronounces cure impossible but with care may live on indefinitely. After his visit Maria and her little girls come for an hour and Hoffmeister returns to me in the evening. During the night think much of the short remainder of my life.

From now onward his time is occupied with arranging and destroying the papers which George Catchpole had brought from Bungay, writing letters and going through accounts connected with the schools, and other business. His cousin Samuel comes from London to help him with the Book Club affairs, Wingfield's, Smith's, and other Charities and the various duties connected with the town of Bungay which he had so long undertaken.

February 26.   Birthday.   Seventy! The age of man completed. What done? Only fragments remain. Even in these good and evil may be effected. A cold, dreary day. Letters to Tarver and Raven. Thoughts of Bungay Grammar School.

February 29.   Hear that the Bungay Book Club at the King's Head is broken up after ninety-two years, on the resignation of J.B.S!

May 6.   At noon Samuel Scott and Alfred Hughes and I receive the Sacrament from the Rev. Silver. Alfred returns to Thorness after a long talk with Dr. Hoffmeister and Samuel about my journey to Bungay.

May 20.   Start with Alfred for London this morning and reach Waterloo at 5.50 where Samuel meets us. Fix at 10, Cecil Street, Strand and all dine there together.

May 21.   Mrs F. Patch to see me this morning, also George and Mrs Sandby (who are now living in London).

May 22.   Return to Bungay, Alfred with me. Mitchell travels with us as far as Chelmsford. Reach home at 5. o'clock. Received at the Bungay station with tears by the old people and cheers from the boys and girls and the music of the Rifle Band, and by universal kind enquiries.

May 23.   See no one of the twenty callers who came today.

On the 25th Alfred Hughes leaves and the next day Samuel arrives. From now until his death in September one or other of them is constantly with him. Scott continues visiting the National Schools almost daily and resumes their management with Samuel's help. He has constant visits from his many friends, usually in the morning, and in the afternoon goes out driving and pays short calls on various neighbours.

The entries are continued in his diaries until the end of August but are often almost, if not quite, illegible. On the 22nd. of this month he records "Very ill in body and mind. To the schools in chair. Exhausted."

Throughout his illness there is no sign of discontent nor regret about his failing health. His interest in life and pleasure in the society of his friends continues to the end.

He died the 10th September in his 71st. year.

PART VII (1852-1862) The Last Ten Years

References

1. Kemble, Frances Anne (Fanny) (1809-1893). Actress and poetess.

2.   Barlee, Mrs Frances (1780-1854). Mrs Frances Barlee lived at Dukes Bridge House. The large family pew had been granted to her ancestor, Gregory Clarke, probably in the early years of the eighteenth century. Mrs Barlee appears to have resisted the removal of the pew during alterations to the church, and, according to Ethel Mann in "Old Bungay", it had to be secretly smuggled out during the night, by order of the churchwardens. Scott records her death in 1854.

3. Childs, John (1784-1853) was born in Bungay and apprenticed to a grocer in Norwich. His obvious abilities were recognised by Charles Brightly, who had a small printing works in Bungay, and he took Childs into his employment. Childs married Brightly's daughter and succeeded to the business when his employer died in 1821. His brother, Robert, and later his son Charles, became partners. The firm prospered, particularly as a result of its production of cheap editions of the Bible and the Imperial Edition of Standard Authors. Childs was a leading member of the Congregational Church, and his clash with the Scott family over his refusal to pay Church Rates, and his subsequent imprisonment, are recorded in the Appendix. He was buried in the Congregational churchyard, where the family tomb can still be seen. There are various mementoes concerning his career in Bungay Museum, including his Bible which he took into Ipswich gaol.

4.   The Misses Owles. "The house late Elswoods" was Linden House in Earsham Street, now St Mary's House, a residential home for the elderly. The school which the Misses Owles established there continued until 1878, when it was sold by Miss Harriet Owles. Later it was taken over by Miss Jane and Miss   Maude Maddle and called St. Mary's Ladies School. It continued as a school for girls and a prep school for boys until 1966.

5.   "Blood" and "Goat Skippen"; both seem to have been notorious characters who were punished in the stocks in Bungay Market Place. They may have been brothers as they died within three years of each other. H.C.Botwright wrote in a letter to the East Suffolk Gazette in 1907 that one reason "Blood" Skippen got his name "may have been the filthy state of his clothes from carrying horse flesh on his back for the dogs he had in training; but the real

210

reason, he believed was the fact that in a fight in our market place "Blood" bit off his opponent's ear. We do not know how "Goat" got his name.

6. The parents of Ethel Mann.

7. This station remained in use until 1933 when it was replaced by a permanent building. This was demolished when the Waveney Valley Line was closed in 1953.

St Mary's Church, c. 1930

APPENDIX I

CONTINENTAL TOURS OF J.B. SCOTT

1814. May 7 - October 25.

Crossed Channel by 'Packet' sailing-boat from Brighton to Dieppe.

France   Toulon, Lyons, Dijon, Paris, Crecy.

Italy   Pisa, Leghorn

Elba   Where he met and talked to Napoleon. (Scott was then aged 22.) Returned Calais - Deal, nearly shipwrecked.

July 10, 1816 - June 21, 1818.

Belgium   Crossed to Ostend. Liege.

Germany   Rhineland. Munich. Dresden for 5 months where he met Schopenhauer & studied German. Leipzig, Berlin, Hanover.

Switzerland   Climbed in the Alps for 2 months.

Italy   Milan, Florence, Rome, Naples, Ancona, Venice, Lake Como, Lugano.

Austria   Tirol, Salzburg, Vienna.

Bohemia   Prague.

Holland   Arnheim, Amsterdam.

1822. February 16 - September 13

Crossed from Dover to Calais.

Paris 7 months

1823. January 17 - April 26

Paris 3 months.

1823 - 1824. November to May

France & Italy

December 18, 1824 - June, 1826

Italy 18 months in Rome.

(All these tours were unaccompanied but after 1840 he took young Alfred Hughes , aged 16 in that year, with him.)

1840. January 12 - May 1

London to Antwerp by steamer, 22½ hours

Liege

The Rhineland   Cologne, Coblenz, Mainz,
                       Frankfurt and Heidelberg.
                       Moselle valley: Trier.

Rhine steamer to Rotterdam. Crossed to Woolwich, 17 hours.

1841. June 12 - October 4

London - Rotterdam.

Germany   Steamed up Rhine to Coblenz. By
                       road to Ems, Wiesbaden, Frankfurt,
                       Nurnberg and Regensburg.
                       Munich, Augsburg, Lake Constance.

Switzerland   Attended Swiss Assembly in Berne.

Zurich.
Climbing in Alps.
Back via Cologne to Brussels.
Visited Waterloo battlefield.
Antwerp to London.

1843. May 4 - June 26

Southampton - Le Havre, 6 hours.

France   Steamer up Seine to Rouen. Paris by
                          new railway. Versailles, Sevres &
                          Fontainebleau.

Boulogne - Dover, 3½ hours.

1844. August 5 - September 26

Sailed from Shoreham, Sussex - Dieppe , 9 hours.

France   Rouen, Paris for 3 weeks. Metz.
                          Luxembourg.

Germany   Trèves. Coblenz. Aachen.

Belgium   By train to Ghent. Bruges.

1851. October 19 - 31

Paris   Paris to London 14 hours.

1855. October 5 - 20

Paris   Visited International Exhibition.

John Barber Scott as a child

Monday 8	**Friday 12**
1799 Feb I took a walk with my Papa and Mama and Mr and Mrs Kingel	1799 Feb I helpt to hack Wool
Tuesday 9	**Saturday 13**
I Plaid about the Tanyard	I helpt to hack Wool again
Wednesday 10	**Sunday 14**
I road to the farm with my Papa and Mama	I took a ride with my Mama to Mr H... ammonds
Thursday 11	**Monday 15**
I took a walk and had my tooth drawn	I went to see our Volunteers Exercise

Two pages of Scott's Diary written when a child of seven

APPENDIX II: THE SCOTT FAMILY OF BUNGAY

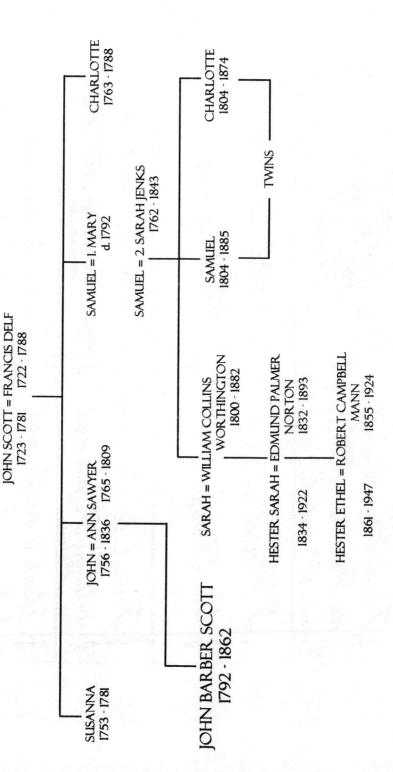

JOHN SCOTT = FRANCIS DELF
1723 - 1781   1722 - 1788

SUSANNA
1753 - 1781

JOHN = ANN SAWYER
1756 - 1836   1765 - 1809

SAMUEL = 1. MARY
d.1792

SAMUEL = 2. SARAH JENKS
1762 - 1843

CHARLOTTE
1763 - 1788

SAMUEL
1804 - 1885

CHARLOTTE
1804 - 1874

TWINS

JOHN BARBER SCOTT
1792 - 1862

SARAH = WILLIAM COLLINS
WORTHINGTON
1800 - 1882

HESTER SARAH = EDMUND PALMER
NORTON
1834 - 1922   1832 - 1893

HESTER ETHEL = ROBERT CAMPBELL
MANN
1861 - 1947   1855 - 1924

Tombstones in St Mary's churchyard

Samuel Scott
Charlotte Scott

John Barber Scott

John Sawyer
Anne, his wife

Samuel Scott in old age

APPENDIX III

JOHN CHILDS AND THE CHURCH RATES CONTROVERSY.

The congregations of Nonconformist churches developed rapidly in the early years of the nineteenth century. With their own buildings and running costs to finance, they began to feel that it was unfair that they were obliged by law to continue paying rates to support the established Church of England. Scott records in his diary, March 21st, 1834, that a Church Rates Abolition Bill was discussed in Parliament. The fact that the Bill was not passed caused growing dissent among the Nonconformist communities, and in Bungay resulted in a head-on clash between Scott and another of the town's leading figures, John Childs.

John Childs was the owner and manager of the prosperous printing works, and a member of the Congregational Church in Upper Olland Street (now the United Reformed Church). Trouble initially flared up when another member of the congregation, Mr. J.C. Morris, refused to pay his church rates; and, as a result, the two churchwardens of St. Mary's, John Bobbit and Samuel Scott, (John Barber Scott's cousin), had items of his furniture seized in lieu of payment. Matters came to a head in 1835 when John Childs also refused to pay the required rate of 17s. 6d. The churchwardens, fearful of dealing with him directly, handed the matter over to the Ecclesiastical Courts in Norwich. The Court issued a writ, summoning Childs to appear before them to explain why he had refused payment. Childs ignored the summons, and consequently was taken into custody, on Tuesday, May 12th, 1835, and imprisoned in Ipswich Gaol.

There was a howl of outrage from all the Nonconformist congregations, and the matter became a subject of national interest. The case was even debated in the House of Commons, when Sir Robert Peel, (then Prime Minister), contemptuously referred to Childs as 'the Bungay Martyr'. The fact that Childs had been in poor health at the time of his arrest increased local agitation, and a group of his supporters organised subscriptions to pay his rates and fines, in order to obtain his early release from prison. He was welcomed back to Bungay as a hero; a dinner was held in his honour, and in the following year he was presented with a silver inkstand bearing the inscription: "Presented to Mr. John Childs by the friends of Civil and Religious Freedom resident in Bungay and its vicinity, as a

224

testimony of their approbation of his conduct in passively resisting the payment of Church Rates in the year 1835, for which he was imprisoned eleven days in Ipswich Gaol."

Although it was the two churchwardens who were instrumental in procuring Childs' arrest and imprisonment, the cartoons relating to this affair (see appendix III), present John Barber Scott as the chief protagonist. As a result he must have suffered considerable personal attack from Childs' numerous supporters. It is therefore intriguing that there are no references to the controversy in the existing diaries, which in fact cease from the winter of 1834, until October 1838, when the conflict was at its height. It seems odd if Scott gave up writing a diary in these years, as he had been an indefatigable diarist from infancy.

In the last months of his life he spent some time in destroying his personal papers; and it is possible that he also destroyed the diaries covering this period, because they brought back painful memories, and could also cause embarrassment to his relatives, apart from possibly presenting his own character to posterity in an unfavourable light. But considerably more research needs to be done before any firm conclusions can be arrived at.

Despite the enmity which must have existed between Scott and Childs, Scott remained on friendly terms with Charles Childs, John's son, as this diary illustrates. There are few references to Childs senior, but following his death in 1853, Scott expresses the bitter feeling that he was a "man of obstinacy, prejudice and forbidding manners". Yet, as a result of this 'obstinacy' Childs is now recognised as both a local and national hero, since it was partly due to his self-imposed 'martyrdom' in Ipswich Gaol, that eventually, in 1868, compulsory church rates were finally abolished.

APPENDIX IV

THE CARTOONS

A *Barber And His Blocks* depicts Scott as the central figure. The title is obviously a pun on his name, and the 'blocks' with which he is threatening his opponent, are the type of dummies which Victorian hairdressers used for displaying wigs. The pun also refers to 'printing blocks', and 'block heads'. Scott's speech-bubble represents him as saying that he "hates" Childs, because "he don't shave in our shop"; in other words, Childs is a member of the Nonconformist, Congregational community, not the Church of England. Scott intends to "crush" Child's printing press, and "tan his hide"; an allusion to the Scott family tanning business from which they derived their fortune.

The curly-headed figure on the right is Samuel Scott, John's cousin, and churchwarden of St. Mary's. He declares that, although he personally would be prepared to grant Childs bail, in order that he might escape immediate imprisonment, "the Barber won't let me". The cartoon thus voices the opinion that it is J.B. Scott who is the chief protagonist, the other opponents merely his 'dummies'. In the bottom left hand corner is John Bobbit, the other churchwarden. He was an ironmonger, and is depicted surrounded with the tools of his trade. He whines to Scott, that, although it may be "sport" to him, "you have broken my stiff neck in the encounter". This may suggest, either that he feared that he might lose his post as churchwarden, or that his local unpopularity as one of Childs's opponents is causing him a loss of trade.

On the right sits General Robert Meade, a great friend of Scott's. He is urging him to continue the attack on Childs - "Annihilate his press, knock his brains out, flay him alive, and give his hide to the boy Sam to tan". The reason given for Meade's enmity is that Childs - "wrote about my pension"; but nothing more is known about this particular issue.

226

Church Rates Prosecution: Cartoon No. 1

The Church In Danger From Her Supporters shows Scott physically 'supporting' St. Mary's Church. With him is Bobbit, crying out against Childs for his "contempt of Court", and two Devils, who represent the officers of the Ecclesiastical Courts at Norwich. Samuel Scott and General Meade are again depicted, and two new characters are the Reverend George Glover, Vicar, and the Reverend Robert Cobb, Deputy Curate, of St. Mary's. Cobb is bemoaning his fate - "At this rate, down will come church, pulpit, steeple, and all! Have mercy on my Deputy Curacy"; while Glover cries - "Down goes St. Mary's. And with my Church, all my blessed hopes of a Bishopric".

The cartoon suggest that even the clergy feel that Scott and his allies are acting in such a pugnacious and uncharitable manner that the Church itself is attracting hostility. This was not just a local concern. Throughout the country, the opinion was being voiced, that unless the Church of England initiated some long needed reforms of its organisation, then it should be 'Disestablished', in other words, it should no longer benefit from state patronage. The growth of the Nonconformist sects was thus an additional cause for alarm among the Church of England's supporters, and any concessions to them, such as the removal of Church Rates, was not to be tolerated. Scott and Childs, in this context, can be seen as representatives of opposing parties in a national conflict; in the end, it was Childs who was heralded as the national hero and 'martyr'.

Church Rates Prosecution: No .2

General the Hon. Robert Meade of Earsham Hall

APPENDIX V

THE WILL OF J.B. SCOTT

John Barber Scott's will consists of five closely-written pages which are unpunctuated, repetitive and difficult to read. It can, however, be summarised as follows:

Executors

His cousin, Samuel Scott of Lincoln's Inn, London, Barrister. Alfred Hughes of Bungay, but then living in the Isle of Wight, Gentleman. The Reverend George Sandby, late Vicar of Flixton, then living in London.

Bequests

£100 to George Sandby for his work as Executor.

£100 to the Bungay National Schools for the Education of Poor Children in the Principles of the Established Church.

£100 to the Norfolk & Norwich Hospital.

£ 50 to the East Suffolk & Ipswich Hospital.

£ 50 to the Suffolk General Hospital, Bury St. Edmunds.

£100 each to the following:

The Corporation for the Relief of Poor Widows and Orphans of Clergymen in Suffolk.
The Incorporated National Society for Promoting the Education of the Poor in the Principles of the Established Church.
The Society for the Promoting of Christian Knowledge.
The Incorporated Society for Promoting the Enlargement, Building and Repairing of Churches and Chapels in England and Wales.

231

Personal Legacies

£ 10 to John Colman, Master of the National School, for every year of his service there.
£5 to Rachel Cornish, Spinster, Mistress of the National School, for every year of her service.

£100 to Fanny Barne of Tiverton, Devon, Spinster, 'in memory of many previous kindnesses rendered to me in my youth from her mother, Mary Barne'.

£500 to the Reverend Charles Thomas Scott, Vicar of Shadingfield, Norfolk.

£500 to John Barber Scott of Great Yarmouth.

£ 50 to Harry Hodgkinson Scott of Great Yarmouth.

£500 to Anna Maria Kilner, formerly Anna Maria Scott, wife of John Kilner of Bury St. Edmunds, surgeon.

£1000 to Hannah Butcher of Bungay, Spinster. If she died before him this legacy to be given to Anna Warmoll Butcher, Spinster, daughter of Stephen Butcher of Anmer, Norfolk.

£ 10 to be given to his man servant, George Catchpole, for every year of his service.

£200 to his wife, Harriet Catchpole 'for her sole and separate use exclusive of her husband'.

£5 to his cook or housekeeper for every year of her service.

£5 to his housemaid for every year of her service.

£3000 to be invested in Government securities to provide income towards the maintenance, education and advancement of his Godson Harry Scott Hughes until the age of 24, when he shall have absolute use of the capital.

£12,000 to Alfred Hughes for his own use.

All the rest of his personal estate he bequeathed to his cousin, Samuel Scott.

The will was signed on March 23rd 1861 in the presence of John James Raven, Master of Bungay Grammar School, and John Crabtree, solicitor of Halesworth, Suffolk.

It was proved at London on the 19th of November 1862.

Index of Persons

235